T0301844

Experiential Exercises in the Classroom

TEACHING METHODS IN BUSINESS

Series Editors: Jeanie M. Forray, *Western New England University, USA*, Jennifer S.A. Leigh, *Nazareth College, USA* and Sarah L. Wright, *University of Canterbury, New Zealand*

Contemporary business education encompasses a wide range of disciplines with all business faculty expected to teach effectively. Yet, in establishing that expectation, business schools don't always consider what resources educators may need to become effective teachers or to continue to develop their craft. The Teaching Methods in Business (TMB) series is designed to address that gap.

Every TMB volume provides focused, informative, and immediately useful coverage of a single active learning method with relevant considerations for any type of business classroom. Authored by interdisciplinary teams of business educators, the series has been planned and edited for a global audience.

Each TMB volume begins with a discussion of a specific teaching method within its theoretical and historical roots. Following this foundation, each volume discusses how the method meets the needs of particular learners in specific ways, offers reflection on the method's strengths and challenges, and provides examples of how the method may be implemented in various contexts. All volumes conclude with a list of annotated references drawn from pedagogical journals in business and related resources. The series is tailored for business educators at all levels of experience, from doctoral students in their first teaching assignment to experienced full-time faculty looking to refresh or expand their teaching repertoire. The series is also intended as a resource for adjunct instructors, libraries and university teaching centers.

The TMB series takes both a scholarly and an applied approach to educator development by providing conceptual grounding along with practical guidance and resources needed to implement the method based on the specific needs of the reader. Regardless of your particular business discipline or your experience with engaged learning, we hope you find the information provided in this and other volumes both inspiring and useful!

Titles in the series include:

Role-Play Simulations
Alex R. Bolinger and Julie V. Stanton

Experiential Exercises in the Classroom
Mary K. Foster, Vicki Fairbanks Taylor and Jennie L. Walker

Forthcoming titles include:

Project and Problem Based Learning
Garth Coombs and Janelle E. Goodnight

Computer Simulations and Gaming
James W. Cooper, Michele E. Yoder and Stacey L. Watson

Group and Team Work
Ricardo Flores and Antonina Bauman

Course Design and Learning Assessment
Kathy Lund Dean, Nancy S. Niemi and Charles J. Fornaciari

Experiential Exercises in the Classroom

Mary K. Foster

Associate Professor, Business Administration Department, Morgan State University, USA

Vicki Fairbanks Taylor

Associate Professor, Department of Management, Marketing and Entrepreneurship, Shippensburg University of Pennsylvania, USA

Jennie L. Walker

Associate Professor of Leadership, University of Arizona Global Campus, USA

TEACHING METHODS IN BUSINESS

Edward Elgar
PUBLISHING

Cheltenham, UK • Northampton, MA, USA

Published by
Edward Elgar Publishing Limited
The Lypiatts
15 Lansdown Road
Cheltenham
Glos GL50 2JA
UK

Edward Elgar Publishing, Inc.
William Pratt House
9 Dewey Court
Northampton
Massachusetts 01060
USA

A catalogue record for this book
is available from the British Library

Library of Congress Control Number: 2021932646

This book is available electronically in the **Elgar**online
Business subject collection
http://dx.doi.org/10.4337/9781789901122

ISBN 978 1 78990 111 5 (cased)
ISBN 978 1 78990 113 9 (paperback)
ISBN 978 1 78990 112 2 (eBook)

Printed and bound in Great Britain by TJ Books Limited, Padstow, Cornwall

This volume has been written in the spirit of collegiality and connection with all those around the world who engage in experiential education. It is first and foremost for you and the students whose lives you touch. May it spark your creativity to design new learning experiences and aide in your facilitation of transformative learning.

With gratitude for my husband Jim and my daughter Jamiee, the loves of my life.
Mary

To my husband Paul and my children Stephanie and Lukas.
Vicki

To my children, Geneva, Deborah, Vienna and Theodore, and to my mother, Deborah, thank you for your patience and support. You are my inspiration to strive for both excellence and genuine connection with others in my work, while sprinkling a little more joy and inspiration in the world.
Jennie

Contents

About the authors   viii
Preface   x

1   Conceptual/theoretical framework   1

2   Considerations for implementing experiential
     exercises in the classroom   50

3   How to prepare and implement   138

Annotated bibliography   198

Resources for experiential exercises   216

References   220

Index   245

About the authors

Mary K. Foster, PhD, MBA, is an Associate Professor at Morgan State University's Earl G. Graves School of Business and Management, USA. She earned a PhD in management from Morgan, an MBA from The Wharton School at the University of Pennsylvania, USA, an MS from Johns Hopkins, USA, and a BS from the University of Maryland, USA. Mary is a dedicated instructor, committed to continuous improvement in her teaching practice. She is actively involved in the experiential learning community at the Eastern Academy of Management and the United States Association of Small Business and Entrepreneurship. Her research interests are the scholarship of teaching and learning and team and organizational effectiveness, particularly in health care, education, and innovation settings. Her research has been published in *Small Group Research, Journal of the National Cancer Institute, Management Teaching Review, SAGE Research Methods Cases, Case Research Journal,* the *CASE Journal,* and the *Journal of Critical Incidents* (best paper award).

Prior to becoming an educator, she was an accomplished business executive who held executive positions at Sylvan Learning, Inc., Riverside Corporation, Mars, Inc., and General Electric. Her areas of expertise and experience in the corporate world included strategy and innovation.

Vicki Fairbanks Taylor, **PhD** earned her doctorate in Human Resource Management from Temple University, USA. She is an Associate Professor of Management at Shippensburg University of Pennsylvania, USA, where she utilizes experiential teaching methods in her undergraduate and graduate classes to build student engagement and promote learning. Vicki is actively involved in the experiential learning community. She serves on the Academy of Management Teaching and Learning Conference Committee and served as co-chair for the Experiential Learning Association. Creating and facilitating experiential exercises to promote student engagement and foster learning from experience is a central component of her scholarship and teaching. She regularly reviews and authors experiential exercises. Many of her exercises have been published in books and journals and she regularly presents experiential activities at regional, national, and international conferences.

Jennie L. Walker, PhD is Associate Professor of Leadership and Lead Faculty at University of Arizona Global Campus' Forbes School of Business and Technology, USA. For the past 20 years, she has specialized in developing people and organizations for success in complex, diverse, and increasingly global environments, within Fortune 500 organizations, as a professor and executive in higher education, and as a consulting partner to many organizations across the world. These efforts have included leading the design of programs, courses and learning experiences that incorporate experiential education. She was awarded Faculty of the Year in 2019 at Indiana Institute of Technology's PhD program in global leadership.

Preface

Each author of this volume traveled a different path on the road to experiential learning. We share our stories and our hope that this volume on experiential exercises in the classroom will provide the reader with guidance on how to use this method in the classroom and helpful information about the pedagogical background of the method.

"As a twenty-something, I dreamed of being a college professor as I strolled around the campus of a small liberal arts college in central Florida. I went on to spend more than 25 years working in business, earning an MBA along the way. As mid-life approached, I re-examined the dream of my twenties: Did I still want to be a college professor? What would it take to make that happen? I decided to pursue my dream and started looking at doctoral programs. I was surprised that most doctoral program descriptions did not mention anything about teaching me how to be an effective educator. I approached my new career as I had approached my business career. I wanted to be effective, to leverage the experience and expertise of others, and to use best practices. I did not want to 'reinvent the wheel' and make all the 'rookie mistakes.' So, I selected a doctoral program that allowed me to learn about the scholarship of teaching and learning, and I have been devoted to actively becoming a better educator, a better designer and creator of effective learning experiences, and a part of the active community of teaching and learning scholars."
Mary K. Foster

"Before beginning my career as a full-time academic, I worked in management development and was schooled in the idea that effective training needed to be interactive, hands-on, relevant, and tied to experience. The training process required as much attention as the curriculum development and developing content also meant addressing how participants would apply new learning and practice new skills. Trainees were expected to acquire knowledge and learn new skills and behaviors that would carry over to their jobs. To accomplish these objectives, I created

learner-center content, worked to identify and build upon learners' existing knowledge and strengths, applied the material directly to their work, facilitated small and large group discussions and above all provided opportunities for practice and reflection. With this background, I entered academia and found that in higher education, content often took priority over the learning process. I quickly found myself connecting with other educators interested in creating learning experiences rather than lecturing, and this peer group proved invaluable as I developed my teaching skills."
Vicki Fairbanks Taylor

"Experiential learning is an intuitive part of my work as a professor and professional trainer, because I was a scuba diving instructor for 12 years. Most of the concepts and skills discussed in the scuba classroom must be physically practiced and then evaluated in both the swimming pool and open water for successful certification. The training is highly experiential: even in the classroom, students work through scenarios. Scuba instruction taught me that student engagement in learning activities is vital in developing the kind of trust and attention that is needed to develop safe, capable, and happy divers. While the curriculum I facilitate in corporations and universities today is different, I still find experiential learning to be of great value in engaging participants and providing rich learning opportunities. Experiential learning activities have a certain spark to them that ignites learning."
Jennie L. Walker

1. Conceptual/theoretical framework

Described as one of the most robust instruments of management development (Holman and Mumford, 2001), experiential learning has emerged as a central instructional resource in business education (Bevan and Kipka, 2012; Tomkins and Ulus, 2016; Wright et al., 2019). Often driven by the desire for enhanced learning outcomes, accreditation requirements, student preference for active learning methods, and demands from the business community for workplace skills, experiential learning methods are increasingly considered a core component of the business curriculum (Bell, 2015; Kolb and Kolb, 2009a; Lund Dean et al., 2019; McNamara and McNamara, 2019). This volume focuses on experiential exercises in the classroom. Classroom-based experiential exercises, a type of active learning, provide students in the classroom with meaningful activities that serve as a basis for reflection and learning, and serve as effective alternatives to traditional, lecture-based methods.

Chapter 1 provides readers with a foundation for understanding classroom-based experiential exercises. The chapter covers definitions of experiential learning and includes a discussion of the characteristics of experiential learning, drawing attention to related constructs and various types of experiential learning activities. Next, the chapter covers the theoretical underpinning of experiential learning along with a discussion of influential educational theorists. Following the history of experiential learning and its use in business education, empirical evidence of effectiveness and evidence-based suggestions and best practices for classroom-based experiential exercises are presented.

DEFINING EXPERIENTIAL LEARNING

Defining experiential learning proves challenging given the vast collections of educational activities associated with experiential learning as well as the number of related approaches, models, programs, and methods with "experience" as their pedagogical base (Johnston and Sator, 2017). Moon (2004) noted the absence of an agreed-upon definition of experiential learning in the literature, and a review of experiential learning definitions finds considerable overlap between definitions of experiential learning and other experience-based methods such as active learning, inquiry-learning, collaborative learning, and discovery learning. The term "pedagogies of engagement" has also been used to capture instructional interventions that increase a student's active involvement in learning and enhance cognitive knowledge acquisition and psychosocial change (Smith et al., 2005). Table 1.1 includes definitions of the various teaching approaches that fall under the umbrella of experiential learning, along with examples of instructional activities associated with the different methods. Not all of the experiential learning methods described are classroom-based.

Hence, experiential learning means different things to different people, and the concept is open to many interpretations (Henry, 1989). Given the extensive use of experiential learning and related concepts encompassing many different pedagogies (Illeris, 2007), some authors find it easier to describe what experiential learning is not rather than settle on a definitive definition. According to Tomkins and Ulus (2016), experiential learning is not the dissemination of information via lecture for the purpose of memorization and testing. Passive lecture methods are what educator and philosopher Freire (1970) termed the "banking" model of education, where students are viewed as empty accounts to be filled by educators. In this volume, the authors use experiential learning as a broad umbrella term to cover the wide variety of approaches to learning-by-doing that engage students in the learning process and enable reflection about their experience as a component of that learning.

CHARACTERISTICS OF EXPERIENTIAL LEARNING

While the traditional lecture is often criticized for its passive style, lack of realism, and failure to provide whole-person, learning-focused outcomes (Godfrey et al., 2005; Hoover et al., 2010; Offstein and Chory, 2019), experiential learning incorporates experiences, reflections, and a learner-centered focus. These characteristics differentiate experiential learning methods from other more passive forms of instruction.

Experience

At its foundation, experiential learning is a constructivist approach to learning where the learner builds new knowledge through the interaction

Table 1.1   *Experiential learning-related concepts and definitions*

Concept	Definition
Action learning	"Action learning is a means of development, intellectual, emotional, or physical, that requires its subjects, through responsible involvement in some real, complex, and stressful problem, to achieve intended change to improve their observable behavior henceforth in the problem field" (Revans, 1982, pp. 626–627).
Active learning	Active learning engages students in the process of learning through activities and exercises that require students to articulate and communicate ideas, explore attitudes and values, and utilize higher-order cognitive strategies such as analysis, synthesis, and evaluation (Bonwell and Eison, 1991).
Case-based learning	A pedagogical approach that engages students in the process of making decisions or solving problems involving authentic workplace situations by applying knowledge gained from the classroom or through additional research (Williams, 2005).
Collaborative learning	Any instructional method in which students work in teams to accomplish a common goal, under conditions that include the following elements: interdependence, individual accountability, face-to-face interactions, collaborative skills, and group processing (Johnson et al., 2000).
Cooperative education	A structured educational method combining classroom-based education with productive work experiences in a field related to a student's academic or career goals (Groenewald, 2004).
Cooperative learning	Instructional techniques involving the use of small groups of students working on learning activities for the purpose of maximizing their own and each other's learning. Cooperative learning requires some degree of interactive interdependence in terms of mutual goals, joint rewards, resources, and roles (Johnson et al., 1991).
Discovery learning	An instructional method involving self-guided learning where students interact with materials, manipulate variables, explore phenomena, and attempt to apply principles for the purpose of discovering patterns, eliciting explanations, and discerning underlying causalities (Alfieri et al., 2011).
Field-based learning	Experiential education programs where students learn as workers or community participants (Eyler, 2009) and interact with professionals in the field (Wurdinger, 2005).
Inquiry-based learning	Inquiry-based learning encompasses a variety of pedagogical approaches such as problem-based learning, project-based learning, discovery learning, certain types of case-based instruction and student research (Prince and Felder, 2006).
Live cases	Team-based experiential project centered on a real company problem where students work in real time with the client to help solve problems. Results in the submission of written analysis and recommendations for the company client and in-class presentation with feedback by the educator and company client (Schramm, n.d.).

Concept	Definition
Outdoor adventure education	Outdoor adventure education incorporates direct and purposeful experience with adventurous activities in an effort to facilitate both intra- and interpersonal growth (Meyer and Wenger, 1998).
Place-based learning	Place-based learning stems from the field of environmental education and focuses on using the local community and environment as a starting point to teach concepts using an interdisciplinary approach to education (Sobel, 2003).
Problem-based learning	An instructional method involving the use of a problem to provide the stimulus for the learning (Boud and Feletti, 1997). This approach requires students to use problem-solving or reasoning techniques, self-directed learning strategies, and knowledge and information to understand the problem and how it might be solved (Barrows and Tamblyn, 1980).
Project-based learning	A method where educators guide students through a problem-solving process which includes identifying a problem, developing a plan, testing the plan against reality, and reflecting on the plan while in the process of designing and completing a project (Wurdinger et al., 2007, p. 151).
Service-learning	A teaching method where guided or classroom learning is deepened through service to others in a process that provides structured time for reflection on the service experience and demonstration of the skills and knowledge acquired (Kaye, 2004, p. 7).
Student-centered learning	A learning process where much of the power during the learning process resides with the student (Estes, 2004), giving them control over such things as choice of subject matter, learning goals, learning methods, and pace of study (Brandes and Ginnis, 1986).
Team-based learning	An instructional strategy that organizes students into permanent groups and promotes active learning through small group activities and assignments across a semester (Michaelsen et al., 2004). The four essential elements are: (1) properly formed and managed groups; (2) student accountability for individual and group work; (3) frequent and immediate student feedback; and (4) assignments that promote both learning and team development (Michaelsen and Sweet, 2008).

of their prior knowledge and experiences rather than receiving knowledge (Hanson, 2015; Mayer, 2009; Richardson, 1997). Through experiences, the learner validates the theory, concept, or practice being studied and constructs new meaning (Beaudin and Quick, 1995). However, what constitutes an "experience" in experiential learning may vary considerably and, according to Dewey (1938), not all experiences are equally educative. What makes an experience educative depends on the quality of the experience, whether or not the experience is engaging to the student, and whether or not the experience is connected with the student's future experiences (Dewey, 1938). According to Andresen et al. (2000), experiences should be direct and meaningful and may consist of past events in the learner's life or current events. Experiences need to be examined by the learner and understood so that learning may be generalized and used again (Crosby, 1995). In the experiential classroom setting, educators provide educative experiences through well-designed activities and the student derives meaning from the experience through subsequent reflection upon the experience. The reflection process is the second characteristic of experiential learning.

Reflection

Defined as a cognitive process through which individuals actively attempt to increase their understanding of personal experiences, reflection enables individuals to learn or create meaning from experiences (Argyris and Schön, 1974; Boud et al., 1985; Mezirow, 1998). The concept of reflection appears consistently in definitions and models of experiential learning (Frontczak, 1998). Schön (1987) identified two types of reflection: reflection-in-action, which entails reflecting in the middle of an experience; and reflection-on-action, which takes place after an experience. A different kind of reflection associated with experiential learning is pre-reflection. Pre-reflection involves identifying one's attitudes, knowledge, and beliefs about a concept, issue, or problem and identifying possible strategies for examining an issue or tackling a problem, before beginning an activity (Slavich and Zimbardo, 2012). Pre-reflection can be conducted individually or collectively. Collective pre-reflection has the added advantage of uncovering the existing attitudes, knowledge, and capabilities of the group at large as well as providing students with differing perspectives on how to tackle problems (Slavich and Zimbardo, 2012). Mezirow (1991) also discussed the importance of reflection, and identified three forms of reflective thinking:

content reflection, process reflection, and premise reflection. Content reflection consists of reflections on "what we perceive, feel or act upon and can be considered reflection on experience" (Mezirow, 1991, p. 107). Process reflection focuses on how one performs the functions of perceiving, thinking, feeling or acting or "reflection on concepts we use to help us understand experiences" (Rodgers et al., 2016, p. 200). Finally, premise reflection focuses on "why we perceive, think, feel or act as we do" (Mezirow, 1991, p. 108). Thus, premise reflection involves a critique of the assumptions held (Rodgers et al., 2016).

Dewey (1938) claimed that for real learning to occur at deeper levels, education needs to be grounded in experience, and experience needs to be accompanied by the student's active reflection on their experience. "Experience alone is insufficient to be called experiential; it is the reflection process which turns the experience into experiential education" (Joplin, 1995, p. 15). In experiential learning, reflection involves thinking about experiences and reflecting critically upon one's assumptions and beliefs (Ng et al., 2009). According to Kolb and Kolb (2005), reflection helps people to describe the situation objectively and to develop an understanding of why things happen. Either individually or collectively, reflection in all forms – pre-, in-action, or on-action (post-) – enables learners to benefit from experiential learning activities (Boud et al., 1985).

Learner-Centered

In addition to emphasizing the construction of knowledge through experience and the importance of reflection to create meaning from experience, experiential learning focuses on the central role of the learner. As a learner-centered method of instruction, experiential learning engages students as "subjects" rather than "objects" of the educational process (Lutterman-Aguilar and Gingerich, 2002), and much of the power during an experiential activity resides with the learner, or the learner and the educator share it (Estes, 2004).

Jarvis and Wilson (1999, p. 120) define experiential learning as an activity "in which the learner has a primary experience with the reality being studied." Learners enter into a learning situation bringing their whole self, which includes their knowledge, skills, competencies, attitudes, values, emotions, identity, beliefs, and senses (Jarvis, 2006). According to Hoover and Whitehead (1975), "experiential learning exists when a personally responsible participant (learner) cognitively, affectively, and behaviorally processes knowledge, skills, and attitudes in a learning situation characterized by a high level of active involvement" (p. 25). The educator's role in experiential learning entails providing learning experiences that require students to formulate and test their ideas, draw conclusions and inferences, and convey and pool their knowledge in a collaborative learning environment (Sunderman, 2006). As the designer of the exercise, educators determine the learning outcomes. However, according to Gosenpud (1990), "the learner often learns things not intended by the designer, and often this unintended learning is more valuable because it is relevant to the learner" (p. 304). Boud et al. (1985) further emphasize the central role of the learner in experiential learning:

> Only learners themselves can learn, and only they can reflect on their own experiences. Teachers can intervene in various ways to assist, but they only have access to individuals' thoughts and feelings through what individuals choose to reveal about themselves. At this basic level, the learner is in total control. (p. 11)

Drawing upon the three characteristics of experiential learning – experience, reflection, and learner-centered pedagogy – we define experiential learning as a process where students actively participate in learning through meaningful experiences and reflection upon those experiences to construct new knowledge, skills, or attitudes. The next section describes various types and categorizations of experiential learning activities.

EXPERIENTIAL LEARNING ACTIVITIES

Experiential learning subsumes a wide variety of activities and engagements. One way of differentiating among experiential learning activities involves categorizing them as field-based or classroom-based (Wurdinger, 2005). Students in field-based experiential education programs learn as workers or community participants (Eyler, 2009) and interact with professionals in the field (Wurdinger, 2005). Examples of field-based experiential learning include apprenticeships, internships, practicums, cross-cultural experiences, and cooperative education. Field-based experiential learning involves varying degrees of time spent outside of the classroom interacting with the community. Quality field-based exercises require careful planning, integration of field experience with curricular goals, faculty supervision to provide continuous monitoring and feedback, and the opportunity for structured reflection to help students link their out-of-classroom experience with the course or program content (Eyler, 2009).

Classroom-Based Activities

Classroom-based experiential learning incorporates direct learning experiences into the classroom and subsumes a wide variety of activities, from short primer activities such as ice-breakers, to semester-long projects. Hamer (2000) classified classroom-based experiential learning activities as semi-structured or loosely structured, based on the level of complexity and degree of ambiguity present in the activity. Semi-structured classroom activities are relatively short and moderately complex. For example, a semi-structured classroom activity might consist of short individual or group problem-solving assignments that give students experience with the application of course materials and builds on their theoretical understanding. Loosely structured experiential activities are typically completed over a longer time frame, are more complex, and ambiguous. Complexity denotes the array of variables that might impact the outcome of a decision (Lainema and Lainema, 2007; Nicolaides and Yorks, 2008), while ambiguity "requires students to think beyond stated facts and examine a range of unspecified influences and potential alternatives" (Hamilton and Klebba, 2011, p. 2). Loosely structured activities give students a great deal of control over what they learn from the activities and the process through which they learn (Hamer, 2000). Examples include computer simulations, debates, semi-structured role plays, various types of case studies, and group projects.

Classroom-based activities may also incorporate contact with the community or practitioners. For example, live cases serve as an example of blending classroom-based activities and direct interaction with practitioners. Live cases consist of a team-based experiential project centered on an organizational problem where students work in real time with clients to help solve problems (Schramm, n.d.). Teams conduct analyses, submit written recommendations to the company client, and conduct in-class presentations with feedback by the educator and company client (Schramm, n.d.). For example, one of the authors had students in her human resource management class consult with a local retirement facility to help determine a recruiting strategy for direct-care workers and nursing staff. Representatives from the retirement facility visited the classroom to describe their organization and a current problem they were experiencing in recruiting qualified applicants. Students then worked in teams to develop a recruiting strategy proposal, which they later presented to organizational representatives in class.

Classroom-based activities may also incorporate elements associated with outdoor adventure education. Schary et al. (2018) provide an example of a classroom-based, adventure education activity in the form of a challenge course. Educators facilitated a series of cooperative physical activities in the classroom, each increasing in complexity, with the goal of helping students to "communicate, work together, and think creatively in a cooperative manner" (Schary et al., 2018, p. 241).

Problem-Based and Project-Based Activities

Wurdinger (2005) categorized classroom-based experiential exercises as project-based or problem-based. With project-based activities, students work individually or cooperatively to create, build, or produce something (Wurdinger, 2005). Project-based activities typically cover the breadth of the curriculum and conclude with a written or oral report (Prince and Felder, 2006). An example of a project-based activity in an organizational behavior class might consist of designing and conducting research to examine the impact of stress on job performance. The findings from the study would be presented at the end of the semester in class, in writing, or both. Problem-based activities tend to be shorter in length than project-based activities and focus on identifying problems and discovering solutions (Wurdinger, 2005). Problem-based activities involve analyses of real or hypothetical scenarios such as the NASA Moon Landing survival exercise (Hall and Watson, 1970). According to Wurdinger (2005), problem-based "activities can be just about anything that requires solving a problem that is relevant to a student's life" (p. 15). While Wurdinger (2005) distinguishes between project-based and problem-based activities, other authors find it difficult to ascertain these differences. For example, Lemar (2016) views problem-based learning as a subset of project-based learning. Both methods fall under inquiry-learning, which begins by presenting students with questions, problems, or a set of observations to provide a context for learning (Prince and Felder, 2006). Furthermore, Wurdinger's (2005) classification of classroom-based exercises as problem-based or project-based could also be applied to experiential exercises outside of the classroom. Thus, we prefer to simply define classroom-based experiential exercises as a wide variety of experiential activities that are facilitated by educators in the classroom.

Classroom-based experiential exercises can cover a single class, a portion of a class, many classes, or a semester. Additionally, classroom-based experiential exercises encompass primer activities such as ice-breakers, or acquaintance exercises designed to introduce a topic, reduce inhibitions, or create trust among students or between students and the educator. In sum, experiential activities differ on a number of dimensions, each with varying degrees of student interaction, environmental contact, ambiguity, complexity, realism, uncertainty, and structure (Gentry, 1990; Hamilton and Klebba, 2011). Classroom-based experiential activities, regardless of their type, scope, or length, entail students actively participating in the learning through meaningful experiences and reflecting upon their experience to construct new knowledge, skills, or attitudes. This volume focuses on the wide variety of classroom-based experiential exercises used in business education to promote learning, with the exception of role plays and cases, which are thoroughly explored in other volumes of this series on *Teaching Methods in Business*. The next section of this chapter addresses the theoretical foundations of experiential learning in the classroom and discusses the history of classroom-based activities in business education.

THEORETICAL FOUNDATIONS OF EXPERIENTIAL LEARNING IN THE CLASSROOM

Experiential education and the practice of experiential learning is frequently associated with the educational reformer John Dewey (Beaudin and Quick, 1995). However, Smith and Knapp (2011) identified 33 key influencers of experiential education along with an additional list of thinkers associated with the pedagogy. The learning theories which undergird experiential methods emphasize a central role for experiences and stand in contrast to other theories that emphasize cognition over affect and neglect the role of the learner's consciousness and subjective experience (McCarthy, 2016). The theoretical foundations of experiential learning encompass constructivism and humanistic theory as well as integrative theories such as Mezirow's (1978) transformative learning theory, Schön's (1983, 1987) theory of reflective practice, and Kolb's (1984) experiential learning theory (ELT). This section provides an overview of the theoretical foundations of experiential learning and discusses how learning theory informs experiential teaching practices.

Constructivism

Constructivism, a theory of human learning that explains how learners acquire new knowledge by building or constructing cognitive structures in their minds (Hanson, 2015), draws from Piaget's cognitive development theories, Vygotsky's sociocultural view of learning, and Bruner's discovery learning (Slavin, 1994). According to constructivism, knowledge does not come from outside people but instead comes from inside them (Schunk, 2012). Constructivist theory advances the idea that students actively construct knowledge (rather than passively receive information) from the interaction of their prior knowledge and their current experiences (Hanson, 2015). Constructivism posits that for information to have meaning, it must be created, interpreted, and reorganized by the individual and reconciled with the learner's existing knowledge (Windschitl, 2002). Constructivism advocates teaching that actively engages learners in structured experiences and situations from which they can make sense of the subject matter through the manipulation of materials and social interaction (Gordon, 2009). Ideally, experiences should challenge learners' thinking and cause them to reconsider their beliefs (Schunk, 2012). Constructivism also emphasizes the importance of prior knowledge or prior beliefs that must be reconciled with experience.

Constructivist views encompass two approaches to learning: cognitive constructivism and social constructivism. In cognitive constructivism, individuals construct personal theories, mental models, and internal explanations (cognitive structures) in reaction to experiences (Hanson, 2015; Prince and Felder, 2006). Learning, from the cognitive constructivist perspective, requires intellectual engagement to assimilate or reconcile experiences with existing knowledge (Hanson, 2015). Without cognitive engagement, learning will not take place. In social constructivism, learners construct knowledge from experience through interactions with others. So, from the perspective of social constructivism, meaning is not simply constructed, it is co-constructed (Prince and Felder, 2006). Social constructivism encourages collaborative learning techniques such as team-based learning, which requires interaction and interdependence among team members to produce skills development and knowledge co-creation (Lohmann et al., 2019).

Both cognitive and social constructivism require experiences that challenge the learner's existing knowledge, intellectual engagement by the learner, and reflection as individuals attempt to resolve their cognitive disequilibrium and construct new meaning and representational models

(Hanson, 2015). According to Noddings (1990), constructivists generally agree upon three points: (1) all knowledge is constructed, at least in part, through a process of reflection; (2) there exist cognitive structures that are activated in the process of construction; and (3) cognitive structures are under continual development (see also Kinsella, 2006). Experiential learning theorists associated with the constructivist view include Donald Schön (1983, 1987), David Kolb (1984), and Jack Mezirow (1978). The following discussion highlights their theories, how they relate to constructivism, and implications for teaching.

Schön's theory of reflective practice
Schön (1983), an educational theorist, introduced the theory of reflective practice encompassing the ideas of reflection-on-action, reflection-in-action, and the reflective practitioner. His views on learning grew out of John Dewey's concept of reflections (Linder and Marshall, 2003) and from his observations of how and when professionals use reflection to build professional knowledge and expertise. He argued that the static knowledge taught in textbooks did not reflect the dynamic, adaptive knowledge that experts use in professional settings. According to Schön, reflection-in-action entails in-process reflection on a situation so that changes can still be made to affect the outcome; versus reflection-on-action, which involves contemplative reflection about something that has occurred (Hedberg, 2009). With reflection-in-action, individuals focus their attention on the moment, collecting their thoughts and reframing the situation. From Schön's perspective, learning is about being able to hold a "conversation with the situation" (Schön, 1983, p. 242) and allowing the experience to teach. According to Schön (1995), the "conversation" begins with a spontaneous action that is interrupted by a surprise. Surprise triggers reflection – What is this? What strategies and understandings have led to this? – and a new understanding of the situation emerges, which stimulates a new plan of action. This type of active experimentation is reflection-in-action and allows for mid-course corrections. Individuals also reflect on the experience (reflection-on-action) after the conversation. Schön (1995) likened this experience to a sportsman reviewing a video of Saturday's game on Sunday morning. Reflection-on-action allows the individual to critique the strategies and assumptions utilized. Together, reflection-in-action and reflection-on-action lead to knowledge and skill development.

The constructivist underpinning of Schön's theory exists in his rejection of the objectivist's view of technical rationality as the only means of problem-solving, and his notion of the reflective practitioner (Kinsella, 2006). According to Schön, through reflection-in-action, practitioners begin the process of remaking (reconstructing) the practice world when a situation arises that is surprising for the practitioner (Kinsella, 2006). Schön's theory of reflective practice, when applied to the education of future business professionals, entails coaching students in professional practice. Students participate in simulated real-world problems or actual work situations (such as a business management simulation, internship, or practicum). The experience should provide a relatively risk-free context that approximates the world of practice, where students can learn by doing (Jordan, 2010). Within the experience, students are directed to reflect-in-action, to question unexpected responses to actions taken (surprises) and to experiment within situations actively. Through reflection-in-action, students engage in iterative analyses and active experimentation that take into account ambiguities, multiple perspectives, and long-term, systemic implications (Inamdar and Roldan, 2013). Experimentation then generates new problems and confusion which becomes material for reciprocal reflection between the student and coach (Schön, 1987). Thus, it is through reflection that students construct meaning from classroom practices and practical experiences (Hedberg, 2009).

Mezirow's transformative learning theory
The theory of transformative learning, first introduced by Mezirow in 1978, is defined as: "The process by which we transform our taken-for-granted frames of reference – perspectives, habits of mind, mindsets – to make them more inclusive, discriminating, open, emotionally capable of change and reflective so that they may generate beliefs and opinions that will prove truer or justified to guide actions" (Mezirow, 2000, p. 7).

According to Mezirow (1991), learning begins with a disorienting dilemma that creates a state of cognitive conflict that causes the learner to critically assess basic assumptions from the individual's upbringing, life experience, culture, or education. If, as a result of critical reflection, learners experience a change in their perspectives and assumptions, they will begin exploring different options and planning their course of action. Next, they begin practicing new skills and building competence and self-confidence in new roles and relationships. The process culminates in a transformed perspective and understanding. Transformative learning involves the following ten phases:

1. A disorienting dilemma.
2. Self-examination with feelings of fear, anger, guilt, or shame.
3. A critical assessment of assumptions.
4. Recognizing that one's discontent and the process of transformation are shared.
5. Exploration of options for new roles, relationships, and actions.
6. Planning a course of action.
7. Acquiring knowledge and skills for implementing one's plan.
8. Provisional trying-out of new roles.
9. Building competence and self-confidence in new roles and relationships.
10. Reintegrating one's life on the basis of the new perspective. (Mezirow, 1991, p. 50; Mezirow, 2000, p. 22)

In the process of transformation, the phases may not occur in the sequence presented above, and learners may experience more than one phase in the process simultaneously (Roberts, 2006). Furthermore, not all disorienting dilemmas result in transformation. The cognitive conflict brought on by the disorienting dilemma may spark anger, humiliation, and resistance to change (Roberts, 2006). According to Bourgeois (2002), interpersonal relations among learners and between educators and learners can support a transitional space where learners can overcome their resistance to change and engage in self-examination and critical reflection on assumptions. Without support, learners can get stuck in the disorienting dilemma and transformational learning will not take place (Wilhelmson et al., 2015).

Constructivist assumptions underlying Mezirow's transformative learning theory include the idea that "meaning is individualist and found inside the student and teacher rather than prescribed by external influences such as written texts and speeches" (Kitchenham, 2008, p. 113). In addition, Mezirow (1991) asserts that "meaning is interpretation, and since information, ideas, and contexts change, our present interpretation of reality is always subject to revisions or replacement" (p. xiv). The implications for teaching according to transformative learning theory are to engage students in learner-centered, participatory, and interactive experiences that require group problem-solving, autonomous thinking, critical reflectivity, and discourse (Mezirow, 1997). Educators can create disorienting dilemmas by exposing students to the limitations of their current knowledge and assumptions. More specifically, Mezirow (1997, 2000) suggests that engaging students with concepts in meaningful and relevant ways – through group projects, role play exercises, case studies, and simulations – promotes changes in attitudes and beliefs (Slavich and Zimbardo, 2012). To mitigate any adverse effects of disorienting dilemmas on students, educators need to provide support for the students during the transformative learning process (Roberts, 2006).

Kolb's experiential learning theory

Kolb's (1984) experiential learning theory (ELT), considered the most influential model in experiential learning (Seaman et al., 2017), posits that learning is "the process by which knowledge is created through the transformation of experience. Knowledge results from the combination of grasping and transforming experience" (Kolb, 1984, p. 41). According to this theory, learners progress through four steps in a learning cycle: concrete experience, reflective observation, abstract conceptualization, and active experimentation where learners "touch all bases" (Kolb, 1984,

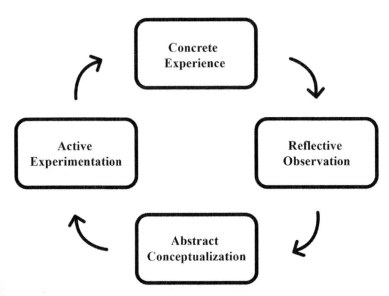

Figure 1.1   Kolb's experiential learning theory

p. 41) in the cycle (see Figure 1.1). In the concrete experience stage, learners encounter a situation that they explore with open-mindedness and adaptability. In reflective observation, the learner reflects on and critically examines the experience from multiple perspectives. Abstract conceptualization entails using logic and reasoning to assimilate knowledge from the experience. Finally, in active experimentation, learners use the knowledge gained to make predictions and test new hypotheses in a new situation. While all steps in the learning cycle are required, the reflection step, according to Desjarlais and Smith (2011), is critical to discovering "insights about one's self, one's behavior, one's values or knowledge gained" (p. 3). In summarizing the theory, Ramburuth and Daniel (2011) state: "not all learners will enter and engage with the learning stages equally, but the model provides for a framework that captures the learning process and enables its re-creation in classroom contexts" (p. 40).

In terms of its link to constructivism, Kolb and Kolb (2009a) state that experiential learning theory builds upon the cognitive constructivist theory of Piaget and the social constructivist theory of Vygotsky, and emphasizes that people construct new knowledge and understanding through experience and reflection. Educators utilizing this theory provide students with experiences such as classroom-based exercises (concrete experiences); educator-facilitated, structured reflection through discussions or other types of reflective assignments such as papers, discussion boards or journaling (reflective observation); conceptual material to help students assimilate their experiences and observations (abstract conceptualization); and a follow-up application assignment (active experimentation). According to Kolb and Kolb (2009a):

> The teacher's role is that of facilitators of a learning process that is basically self-directed. They help students to experience in a personal and immediate way the phenomena in their field of specialization. They stand ready with alternative theories and concepts as students attempt to assimilate their observations into their own conception of reality. They assist in deducing the implications of the students' concepts and in designing new "experiments" to test these implications through practical, real-world experience. (pp. 57–58)

Humanistic Learning Theory

Humanistic learning theory focuses on personal growth, well-being, autonomy, and full development of each person's potential (Chen and Schmidtke, 2017). Humanistic theory incorporates insights from psychotherapy and group dynamics into the learning environment (Boud,

1989), and proposes natural learning experiences based on the idea that all humans possess the tendency to grow, learn, and fully develop. According to Rogers (1969), people have a natural potential for learning and are eager to learn. Humanistic education largely builds on constructivist theories of learning (Herman, 1995; Slavin, 1994). However, it differs from constructivism by emphasizing respect for human dignity and the uniqueness of the individual, personal freedom of choice with responsibility for actions, and the viewpoint that motivation is optimal when students perceive personal meaning in learning (Herman, 1995). According to Rogers (1983), motivation to learn comes from the individual. Therefore, the responsibility for setting the direction of learning rests as much with the student as with the educator. Hence, in humanistic pedagogies, the individual is prioritized over the subject matter, teaching methods, and academic achievement: the holistic development of the individual takes on central importance (Chatelier, 2015). Furthermore, the educator plays a supporting role, helping the student to grow emotionally and intellectually to become an independent and self-directed learner (Aloni, 2011).

To align with humanistic theory, educational experiences should: (1) revolve around the student's interests; (2) be as self-directed as possible; (3) take place in an interactive, cooperative and supportive environment; (4) involve the whole human in the learning experience, addressing affective, cognitive, physiological, and contextual aspects; and (5) operate under the goal of producing individuals who want to and know how to learn (Johnson, 2012). Educators following this theory function as facilitators of learning (rather than educators), demonstrating respect for the student's whole person (Khatib et al., 2013), and creating the environment, climate, and conditions for natural learning to take place (Rogers, 1983).

Knowles's theory of adult learning
Knowles, best known for his theory of adult learning (Knowles, 1970), is an educational theorist closely associated with the humanistic learning theory. The strong influence of humanistic learning theory revealed itself when Knowles argued for a learner-centered educational process characterized by self-directed learning where educators function as facilitators and learners function as co-determinants of course goals and materials (Fenwick, 2001). Knowles conceptualized a continuum of learning from childhood to adulthood where younger learners might learn better "when their needs and interests, life situations, experiences, self-concepts, and

individual differences are taken into account" (Knowles et al., 2005, p. 40). According to Knowles et al. (2005), the biological, legal, and social definitions of "adult" matter less than the psychological definition, where adulthood means arriving at a self-concept of being responsible and self-directed. Thus, the theory of adult learning is relevant to the practice of teaching and the role of the educator in elementary, secondary, tertiary, and professional education (Knowles et al., 2005).

According to Knowles (1989, 1990), the theory of adult learning is based on the following assumptions:

1. The need to know. Adults learn best when they understand why they need to learn something before undertaking to learn it.
2. The learner's self-concept. Adults possess a self-concept of being responsible and a need to be seen by others and treated by others as being capable of self-direction.
3. The role of the learner's experience. The wide range of individual differences and experiences of the adult learner means that the most abundant resources for learning reside in the adult learners versus with the educator. Thus, the emphasis in adult education is on individualized instruction, experiential techniques, and self-reflection to help learners examine their assumptions.
4. Readiness to learn. Adults become ready to learn those things that are meaningful and relevant to coping effectively with their real-life situations.
5. Orientation to learning. Adults possess a life-centered orientation to learning. Adults desire instrumental, applied learning that addresses the problems learners experience in real life.
6. Motivation. Adults respond to some external motivators, but the most potent motivators are internal, and include such things as the desire for increased job satisfaction, self-esteem, and quality of life. (Knowles et al., 2005, pp. 64–69)

Based on these assumptions, Knowles proposed a process model for adult learning that encompasses the following steps: (1) preparing the students; (2) establishing a climate conducive to learning; (3) creating a mechanism for mutual planning; (4) diagnosing the needs for learning; (5) assessing discrepancies; (6) designing a pattern of learning experiences; (7) conducting learning activities; and (8) evaluating the program. Of these eight steps, Knowles considers establishing a climate conducive to learning to be the most crucial element in the entire process (Knowles et al., 2005). For an in-depth discussion of each of the steps in this process model, see *The Adult Learner* (Knowles et al., 2005).

Educators bring underlying assumptions (theories) about students and learning to the practice of teaching. Understanding the constructivist and humanistic underpinning of experiential learning will help educators more effectively design and facilitate pedagogical interventions. It is also important to understand, from an historical perspective, how experiential learning came to be incorporated into business education. The history and future of experiential learning in business education is discussed in the next section.

HISTORY AND FUTURE OF EXPERIENTIAL LEARNING IN BUSINESS EDUCATION

When discussing the history of experiential learning, many writers cite progressive educator John Dewey, and his seminal work, *Experience and Education*, published in 1938. A review of the scholarly record shows that the concept of experiential learning began circulating in the mid-20th century (Seaman et al., 2017) with the rise of humanistic psychology (Fenwick, 2001). According to Seaman et al. (2017), the concept of experiential learning "began in 1946 as a form of social practice influenced by Kurt Lewin's action research agenda applied to problems of intergroup conflict" (p. 24). Initially, experiential learning challenged prevailing norms regarding where and how education took place. However, over time, educators began developing and adopting a variety of experiential methods.

One of the earlier experiential methods, problem-based learning (PBL), was developed in 1969 by Barrows and colleagues in the School of Medicine at McMaster University in Canada (Ungaretti et al., 2015). The curriculum focused on small groups of students using real patient problems and simulated patients as a means of acquiring both medical knowledge and medical skills (Ungaretti et al., 2015). Research on PBL found it to be as effective as traditional educational approaches in terms of achieving objective learning outcomes (medical board examinations) and superior in developing clinical problem-solving skills (Vernon and Blake, 1993). From there PBL spread to other schools and universities across various subject domains. By the late 1970s, experiential learning was elevated to the status of a general theory and writers began grappling with how to transform the ideals and assumptions of experiential learning theory into techniques to enhance learning from experience (Seaman et al., 2017). By the early 1990s, assumptions about teaching effectiveness began to shift in favor of experiential methods (Fenwick, 2001), and by the late 1990s, experiential learning methods had made solid inroads into higher education (Bobbitt et al., 2000; Saunders, 1997).

History of Experiential Learning in Business Education

Business education has been dominated by two arguments. The first is that business education is too vocational and lacks academic rigor, and second is that business education is too academic and lacks relevance (Augier and March, 2007). While the United States (US) business school model is dominant (Pfeffer and Fong, 2002), the European models are more strongly rooted in social constructionism, and differ from their US counterparts by their emphasis on reflective, integrative, and experience-based learning; public-sector management and public policy issues; and greater sensitivity to international relations (Antunes and Thomas, 2007).

Many business academics consider discipline-based content the primary objectives of their programs (Crossan et al., 2013), resulting in a curriculum that is highly cognitive and heavily quantitative (Colby et al., 2011). Conventional business disciplines such as accounting, economics, finance, marketing, operations, and organizational behavior often exist in separate silos in terms of both research and teaching (Pfeffer, 2018). Both US and European business schools share similar histories (Augier and March, 2007). During the first half of the 20th century, business schools or "schools of commerce" sought to prepare students for careers in the business community, and the emphasis on scholarship was less prominent (Augier and March, 2007). Experienced executives served as faculty, and the primary teaching methods included the case study approach, established in 1908 in Harvard's Graduate School of Business Administration (Merseth, 1991), and cooperative education where students work part-time in the business community (Augier and March, 2007). Business schools focused on best practices (Gordon and Howell, 1959) and early business writers such as Frederick Taylor were more likely to be practitioners than doctoral-qualified business educators (Edfelt, 1988).

Introduction of business games and simulations
The post-World War II (WWII) era ushered in a focus on objective data, rational approaches to managing corporate enterprises, and abstract

skills such as forecasting, planning, decision-making, and coordination (Khurana and Spender, 2012). Business games and simulations – made possible by the integration of military war games, operational research, computer technology, and educational theory – were among the initial experiential methods adopted in business education (Keys and Wolfe, 1990). The University of Washington was the first university in the US to utilize a business game in the college classroom, in 1957 (Watson, 1981). Created mainly by organizations for use in managerial training, business school educators saw the advantages that games and simulations offered students, and began incorporating them into their courses (Keys and Wolfe, 1990). By 1961, more than 100 business games had been created (Kibbee et al., 1961) and in 1987, a study conducted by Faria estimated that approximately 8,755 educators in over 1,900 four-year business schools had adopted business games in their curricula (Keys and Wolfe, 1990). As more business educators embraced classroom-based simulations and games, organizations supporting the development and use of business games came into existence (Faria et al., 2009). In 1974, the Association for Business Simulation and Experiential Learning (ABSEL) was formed. By the end of the 20th century, more than 95 percent of schools accredited by the Association to Advance Collegiate Schools of Business (AACSB) were using business simulations in their programs (Faria, 1998).

Early experiential learning movement
The post-WWII era also witnessed the emergence of experiential approaches to management education based on Lewin's (1951) change theory, sensitivity training and T-group methods developed by the National Training Laboratories (Keys and Wolfe, 1990; Whetten and Cameron, 1983). Other influencers included the work conducted at the Tavistock Institute of Human Relations in the United Kingdom on group therapy techniques (Highhouse, 2002). While these methods are most often associated with organizational behavior and organizational development, their influence on business education included a movement from the traditional, lecture-based model of education to learner-centered experiences where, according to Whetten and Cameron (1983), "lectures were kept to a minimum, empirical research was deemphasized, and theory was introduced only to validate the personal experiences of the participants" (p. 13).

Focus on research and scholarship

During this same period, efforts to reform business education took root, mostly in response to criticism in the Ford Foundation's Gordon/Howell Report (Gordon and Howell, 1959) that "described American business education as a collection of trade schools lacking a strong scientific foundation" (Zimmerman, 2001, p. 2). As a result, over the next two decades, an emphasis on the scientific method, research and knowledge creation and a strong focus on graduate education emerged (Antunes and Thomas, 2007). As scholarship rose to prominence in US business schools, faculty were recruited based on the significance of their research rather than their teaching skills (Augier and March, 2011). According to Whetten and Cameron (1983), the transition from practitioner-as-educator to researcher-as-educator significantly altered US classroom instruction from an anecdotal, best-practice focus to an emphasis on theoretical models and research-based teaching. By the 1970s, American business schools were dominated by an analytical perspective where academic research was rewarded, and educators who preferred to think and teach in other ways were disenfranchised (Leavitt, 1989).

Calls for reform

Beginning in the 1980s, concerns emerged that North American business education had distanced itself from business practices and did little to prepare graduates for successful careers in business (Cameron and Whetten, 1983). According to critics, the overly vocational business schools of the early 20th century were now "too academic and not producing the managers needed by American business" (Cheit, 1985, p. 44). Similarly, Whetten and Cameron (1983) claimed that management education lacked relevance, and "the key problem seems to be an overemphasis on analytical techniques and theory devoid of application" (p. 11). Numerous others concurred with the criticism that business schools overemphasized quantification and specialization to the point of being irrelevant to the world of business practice (e.g., Bickerstaffe, 1981; Leavitt, 1989; Mandt, 1982; Miles, 1985; Muller et al., 1988).

The call for reform led some business schools to increase their emphasis on experiential learning (Augier and March, 2007) and skill development in the application of knowledge (Wren et al., 1994). Despite efforts to integrate more experiential methods into the business curriculum, business education scholars continued to point to the failure of business schools in preparing graduates for careers in business (e.g., Arbaugh and Hwang, 2015; Datar et al., 2011; Mintzberg, 2004; Pfeffer and Fong,

2002; Salas et al., 2009; Ungaretti et al., 2015). With the exception of the frequently utilized Harvard Business School case method of teaching, lecture-centered approaches to business education remained the norm (Farashahi and Tajeddin, 2018; Hay and Samra-Fredericks, 2019; McNamara and McNamara, 2019; Ungaretti et al., 2015). Pfeffer and Fong (2002) noted "little evidence that mastery of the knowledge acquired in business schools enhances people's careers, or that even attaining the MBA credential itself has much effect on graduates' salaries or career attainment" (p. 80). Institutional pressure to publish in high-ranking journals (Vogel et al., 2017) focused educator efforts on research rather than teaching and learning, especially when tenure and promotion decisions were determined by publication records (Harley, 2018). Even though the most highly regarded accreditation body in business education, AACSB, called for experiential learning, it has not been wholeheartedly adopted into the business curriculum (Billsberry et al., 2019; Hanson, 2015; Pettigrew and Starkey, 2016).

Demands for learning outcomes
While the importance of content knowledge remains an integral part of business education (Colby et al., 2011), increasingly stakeholders express a need for learning outcomes in terms of skill development and applied learning experiences (Hanson, 2015; Mintzberg, 2004; Ungaretti et al., 2015). According to a 2017 National Association of Colleges and Employers (NACE) survey, the top four attributes employers seek most in job applicants include problem-solving skills, the ability to work in a team, communication skills (written), and leadership. Despite business schools recognizing the importance of the competencies desired by employers, many fail to incorporate those same competencies into their curricula (Abraham and Karns, 2009; Rubin and Dierdorff, 2013).

Educational accrediting bodies such as AACSB, The European Quality Improvement System (EQUIS), and the Association of MBAs (AMBA) also call for business schools to deliver learning outcomes beyond discipline-specific content. AACSB, in its 2013 accreditation standards, highlights the need for creative and innovative student projects that engage and deepen student understanding of the course content and provide students with job-specific skills (Gundal et al., 2018). AACSB's 2019 standards regarding obligatory elements in curricula of accredited business programs include the ability to communicate effectively orally and in writing; ethical understanding and reasoning; analytical thinking; the ability to work effectively with others and in team environments; the ability to work effectively in diverse environments; reflective thinking (ability to understand oneself in the context of society); the ability to translate knowledge of business and management into practice (application of knowledge); and the integration of real-world business experiences (AACSB, 2018). In its 2019 standards and criteria, EQUIS identified similar outcomes which it divides into two categories: intellectual skills (for example, the ability to analyze, synthesize, and critically assess complex material; the ability to formulate and defend independent judgments; the ability to conceptualize and to communicate effectively in writing and orally) and managerial skills (for example, teamwork, interpersonal skills, presentation skills, project management, and leadership skills) (EFMD, 2019). According to Beck-Dudley (2018), Vice-Chair of AACSB and Dean of the Leavey School of Business at Santa Clara University, California, business courses and curriculum can no longer be informed only by the academic disciplines: the traditional lecture needs to be replaced with "content that is about doing and not just about listening" (p. 168).

Increased emphasis on experiential methods

A growing body of literature calls for experiential pedagogy in business education (Cunliffe, 2008; Dehler and Welsh, 2014; Hanson, 2015; Petriglieri and Petriglieri, 2010). Roberts (2018) argues that a "great disruption" in higher education, caused by: (1) increased competition for students; (2) critiques that traditional educational methods do not provide students with necessary work skills; and (3) evidence that experiential approaches contribute to post-graduation success and the development of skills required by employers, has resulted in an increased emphasis on experiential learning methods. The disconnect between business education and the skills that future employers look for in graduates (Abraham and Karns, 2009; Pfeffer and Fong, 2002; Rubin and Dierdorff, 2013; Ungaretti et al., 2015); the characteristics and needs of today's business students (George, 2015; Neves and Hillman, 2019); the demands of accrediting bodies such as AACSB, EQUIS, and AMBA; and competition from alternative sources of business knowledge and business education (Pfeffer and Fong, 2002), have ushered in greater demand for pedagogical approaches based on experiential learning (Brown et al., 2013; Forster and Robson, 2019). An emerging consensus exists regarding the importance of experiential learning as a core and integrated component of the business curriculum (Caza et al., 2015; Hodge et al., 2014; Kolb and Kolb, 2005; Waddock and Lozano, 2013; Wright et al., 2019) and as a means for providing students with the competencies employers seek in graduates (Armstrong and Mahmud, 2008; Devasagayam et al., 2012; Forster and Robson, 2019; Roberts, 2018).

Proponents of experiential learning argue that students learn best through direct experience and that experiential learning is more effective in generating cognitive, behavioral, and attitudinal outcomes than more passive methods of instruction (Farashahi and Tajeddin, 2018; George, 2015; Hanson, 2015; Prince and Felder, 2006). Forster and Robson (2019) contend that experiential learning can enhance the development of students' employability skills and attributes. Reynolds (2009) states that "the benefits of experiential learning lie in its connectedness to the social and political aspects of work as well as to the dilemmas and problems that form the stuff of work experience" (p. 390). According to Kosnik et al. (2013), outcomes of an effective business curriculum include business knowledge (concepts, models, and theories), business skills (communication, decision-making, teamwork, emotional intelligence, leadership), and character (integrity, social responsibility, and citizenship). These outcomes align with the content areas included in the AACSB Standards for Business Accreditation, with the exception of the new AACSB content area of 'Technology Agility.' According to AACSB (2013), evidence of a business school fulfilling its teaching responsibilities include student engagement in "experiential and active learning designed to be inclusive for diverse students and to improve skills and the application of knowledge in practice" (p. 32).

Thus, the call for experiential learning in business education is clear. In order to prepare business students for the realities of organizational life and to achieve desired learning outcomes, students need to participate in experiential learning opportunities (e.g., Clark and White, 2010; Reynolds, 2009; Tomkins and Ulus, 2016). A body of compelling evidence both within and outside of business education points to the efficacy of experiential learning methods. The next section examines the results of meta-analyses, systematic reviews, and a sampling of individual studies demonstrating the positive outcomes associated with experiential learning.

EVIDENCE OF EFFECTIVENESS

The body of evidence on the effectiveness of experiential learning can be broken down into individual studies of experiential activities, courses, or programs; comparative studies involving one or more experiential methods; comparative studies examining traditional lecturing and one or more experiential methods; contingency studies examining the impact of moderating variables such as learner characteristics or exercise features; summary narratives of experiential learning methods by type (for example, problem-based learning), by academic discipline (for example, entrepreneurship), or by curriculum (for example, business); and systematic reviews and meta-analyses of one or more types of experiential pedagogies in one or more curricula. This section first summarizes the findings on the effectiveness of experiential learning methods in business education. While a collection of individual studies from various business disciplines will be discussed, the primary focus is on systematic reviews and meta-analyses. After discussing the evidence of effectiveness in business education, systematic reviews and meta-analyses of different types of experiential learning methods from disciplines outside of business are highlighted. The research on how an educator might best facilitate experiential learning are discussed later in this chapter in the "Best Practices for Classroom-Based Experiential Exercises" section and will be delved into even more deeply in Chapter 2.

Evidence of Effectiveness in Business Education

There exists an extensive collection of individual studies demonstrating the positive outcomes associated with experiential learning in business education. Reviews of studies examining the effectiveness of classroom-based experiential exercises in business education find educators deploying a variety of experiential methods across multiple business disciplines. Learning outcomes in these studies vary, and fall into knowledge, skill, and affective domains. Audet and Marcotte (2018) summarized some of the more frequently observed learning outcomes associated with experiential learning in the literature: critical thinking (Austin and Rust, 2015; Kosnik et al., 2013), global business mindset (Chmielewski-Raimondo et al., 2016; Le and Raven, 2015), entrepreneurial mindset (Splan et al., 2016), teamwork (Austin and Rust, 2015; Bell and Bell, 2016; Chmielewski-Raimondo et al., 2016; Kosnik et al., 2013), confidence/self-efficacy (Splan et al., 2016), self-improvement (Chmielewski-Raimondo et al., 2016; Le and Raven, 2015), interpersonal skills (Austin and Rust, 2015; Bell and Bell, 2016; Kosnik et al., 2013; Splan et al., 2016), sales skills and knowledge (Deeter-Schmelz, 2015), ethical literacy (Le and Raven, 2015), cultural intelligence (Le and Raven, 2015), and community citizenship (Austin and Rust, 2015; Kosnik et al., 2013; Le and Raven, 2015).

Audet and Marcotte's (2018) summary covered a wide variety of in-class and field-based experiential exercises in business education. In Table 1.2 a selection of research about the efficacy of classroom-based experiential exercises is presented by business discipline. These classroom-based exercises were identified using Google Scholar and EBSCO Business Source Premier. Exercises were selected to demonstrate how learning outcomes are associated with classroom-based experiential exercises in a variety of business disciplines. Computer games and simulation are not included among these classroom-based experiential exercises due to their coverage in another volume of this series.

When reviewing authors' rationale for adopting experiential learning activities across different business disciplines, it becomes apparent that educators are responding to compelling factors such as accreditation requirements, mounting evidence of the effectiveness of experiential methods, students' interest and preference for experiential methods, the need to provide students with the business competencies desired by employers, as well as educators' beliefs that experiential learning is theoretically sound and pedagogically superior to traditional lecturing. An examination of the learning goals of the selected exercises in Table 1.2 shows that the learning outcomes include specific types of business knowledge (for example, accounting), business skills (for example, critical thinking), and affective outcomes (for example, student engagement and an entrepreneurial mindset). In terms of results, the various experiential learning methods utilized were positively related to cognitive, behavioral, and affective outcomes as measured by student performance on written assignments, objective exams, perceived learning, student reported satisfaction, and perceived effectiveness of the learning activity. In sum, a wide collection of individual studies conducted in various business disciplines add to the growing body of knowledge supporting the efficacy of experiential exercises in business education. The use of various measures of learning suggests that improvements in student performance can be objectively measured and subjectively experienced and observed.

While individual studies provide educators with feedback on experiential activities deployed in the classroom, help to disseminate experiential activities to other educators interested in adopting experiential learning methods, and contribute to the body of evidence on the efficacy of experiential learning methods in business education (Priem, 2018),

Table 1.2   Empirical experiential learning studies in business education

Study	Business discipline	Learning goal	Assessment measures	Summary findings
Teaching tip "the data shuffle": Using playing cards to illustrate data management concepts to a broad audience. Agogo and Anderson (2019)	Data management	Knowledge of business concepts related to data management, knowledge of technical concepts related to the management, storage and processing of data	• Objective quiz scores • Self-reported confidence with understanding concepts • Self-assessed learning • Student reported satisfaction with the activity	• Significant increase in average test scores between pre- and post-tests • No difference between post-test scores and follow-up test scores • Participants' confidence with understanding of the concepts significantly increased between pre- and post-tests • Marginally significant reduction in confidence between post-test scores and follow-up test scores • Participants reported (perceived) learning and enjoyment with the experiential activity • Participants reported high levels of broad recall of the concepts learned
Developing the next generation of entrepreneurs: Giving students the opportunity to gain experience and thrive. Bell (2015)	Entrepreneurship	Entrepreneurial mindset: preference for innovation, proactive disposition, positive self-efficacy, positive attitude toward risk taking	• Reflective essay assessed by educator • Student reported satisfaction and engagement	• Student feedback indicated a high level of student satisfaction and engagement • Reflective essays indicated that students had developed entrepreneurial traits (preference for innovation, proactive disposition, self-efficacy, attitude toward risk taking)
Negotiation skill development exercise. Benson and Chau (2017)	Marketing	Negotiation skills	• Student-assessed learning • Student-reported satisfaction	• Students' satisfaction and perceived learning from the course were consistently higher than the control group • Students reported that the exercise improved their ability to: (1) think more objectively; (2) communicate more effectively; (3) understand and select an appropriate negotiation approach; and (4) be more creative in their solution development

Study	Business discipline	Learning goal	Assessment measures	Summary findings
How instructional methods influence skill development in management education. Cajiao and Burke (2016)	Leadership	Learning behaviors and managerial skill development: social interaction, student reflection, teamwork, communication, influence and work proficiency effort	• Self-reported learning behaviors (dialogue and reflection) • Learning goal orientation • Self-efficacy for class performance • Psychological safety • Educator-assessed skill demonstration (composite score for teamwork, communications influence, work proficiency and effort)	• Students participating in an instructional condition that promoted higher levels of social interaction and reflective activities exhibited considerably greater learning behaviors (student–student dialogue, educator–student dialogue, and reflective activities) than students participating in instructional conditions with less of these activities • Students in the experimental condition reported enhanced self-efficacy for class performance and skilled activity • Students' perceptions of psychological safety partially mediated the relationships between instructional method and students' reflective and dialogical activities • Learning behaviors directly influenced skill demonstrations
The effect of contemporary learning approaches on student perceptions in an introductory business course. Coakley and Sousa (2013)	Introductory business course	Business concepts, business plan concepts, student interest in business education	• Self-assessed learning • Student reported interest in business education	• Students perceive knowledge of business concepts and business plan concepts increased significantly • For the majority of the respondents, interest in business education did not change as a result of experiential-based methods
Experiential learning: Improving the efficacy of an undergraduate business degree. DeSimone and Buzza (2013)	Entrepreneurship and marketing	Critical thinking and decision-making skills	• Scores on educator-graded written assignments	• Students in the marketing experimental group scored higher on average than the control group on end-of-semester, written assignments assessing critical thinking skills • Entrepreneurial students' end-of-semester scores indicate a statistically significant improvement in critical thinking scores from the beginning of the semester (no control group)

Study	Business discipline	Learning goal	Assessment measures	Summary findings
Experiential learning in management education. Eckhaus et al. (2017)	Accounting	Business knowledge – cost accounting	• Exam scores • Final grades	• Students who won in the board game earned higher exam scores and higher final grades than students who lost the game or did not play the game • Taken as a single group, students who won and students who lost in the game earned higher mean course grades than students who did not play the game • The level of perceived entertainment and comprehensibility of the board game was positively related to understanding of the course material
Authentic simulated startups: Bringing the real world into the classroom. McNamara and McNamara (2019)	Organizational behavior	15 skill-based competencies (teamwork, creativity, problem-solving, etc.)	• Self-assessed learning	• In data from 151 closed- and open-ended surveys of undergraduate students across six semesters, students reported developing the ability to work on a team, the ability to work with diverse people, an increased understanding of oneself and how to apply business concepts to real-world situations • Students overwhelmingly agreed that the course helped them learn new skills related to their success after graduation

Study	Business discipline	Learning goal	Assessment measures	Summary findings
The effect of using case studies in business statistics. Pariseau and Kezim (2007)	Business statistics	Critical thinking skills	• Exam scores • Self-assessed learning	• Students in experimental groups received significantly higher grades on their comprehensive final examination • Student perceptions of learning in the experimental groups were significantly higher with respect to communication, software use, and the ability to apply statistics to business decisions
Active learning, cooperative learning, and passive learning methods in an accounting information systems course. Riley and Ward (2017)	Accounting	Business knowledge: accounting	• Exam scores • Student-reported satisfaction • Student-assessed learning • Perceived effectiveness of the method	• Students working individually in active learning conditions (in-class research project) scored higher on examinations than students in passive lecture learning conditions • Students in the cooperative active environment (in-class group research project) posted exam scores that were not statistically different from passive participants' scores • Students in both individual and cooperative active environments reported positive feedback on satisfaction, perceived learning, and effectiveness of the method

meta-analyses and systematic reviews may prove more instructive when attempting to draw general conclusions about the effectiveness of experiential learning methods in the classroom. The next section summarizes the results from systematic reviews and meta-analyses of experiential learning in business education and presents a summary of meta-analyses of experiential methods used in other professional fields.

Systematic Reviews and Meta-Analyses in Business Education

In 1990, Gosenpud published a review of the literature on the assessment of experiential instructional methods to draw conclusions on the effectiveness of experiential learning in business education. The review included studies of experiential exercises, courses, or programs taught entirely or in part with the experiential method; part-time, long-term, or short-term experiential management development programs relevant to the business school setting; and some laboratory experiments generalizable to the business classroom. The review excluded studies involving the case method (except where the purpose of the case method was to develop case-related skills such as problem-solving) and traditional active teaching methodologies such as solving accounting problems in an accounting course. The review covered relevant dependent variables presumed to be influenced by experiential learning (cognitive learning, attitude changes, behavioral changes, and skill development) as well as contingency variables such as learner characteristics and experiential learning features.

Regarding cognitive learning, the data from 14 articles, yielding 23 comparisons of objective exam results between experiential and other teaching methods, suggested that experiential methods were neither superior nor inferior to other methods in helping students to learn cognitively. However, two of the studies examined showed that experiential learning was significantly more effective than non-experiential methods when assessments, in the form of tests, covered material included in the activity. While these results serve as an insufficient basis for drawing conclusions, Gosenpud (1990) suggests that when assessing the effectiveness of an experiential activity relative to cognitive outcomes, educators should use targeted assessments covering the specific concepts learned in the experiential exercise rather than general conceptual exams.

In terms of affective outcomes, 19 studies assessed experiential learning in terms of students' attitudes towards participating in experiential activities and 12 studies assessed experiential learning in terms of changes in attitude from before to after participating in experiential learning. In terms of attitudes toward experiential learning, students expressed significantly more positive general attitudes towards their learning experience than students exposed to more passive, traditional teaching methods such as lectures. Positive general attitudes assessed included greater course benefits, a higher-quality educator–student relationship, greater student satisfaction, or a greater feeling that skills were acquired. Under the conditions of role playing and on-the-job training, positive attitude changes were observed from before to after experiential learning. While too few studies assessed specific attitudes for conclusions to be drawn, these findings suggested that experiential learning results in positive attitude changes.

Eighteen studies assessed the effectiveness of experiential learning in regard to behavioral changes, skill acquisition, or skill development. Results from the review of studies focused on behavioral changes and skill acquisition showed positive results in 17 of the 18 studies, suggesting that experiential learning methods are effective in terms of promoting behavioral outcomes. Behavioral changes were noted in all nine of the studies assessing sensitivity training, two of the three role playing studies and both multifaceted programs and general on-the-job managerial training programs. While some of the studies were methodologically flawed in terms of not pre-specifying or hypothesizing the expected nature of the behavioral change, overall results indicate that experiential methods are effective in helping individuals to acquire new skills or change their behavior in desired directions.

Regarding contingency variables, six out of nine studies examining the influence of learner characteristics found that either learner personality or learner capability influenced experiential learning outcomes. Additionally, management support of training influenced the degree of positive change in trainees. Implications regarding the effect of features of experiential learning on the effectiveness of experiential learning were also gleaned from Gosenpud's (1990) review. The influential features include feedback, the meaningfulness of the exercise, and the meaningfulness of the concepts to the student. The level of involvement or engagement in the activity also enhances learning. These results point to the influence of moderating or mediating variables on the relationship between experiential learning activities and cognitive, behavioral, and affective outcomes. In discussing the results from his review, Gosenpud (1990) stated, "the most obvious problem with experiential learning evaluation research is the lack of rigorously designed studies" (p. 303).

However, he noted that the traditional lecture method also suffers from a similar lack of rigorous research and theoretical grounding.

In another review of 39 published studies, Gosen and Washbush (2004) found clear support for the effectiveness of computer-based simulations and experiential exercises. In addition, students reported learning and positive responses to both experiential methods. Students also reported positive attitude changes, and changes in behavior and intrapersonal effectiveness. However, given the lack of rigorous research design in the studies, the authors viewed their conclusions as tentative. Of the more than 115 articles read by the authors, 39 came close to meeting the research standards needed to support validity claims, and none of the 115 studies considered met all of the criteria for sound research (Gosen and Washbush, 2004). However, Gosen and Washbush (2004) point to the parallel field of management training to support the efficacy of experiential learning in business education. They referred to a meta-analysis of 70 studies measuring the effectiveness of six types of management training (Burke and Day, 1986). The findings demonstrated the effectiveness of different experiential methods based on the use of subjective learning (trainee or trainer perceptions of learning) and objective behavioral outcomes (such as reduced number of errors) and a small training effect (13.8 percent of the observed effect size variance) based on the use of objective learning outcomes (for example, knowledge tests) or subjective behavioral outcomes (perceived changes in on-the-job behavior by the trainee, peer, or supervisor). Gosen and Washbush (2004) argue that business educators should find encouragement in the results from Burke and Day's (1986) meta-analysis in terms of findings, and move forward with assessing the effectiveness of experiential programs using accepted research standards.

In an attempt to determine whether including experiential exercises in business courses results in increased learning or the development of skills, Burch et al. (2014) conducted a quantitative review of the four decades of research on experiential learning published in the annual proceedings of ABSEL. Their research focused on empirical studies involving stated learning objectives and the use of treatment and control groups. In addition, they examined studies that evaluated students' perceptions of learning. In terms of increased learning, while individual studies varied in how experiential learning was measured, and the possibility of moderating variables existed, the result of the meta-analysis showed a significant improvement in the means of the experiential learning groups as compared to the control groups. In terms of perceptions of learning, the results showed a significant positive effect of experiential learning on student perceptions of learning. Also, the results demonstrated that students' perceptions of learning aligned with the level of demonstrated learning (according to tests and evaluations). In other words, experiential learning activities increase student learning and student perceptions of learning similarly (Burch et al., 2014).

In a second meta-analysis examining 53 studies involving 6,768 individuals published over a period of 40 years, Burch et al. (2016) examined the effect of experiential learning methods on learning outcomes as well as the influence of moderating variables. In terms of learning effects, experiential learning had a significant positive effect on student learning across all studies. Furthermore, in those instances when specific learning outcomes were examined, experiential learning was found to have a positive impact on the understanding of social issues, the development of personal insight, and cognitive development. However, the results indicated greater learning outcomes for cognitive and personal insight measures than for social issue measures. The examination of moderators showed that learning outcomes did not vary as a function of whether learning activities focused on knowledge or application outcomes; objective assessment of learning outcomes produced higher learning outcomes than subjective (self-assessed) assessments; and feedback moderated the relationship between experiential learning activities and learning outcomes such that activities with feedback had a greater learning effect than exercises without feedback. Also, the findings indicate that the duration of the experiential activity did not significantly improve learning outcomes. The difference in results between subjective and objective assessments of learning demonstrates that students underestimated their learning relative to the outcomes assessed. The study also emphasizes the critical role that feedback plays in enhancing learning outcomes. Given the robust results, the authors of the study question the ethics of depriving students of opportunities for experiential learning in future studies comparing the effects of experiential learning with traditional lecturing.

Evidence from Outside of Business Schools

The limited number of meta-analyses, systematic reviews, and empirical studies conducted in business education require educators to examine research from other disciplines to glean additional insights about the effectiveness of experiential learning. Priem (2018) draws attention to the deficiency in empirical studies focused on teaching strategic management. In terms of specific experiential methods, Hmelo-Silver (2004) notes the scarcity of research of problem-based learning in managerial education. In discussing the results of their meta-analysis examining the efficacy of experiential learning in business education, Burch et al. (2016, 2019) lament the limited number of usable empirical studies with experimental and control groups, reinforcing comments made by earlier authors reviewing the body of experiential learning literature in business (Gosen and Washbush, 2004; Gosenpud, 1990). Hence, we turn to meta-analyses and systematic reviews conducted outside of business schools to further examine the efficacy of experiential learning over traditional lecturing.

In a meta-analysis examining a 43-year span and 13,626 journal articles, dissertations, thesis articles, and conference proceedings concerning experiential learning in higher education, Burch et al. (2019) found 89 studies containing empirical data with both a treatment and a control group. A meta-analysis of these in-class and out-of-class studies show that students experienced superior learning outcomes when experiential pedagogies were employed. Furthermore, learning outcomes in classes employing experiential learning methods versus traditional learning approaches such as lecturing were almost half a standard deviation higher (Burch et al., 2019). Learning outcomes were categorized as understanding a social issue, developing personal insight, and cognitive development; cognitive development and understanding social issues had the strongest effects. The study also revealed that the difference between objective and subjective assessments of learning outcomes was not statistically different. According to Sitzmann et al. (2010), "self-assessed knowledge is generally more useful as an indicator of how learners feel about a course than as an indicator of how much they learned from it" (p. 180). However, in a meta-synthesis examining the overall relationship between self-assessments of ability and objective performance across 22 meta-analyses, Zell and Krizan (2014) found that the relationship between self-assessed ability and objectively measured performance strengthened when self-evaluations focused on specific rather than broad skills. Furthermore, the accuracy of self-assessments of learning increases under conditions of external feedback. Without feedback, students may over- or underestimate their learning (Gosenpud, 1990). Hence, educators using self-assessments to measure cognitive outcomes should provide students with feedback to assist them in accurately gauging their knowledge (Sitzmann et al., 2010).

In terms of moderating variables, learning outcomes did not vary with activity duration and the presence of feedback did increase learning.

However, studies without feedback performed well, indicating that student learning was enhanced by experiential activities even if feedback was not provided. In their post hoc analysis of 20 studies conducted in business courses, 95 percent of the studies revealed that cognitive outcomes significantly outperformed the cognitive outcomes achieved in non-business disciplines. The authors find these results a clear affirmation of the efficacy of experiential learning in producing desired learning outcomes in business education, given that many business topics are evaluated using cognitive measures (Burch et al., 2019).

Meta-analyses examining the influence of different instructional strategies on the achievement of specific learning outcomes provide additional evidence of the effectiveness of experiential learning. For example, Abrami et al. (2008) conducted a meta-analysis on the effect of instructional strategies on the development and enhancement of critical thinking skills and dispositions (for example, open-mindedness; self-confidence in one's own ability to reason; and prudence in suspending, making, or altering judgments). Critical thinking entails consciously controlled, higher-order reflective thought utilizing lower-order cognitive processes such as perception, attention, and memory (Smith, 2003). It resides as a principal component of business school pedagogy, and there have been consistent calls to research instructional methods in business education capable of developing critically thinking professionals (Khurana and Spender, 2012; Rousseau, 2012; Vaara and Faÿ, 2012). Thus, studies examining effective instructional strategies for teaching critical thinking skills should be of interest to business faculty. The results from their study showed a significant effect for active instructional methods such as educator-led discussions, and experiential methods such as applied problem-solving and role playing, on generic and specific critical thinking skills and dispositions. Furthermore, when a combination of instructional methods was deployed (discussions, authentic role play, and problem-solving situations and mentorship), larger effect sizes resulted. These results support active and experiential learning methods as a means for developing students' critical thinking skills and dispositions as measured on critical thinking tests and disposition measures.

Relative to the examination of specific experiential pedagogies, problem-based learning (PBL), which first emerged in medical training, is one of the more widely researched, experiential learning methods. According to Barrows (2002), a key component of PBL includes the introduction of unresolved, ill-structured, "real-world" problems that can generate multiple thoughts about the causes of the problem and multiple ideas on how to solve it. In addition, PBL is a learner-centered approach where the student determines what they need to learn to solve the problem, and the educator acts as a facilitator or tutor helping the student to identify the knowledge gap and asking students metacognitive questions that they want students to explore (Barrows, 2002). Ungaretti et al. (2015) view PBL as an important pedagogical tool to complement or substitute other pedagogies to achieve learning goals in business education. Furthermore, they assert that PBL seems especially well suited to business education, as it offers the opportunity for students to develop content knowledge and relevant business skills (Ungaretti et al., 2015). Thus, meta-analyses examining the effectiveness of PBL in influencing cognitive, behavioral, and affective outcomes deserve consideration in the quest to identify useful classroom-based experiential methods for business education.

Strobel and van Barneveld (2009) conducted a meta-synthesis examining the findings of meta-analytical research and systematic reviews on the effectiveness of PBL in an attempt to determine generalizable findings. Their sample included eight meta-analyses and systematic reviews. Results for cognitive outcomes, and knowledge acquisition and retention were mixed, but tended to favor traditional learning approaches. However, the method used to assess knowledge influenced outcomes. Both free recall and long-term knowledge retention results favored PBL. Also, the more an assessment instrument evaluated the students' application of knowledge in solving problems, the larger the effect of PBL. Relative to skill or performance, learning results as assessed by educators' observations in clinical settings and educator-assessed case analyses favored PBL. In terms of affective outcomes, students and educators indicated greater satisfaction with the PBL approach to learning, with the exception of studies where knowledge was measured using standardized tests focused on short-term knowledge acquisition and retention. Hence, when academic success is measured in terms of standardized test results, it appears that students prefer traditional educational methods that increase their likelihood of academic achievement. In summarizing their findings, Strobel and van Barneveld (2009) state, "PBL is significantly more effective than traditional instruction to train competent and skilled practitioners and to promote long-term retention of knowledge and skills acquired during the learning experience" (p. 55).

Other meta-analyses focused on different types of experiential learning methods across various academic disciplines also yield encouraging results relative to the effectiveness of experiential learning over traditional lecturing. Table 1.3 summarizes the results of meta-analyses based on the type of experiential activity. Where possible, meta-analyses involving different types of experiential learning methods conducted in business education are cited.

Despite a compelling and growing body of evidence on the effectiveness of experiential learning, critics remain. The next section reviews their arguments.

Critics of Experiential Learning Methods

Some critics question whether experiential learning methods contribute to student learning, and point to studies that reveal mixed results regarding the effectiveness of experiential learning methods (Kirschner et al., 2006; Michel et al., 2009). Others argue that experiential coursework is less rigorous than traditional teaching methods and that conclusions cannot be drawn on the efficacy of experiential learning due to: (1) flawed research designs (Gosen and Washbush, 2004); (2) assessments derived from student satisfaction surveys or course evaluations (Serva and Fuller, 2004; Stewart et al., 2012); and (3) self-reported measures of perceived learning rather than objective outcomes (Benek-Rivera and Mathews, 2004; Hackathorn et al., 2011). In their systematic review of experiential learning, Gosen and Washbush (2004) called attention to the number of studies that failed to meet the highest standards of research design and measurement, thus making it difficult to conclude definitively that experiential teaching methods are effective. Gosenpud (1990) and Burch et al. (2014, 2016, 2019) came to the same conclusion.

Admittedly, there is a dearth of studies involving: (1) experimental and control groups; (2) objective measures of learning; and (3) comparison of instructional methods. And there have been numerous calls for additional qualitative and quantitative research to assess the legitimacy of experiential learning (Burch et al., 2014, 2016, 2019). Given that studies of the effectiveness of experiential learning are performed by different scholars, on different campuses, with different types and groups of students, in different courses, using different types of exercises, pursuing the rigorous validation of learning remains a continuing challenge (Gosen and Washbush, 2014). This challenge is unlikely to be overcome unless there are broad-based, large-scale projects involving many scholars from a wide variety of disciplines and educational settings participating in carefully designed studies to assess the effectiveness of experiential methods. As suggested by Burch et al. (2019), scholars should design

Table 1.3   *Meta-analyses based on type of experiential learning methods*

Study	Experiential activity type	Summary of findings
Springer et al. (1999)	Collaborative (small group) learning	A meta-analysis of 37 studies involving various forms of small-group learning in science, technology, engineering, and mathematics (STEM) courses and programs found small group learning was positively related to greater academic achievement, more favorable attitude toward learning, and increased persistence in STEM courses. The magnitude of the effects exceed effects for educational innovations generally, which suggests that more widespread implementation of collaborative learning would be desirable.
Nesbit and Adesope (2006)	Concept mapping	A meta-analysis of 55 studies involving 5818 participants across several instructional conditions found that the use of concept maps was associated with increased knowledge retention. Use of concept maps enhanced knowledge retention when compared to reading, traditional lecture, or class discussion. The strategy was slightly more effective in terms of knowledge retention than writing summaries or outlines.
Johnson et al. (2000)	Cooperative learning	A meta-analysis of 164 studies (yielding 194 independent effect sizes) involving eight cooperative learning methods found that all eight methods had a significant positive impact on student achievement and were more effective than competitive or individualistic approaches to learning.
Hew and Lo (2018)	Flipped classroom	A meta-analysis of 28 eligible comparative studies showed an overall significant effect in favor of flipped classrooms (videotaped lectures provided before interactive class sessions) over traditional classrooms for health professions education (medical students, residents, doctors, nurses, or other health care professions and disciplines) with no evidence of publication bias. Further, the flipped classroom approach yields even higher learning when instructors use quizzes at the start of each class session. Most students preferred flipped to traditional classrooms.

Study	Experiential activity type	Summary of findings
Strobel and van Barneveld (2009)	Problem-based learning	A meta-synthesis of eight meta-analyses and systematic reviews of the effectiveness of problem-based learning (PBL) found that PBL is superior when it comes to long-term retention, skill development, and satisfaction of students and teachers, while traditional approaches are more effective for short-term retention as measured by standardized board exams.
Yorio and Ye (2012)[a]	Service-learning	A meta-analysis of 57 studies involving 5495 unique subjects found that service-learning has a positive effect on understanding of social issues, personal insight, and cognitive development. Significant moderating effects exists for research design, type of reflection, type of measurement, and the service experience as optional or required.
Swanson et al. (2019)	Team-based learning	A meta-analysis of 17 studies at the post-secondary level found a moderate positive effect of team-based learning (TBL) on content knowledge when compared to non-TBL groups.

Note:
[a] Meta-analysis conducted in business education.

studies to address questions of importance in higher education, use control groups whenever possible, take care to elucidate characteristics of the research setting and design, and conduct longitudinal research to address learning retention over time.

However, when taken in their totality, the findings from individual studies, systematic reviews, meta-analyses, and meta-syntheses provide strong evidence of the effectiveness of experiential learning activities in positively influencing cognitive, behavioral, and affective learning outcomes. Business educators, interested in improving the quality of business education, should view experiential learning methods as effective means for equipping students with the business knowledge and skills required by employers, and for creating the high-impact learning environment desired by students (Kniffin et al., 2017). The question is not whether business educators should use experiential learning activities, but how educators effectively design and implement experiential learning activities in their courses to engage students and facilitate learning.

We suggest that educators integrate various experiential approaches, select targeted assessments of learning, and consider context (learner, educator, instructional methods, subject, and other situational factors) when deploying experiential learning activities in order to maximize student learning and preparedness for future performance in organizations. For insights on implementing experiential learning, the next section addresses best practice and evidence-based recommendations on how to facilitate experiential learning. Chapter 2 provides detailed guidance on how to develop and implement evidence-based experiential exercises for the classroom.

BEST PRACTICES FOR FACILITATING EXPERIENTIAL LEARNING ACTIVITIES

For those new to experiential methods, it is important to recognize that experiential modalities require a unique set of teaching skills, entail risks, and raise the possibility of ethical issues that are otherwise absent in didactic pedagogies (Lund Dean et al., 2019). While professional standards and credentialing for experiential teaching are lacking in business education (Wright et al., 2019), we are able to glean from the experiential learning literature and organizations such as the National Society for Experiential Education (NSEE) and the Association for Experiential Education (AEE) guidance on best practices in experiential learning.

The NSEE's mission is to "cultivate educators who effectively use experiential education as an integral part of personal, professional, civic and global learning" (National Society for Experiential Education, n.d.). In 1998, NSEE convened a task force of 115 global experiential practitioners and adopted the Eight Principles of Good Practice for All Experiential Learning Activities (National Society for Experiential Education, 2013). NSEE's principles of practice outline the conditions, steps, and actions necessary for successful experiential learning (see Table 1.4).

AEE, founded in 1972, supports professional development, theoretical advancement, and the evaluation of experiential education worldwide (Association for Experiential Education, n.d.). AEE's principles of practice address multiple facets of experiential learning, including the importance of supporting experiences with reflection, critical analysis, and synthesis; learner initiative, engagement, and accountability; and the role of the educator in setting experiences, posing problems, establishing boundaries, supporting learners, insuring physical and emotional safety, and facilitating the learning process (Association for Experiential Education, 2012).

Recommendations Based on the Experiential Learning Literature

The literature on experiential learning provides additional insights to guide the practice of experiential teaching. Grabinger and Dunlap (1995) focused on principles for creating a learner-centered educational environment, which they refer to as rich environments for active learning (REALs). These principles include providing learning experiences in complex and authentic contexts; encouraging students to be responsible, take initiative, and make decisions; using dynamic, cross-disciplinary learning exercises where students can integrate acquired knowledge with previous knowledge and experiences; evaluating student progress in course content through realistic activities; and fostering an attitude of knowledge-building where students and educators learn collaboratively. In his model for teaching experiential education, Warren (1995) elucidates the role of the educator in experiential learning as follows:

1. Informed consent. An instructor should provide "a precise course description and a detailed introduction to both the potentials and perplexities of the class."

Table 1.4   *National Society for Experiential Education (NSEE): eight principles of good practice for all experiential learning activities*

Principle	Practice
Intention	All parties must be clear from the outset why experience is the chosen approach to the learning that is to take place and to the knowledge that will be demonstrated, applied, or result from it. Intention represents the purposefulness that enables experience to become knowledge and, as such, is deeper than the goals, objectives, and activities that define the experience.
Preparedness and planning	Participants must ensure that they enter the experience with sufficient foundation to support a successful experience. They must also focus from the earliest stages of the experience/program on the identified intentions, adhering to them as goals, objectives and activities are defined. The resulting plan should include those intentions and be referred to on a regular basis by all parties. At the same time, it should be flexible enough to allow for adaptations as the experience unfolds.
Authenticity	The experience must have a real-world context and/or be useful and meaningful in reference to an applied setting or situation. This means that is should be designed in concert with those who will be affected by or use it, or in response to a real situation.
Reflection	Reflection is the element that transforms a simple experience into a learning experience. For knowledge to be discovered and internalized the learner must test assumptions and hypotheses about the outcomes of decisions and actions taken, then weigh the outcomes against past learning and future implications. This reflective process is integral to all phases of experiential learning, from identifying intention and choosing the experience, to considering preconceptions and observing how they change as the experience unfolds. Reflection is also an essential tool for adjusting the experience and measuring outcomes.
Orientation and training	For the full value of the experience to be accessible to both the learner and the learning facilitator(s), and to any involved organizational partners, it is essential that they are prepared with important background information about each other and about the context and environment in which the experience will operate. Once that baseline of knowledge is addressed, ongoing structured development opportunities should also be included to expand the learner's appreciation of the context and skill requirements of her/his work.

Principle	Practice
Monitoring and continuous improvement	Any learning activity will be dynamic and changing, and the parties involved all bear responsibility for ensuring that the experience, as it is in process, continues to provide the richest learning possible while affirming the learner. It is important that there be a feedback loop related to learning intentions and quality objectives and that the structure of the experience be sufficiently flexible to permit a change in response to what that feedback suggests. While reflection provides input for new hypotheses and knowledge based on documented experience, other strategies for observing progress against intentions and objectives should also be in place. Monitoring and continuous improvement represent the formative evaluation tools.
Assessment and evaluation	Outcomes and processes should be systematically documented with regard to initial intentions and quality outcomes. Assessment is a means to develop and refine the specific learning goals and quality objectives identified during the planning stages of the experience, while evaluation provides comprehensive data about the experiential process as a whole and whether it has met the intentions which suggested it.
Acknowledgement	Recognition of learning and impact occur throughout the experience by way of the reflective and monitoring processes and through reporting, documentation and sharing of accomplishments. All parties to the experience should be included in the recognition of progress and accomplishment. Culminating documentation and celebration of learning and impact help provide closure and sustainability to the experience.

Source: National Society for Experiential Education, https://www.nsee.org/8-principles.

2. Establishing a concrete vision. The instructors must "provide some initial structure and focusing" and provide a "concrete vision of the class by suggesting the course goals and what the students might expect from such an endeavor."
3. Setting ground rules. The instructor needs to create a safety net for students by setting basic operating principles by both statement and example, thus empowering them to take risks. Some potential ground rules are: "the use of 'I' statements to express feelings, active listening, the use of inclusive language, constructive feedback, and intolerance of oppression."
4. Providing process tools. Instructors should ensure students possess the appropriate skills – such as brainstorming, consensus decision-making, group roles, and problem-solving – to effectively participate in collaborative projects.
5. Feedback and debriefing. Experiential learning requires evaluation and reflection. The instructor must ensure that feedback and debriefing occurs. (Warren, 1995, p. 251)

In a report on experiential education in post-secondary institutions in British Columbia, Canada, Johnston and Sator (2017) summarized from the literature the following practices associated with successful student learning outcomes:

- Throughout the experiential learning process, the learner is actively engaged and helps develop the curriculum;
- The learner is engaged intellectually, emotionally, socially and/or physically;
- The results of the learning are very personal and form the basis for future learning;
- The learner is prompted to reflect in and on their experience, before, during and after the learning event;
- Relationships and connections are developed and nurtured between learner and self, learner and others and learner and the world at large;
- There is acknowledgement that the experiences and learning cannot totally be predicted;
- Disruptive opportunities during and after the experience are nurtured and learners (and educators) are supported to explore and examine their own values and beliefs; and
- The design must incorporate educator recognition of learner input, multiple possible outcomes, and the need for customizable teaching

and assessment, tools and techniques. (Johnston and Sator, 2017, pp. 2–3)

To address the ethical dilemmas that may accompany the activation of the emotional process during experiential learning, Maddox et al. (1991) suggest, firstly, that educators reflect upon their values and perspectives to determine their impact on their teaching. Secondly, they highlight the importance of explaining to students the underlying values of experiential learning and the types of activities they will encounter in the class. In addition, they recommend educator self-disclosure, modeling authenticity and respect, exemplifying coaching behaviors in support of student development, encouraging open dialogue and feedback, managing classroom power struggles, and discouraging student dependency. Lastly, they stress the importance of continuing education and training through conferences, professional development workshops, and classes.

Wright et al. (2019) also address the ethical challenges of experiential learning by advocating for value-based practice standards to support teaching and learning; lowering the risks to instructors, institutions, and students; and increasing the probability that learning outcomes are achieved. Their recommendations encompass the following:

1. Competence of the educator to deliver, facilitate and debrief course design;
2. Accurate and transparent course descriptions (including the rationale for including experiential learning activities);
3. Informed consent (especially when deception is required to achieve meaningful learning outcomes);
4. Opt-in/out choices (with a rationale if there is no choice and/or alternative assessment to the experiential activity if appropriate);
5. Confidentiality expectations stemming from the activity;
6. Processes in place to identify and respond to student distress (p. 276).

Additionally, they advocate for mandated (and supported) continuing professional development for experiential educators.

Figure 1.2 summarizes best practices for experiential learning based on the experiential learning literature and the practices articulated by NSEE and AEE.

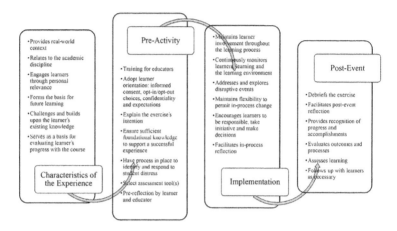

Figure 1.2   Best practices for experiential learning

RECAP

Broadly defined as a process where students actively participate in learning through meaningful experiences and reflection upon those experiences to construct new knowledge, skills, or attitudes, experiential learning encompasses a vast array of approaches to "learning by doing." Classroom-based experiential learning subsumes a wide variety of activities that vary in length, complexity, and ambiguity. Educational theorists such as Schön, Kolb, Mezirow, and Knowles offer theories and models to explain the process by which individual learners acquire new knowledge, skills, and attitudes along with implications for teaching.

A compelling body of evidence exists in support of experiential learning methods. Both individual studies and meta-analyses find support for the efficacy of experiential learning in producing cognitive, behavioral, and affective outcomes. Best practices and evidence-based suggestions for facilitating experiential learning in the classroom stress the important characteristics of meaningful experiences, pre-event actions, implementation guidelines, and post-event activities. Educators incorporating experiential exercises in the classroom may face many challenges. Moving forward requires a concerted effort by all stakeholders and a willingness to engage, experiment, and reflect upon learning by doing in the classroom.

Chapter 2 introduces educators to the process of designing, modifying, and adopting experiential exercises in the classroom. The models, checklists, worksheets, and practical instructions provided will help educators effectively incorporate classroom-based experiential learning exercises in their courses using evidence-based best practices.

2. Considerations for implementing experiential exercises in the classroom

When educators design courses, create syllabi, develop a lesson plan, or plan an experiential exercise, one of their goals is to create effective learning experiences. Educators plan, develop, design, organize, create, and deliver experiential experiences, with the hope of helping students to construct new knowledge from their experiences. For educators to be effective creators of learning experiences, they need to understand not only the content to be taught but also the context in which they teach. They should also understand what does and does not work in instructional design, development, and implementation. The purpose of this chapter is to provide educators with the tools needed to effectively design learning experiences, specifically experiential exercises for the classroom. Targeted toward university educators who are responsible for designing and executing courses consistent with their university's catalog and instructional policies, this book assumes that educators are subject matter experts for the courses they teach. This chapter focuses on the processes and best practices for developing and implementing effective experiential exercises in different contexts. Whether educators use an existing experiential exercise, adapt an existing exercise, or create an original exercise, this chapter offers the resources needed to develop and implement effective evidence-based learning activities in their courses.

The chapter starts with a review and critique of a few key classroom-oriented instructional design models: that is, the Integrated Design; Backward Design; Planning, Implementing and Evaluating (PIE); Systematic Planning; and the Analysis, Design, Development, Implementation, and Evaluation (ADDIE) models. Then a prescriptive procedural model and checklist for developing and implementing effective experiential exercises are introduced: the Effective Experiential Exercise Design Model and Checklist. These tools provide educators with a "how to" roadmap for designing and implementing experiential exercises in the classroom. Then contextual factors, variables in a situation which may have an impact on learning and should be taken into consideration when designing an exercise, are discussed: (1) the specific context of the learning situation; and (2) the general context of the learning situation. Finally, the chapter concludes with a summary of essential insights and practical recommendations for creating experiential exercises.

GETTING STARTED

So, you want to create an effective experiential learning exercise. Where do you start? The number of design resources available is overwhelming. Instructional systems design models first appeared in instructional technology journals and related instructional design and education literature in the 1960s (Branch and Dousay, 2015, p. 13). Currently, more than 100 models of instructional systems design exist (Branch and Dousay, 2015). Many of these models were developed by and for instructional design professionals, people who use a systematic approach to develop education and training programs for organizations such as the military or businesses, rather than for classroom educators (Branch and Dousay, 2015; Molenda, 2015). Some instructional design models have been developed specifically for use by classroom educators: the Integrated Design model by Fink (2003a, 2003b), the Backward Design model by Wiggins and McTighe (McTighe and Wiggins, 2004; Wiggins and McTighe, 2005), the Planning, Implementing, and Evaluating (PIE) model by Newby et al. (2000), and the Systematic Planning model by Gerlach and Ely (1980) are some of the more well-known ones. Another model, the Analysis, Design, Development, Implementation, and Evaluation (ADDIE) model, is widely referred to and often spoken of as the generic model of a systems approach to instructional design; however, its origins, definition, and therefore focus are unclear (Molenda, 2015). See the entry in the Annotated Bibliography near the end of this book, on Branch and Dousay's (2015) *Survey of Instructional Design Models* for an overview of the field. In the next section, the best-known classroom-oriented design models are briefly described and reviewed.

Classroom-Oriented Design Models

Integrated Design
Fink's (2003a, 2003b) model integrates active learning, educative assessment, a taxonomy of significant learning objectives, and the concept

of a teaching strategy to develop a model which university educators can use to design courses featuring significant learning experiences. He argues that the integration or alignment of learning goals, feedback/ assessment, and learning activities is essential to create credible, motivating, significant learning experiences. He also encourages educators to take into consideration situational factors, such as:

- the specific context of the teaching and learning situation;
- expectations of external groups;
- the nature of the subject;
- characteristics of learners;
- characteristics of the educator; and
- any special pedagogical challenges.

However, he provides little specific or evidence-based guidance on how to respond to these situational factors. This issue is addressed in the "What We Know About What Works" section where both specific and evidence-based guidance for responding to contextual factors are provided.

Backward Design

Wiggins and McTighe (McTighe and Wiggins, 2004; Wiggins and McTighe, 2005) offer a conceptual framework, a design template, and design standards, originally targeting primary and secondary school educators and now targeting primary through tertiary school educators. Their premise is that if educators focus, first, on what they want students to learn, and second, on how they will observe or recognize what students have learned, then the curriculum (that is, lessons, units, courses) can be developed to achieve the learning ends sought. They argue that this is a superior method of teaching compared to the conventional coverage or activity approaches. In the coverage approach, the content in textbooks guides the teaching or design process, and educators and students may lose sight of the learning outcomes intended. In the activity approach, where the focus is on creating engaging, hands-on activities, educators and students may also lose sight of the learning outcome. While students may have fun, the activity may not lead to any insights or learning. Wiggins and McTighe argue that students should not just make connections between new knowledge and old knowledge, but must also be able to wisely and effectively use what they know, in context. In other words, students must be able to apply knowledge and skill effectively in realistic tasks and settings. The authors contend that backward design, with its focus first on the desired results, is a superior approach to achieving fluent, fluid understanding. They address context obliquely; embedded in the goals section of the design template are references to institutional standards, and in the learning activities section is a reference to the different needs, interests, and abilities of students.

Planning, Implementing, and Evaluating (PIE)

Newby et al. (2000) maintain that learning is the result of change in knowledge, performance, or behavior caused by interaction with the environment. They argue that the educator, the instruction (instructional methods, techniques, and activities; instructional technology; and instructional media), and the learner interact to yield learning. They recommend that educators and students use the Planning, Implementing, and Evaluating (PIE) model to identify actions which they can take to improve learning. The focus of planning is to ensure that instruction is in an order that learners can effectively process; the goal of implementation is to put the plan into action; and the intent of evaluation is to assess the effectiveness and efficiency of instruction and the learning achieved by students. This model stresses the role of students as active expert learners engaging in a learning environment. The educator's role is to develop or select instructional materials and activities to increase student learning. This model very broadly defines the educator and instruction as the context in which students learn.

Systematic Planning

Gerlach and Ely (1980) encourage primary, secondary, and tertiary educators to take a systematic approach to planning lessons. They encourage the definition of learning objectives first; however, they accept that many educators start with a content approach, a list of topics that must be covered in a certain order and time frame. Either way, they argue that content and learning objectives are interconnected and should be defined concurrently before moving on to other aspects of planning. The next step involves assessment of students' readiness and need for instruction, typically via pre-existing records or a pre-test. Then the educator selects a strategy, determines whether and how to use groups, allocates time, allocates space, and selects resources. These planning steps are considered to be interdependent and should be done concurrently. This design model focuses on identifying and selecting resources as opposed to creating them. Gerlach and Ely argue that a typical classroom educator does not have the time to create resources. The next step is to evaluate what students have learned (evaluation), and the final step is to determine the effectiveness of the instruction (feedback for improvement next time). This systematic planning model takes context into consideration in two key ways: (1) by assessing entering behaviors, the model takes into consideration some characteristics of the student; and (2) by noting the interaction between instructional factors such as choice of strategy, use of groups, time, space, and materials, the model takes into consideration some aspects of the instructional context.

Analysis, Design, Development, Implementation, and Evaluation (ADDIE)

The ADDIE model (Branch and Dousay, 2015; Molenda, 2015) is a well-known generic design model of unknown provenance with widely varying descriptions. Molenda (2015) concludes that ADDIE is a colloquial term used to describe a systematic approach to instructional development or instructional systems development. The five underlying concepts of the ADDIE model can be traced to a model developed by Florida State University for the United States armed forces: the Interservice Procedures for Instructional Systems Development (IPISD) model:

- Analysis of the contexts and needs of the learner.
- Design of a set of specifications for an effective, efficient, and relevant learning environment.
- Development of all student and course management materials.
- Implementation of the planned instruction.
- Evaluation of the results of the design processes, both formative and summative. (Branch and Dousay, 2015; Molenda, 2015)

The ADDIE model is not specifically intended for use by classroom educators; however, as a generic instructional design model, it could be adopted by classroom educators. Branch and Dousay (2015) argue that the ADDIE model assumes that: (1) educational context includes things inside and outside the classroom such as human resources, technology resources, financial support, infrastructure, and curriculum planning; and (2) instructional design models work best when they are matched to a corresponding context.

Strengths and weaknesses of current classroom-oriented design models

This brief survey of classroom-oriented instructional design models indicates how diverse they are in terms of target audience, design focus, assumptions, and approach. See Table 2.1, "Summary comparison of key classroom-oriented experiential learning design models" for a summary comparison of each model, including a new model which we will introduce shortly. Three of the four classroom-oriented models (that is, Backward Design, PIE, and Systematic Planning) target primary, secondary, and tertiary school educators; the Integrated Design model targets higher education or tertiary school educators. The ADDIE model targets instructional designers generally, not classroom educators per se. All the classroom-oriented models focus on curriculum and/or course development as opposed to experiential exercise development. None of these models is specifically designed to help university educators design experiential exercises for the classroom, although arguably they could be adapted for that purpose.

Each model has its strengths. The Integrated Design model with its emphasis on alignment among learning objectives, assessment/feedback, and learning activities encourages the development of authentic, credible learning experiences. Fink's (2003a) development of a taxonomy of significant learning experiences encourages educators to expand their conceptions of desirable learning outcomes. The Backward Design model also focuses on the importance of learning objectives, suggesting that learning objectives should drive the design process. The PIE model is a general conceptual model; it is unique in its focus on students as active expert learners. Essentially the PIE model encourages students to become self-directed learners, using metacognitive techniques to increase their learning. The Systematic Planning model has a pragmatic focus; the authors understand and accept educator resistance to starting the planning process by defining the learning objectives. They acknowledge and accommodate content definition as the starting point of the planning process. They also accept that most classroom educators will not be developing instructional materials, they will be finding them. The ADDIE model is a generic term for instructional design. This is both its appeal and a limitation, since every description of it is different.

Each model also has its limitations, generally and specifically in relation to the development and implementation of experiential exercises for the classroom. Other than the Integrated Design model, none were developed specifically for university educators. None of these models was

Table 2.1   *Summary comparison of key classroom-oriented experiential learning design models*

Models	Overview	Design focus	Target audience	Unique contributions
Effective Experiential Exercise Design (this volume)	Assess the context (specific and general); define learning objectives; select or create assessments for learning objectives; select or create learning activities; ensure that learning objectives, assessments, and activities are tightly aligned; implement, adjust, and adapt "on the fly" while designing and implementing; reflect and revise after implementation.	Experiential exercises	University educators	An exercise is the design focus, not the course or syllabus. Focus on context. Useful whether adopting or designing an exercise. Checklist.
Integrated Design or Creating Significant Learning Experiences (Fink, 2003a)	Learning goals, teaching and learning activities, and feedback and assessment must be aligned to create significant learning experiences. Situational factors must be taken into consideration when selecting and aligning goals, activities, and assessments.	Course development	University educators	Taxonomy of significant learning. Integrated course design.
Backward Design or Understanding by Design (Wiggins and McTighe, 2005)	Identify desired results, determine acceptable evidence of desired results, then plan learning experiences and instruction to achieve the desired results and deliver the acceptable evidence.	Design of curriculum, assessment and instruction	Primary, secondary, and tertiary educators	Design Template. Focus on essential questions. Design Standards. WHERETO[a] rubric for organizing and assessing a learning plan. "Twin sins."[b]
Planning, Implementing, and Evaluating (PIE) (Newby et al., 2000)	Planning focuses on creating an outline, lesson plan, or blueprint to address a desired goal. Implementing focuses on how to enact the plan using various media and methods. Evaluation focuses on assessing learner performance and using the data to continuously improve teacher and student performance.	Integrating computers and other technology into the curriculum	Pre- and in-service primary and secondary school teachers	PIE checklist for lesson planning. Emphasis on what learners and teachers can do to affect learning.

Models	Overview	Design focus	Target audience	Unique contributions
Systematically Planning Instruction (Gerlach and Ely, 1980)	A ten-step process for clearly defining learning goals and developing methods for reaching those goals: (1) specify content; (2) specify objectives; (3) assess entering behaviors; (4) determine strategy; (5) organize groups; (6) allocate time; (7) allocate space; (8) select resources; (9) evaluate performance; (10) analyze feedback.	Unit, module, lesson, course	Primary, secondary, and tertiary classroom teachers, working alone as both designer and deliverer of instruction	Emphasis on systematic approach to planning. Recognizes content orientation of many educators. Emphasis on selecting rather than developing materials.
Analysis, Design, Development, Implementation, and Evaluation (ADDIE) (Branch and Dousay, 2015; Molenda, 2015)	An acronym referring to the major processes that comprise the generic instructional systems development/design (ISD) approach: analyze, design, develop, implement, and evaluate. Analyze the situation and learners to identify probable causes for a performance gap; design a set of specifications for an effective, efficient, and relevant learning environment; develop all student and course management materials; implement the planned instruction and evaluate the results.	Curriculum/ program, curriculum product or system	Instructional designers, curriculum designers	Generic instructional design process. Deliverables include: analysis summary, design brief, learning resources, implementation strategy, evaluation plan.

Notes:
[a] WHERETO = W = Where is the unit going? What is expected? Where are the students coming from?; H = Hook all students and Hold their interest; E = Equip students, help them Experience the key ideas and Explore the issues; R = Provide opportunities to Rethink and Revise understandings and work; E = Allow students to Evaluate their own work and its implications; T = Tailored to the different needs, interests, and abilities of learners; O = Organized to maximize initial and sustained engagement and learning.
[b] "Twin sins" = The use of content or coverage-based design and activity-based design.

designed to help university educators develop and implement classroom experiential exercises. And even though a key assumption underlying instructional design models is that the design model should be selected to fit the context, these models do not take a comprehensive approach to addressing context or provide guidance as to what to do in a given situation. See Table 2.2, "Summary of contextual factors considered by model" for a summary of the contextual factors explicitly or implicitly addressed by each model. The Integrated Design model explicitly identifies a fairly comprehensive list of situational factors that should be taken into consideration when designing a course. The other models do not. Even so, Fink provides little guidance as to the implications of the situational factors, or advice about what is appropriate and effective in specific contexts. All the models suggest that characteristics of the learners be taken into consideration; yet, none provide recommendations for how to do that.

The Effective Experiential Exercise Design Model and Checklist

Based on our review and critique of these classroom-oriented instructional design models, plus our research and experience, we developed an experiential exercise design model which addresses the shortcomings of these models. The Effective Experiential Exercise Design Model and Checklist are specifically designed for university educators who are responsible for creating and delivering their own instructional activities. This model may be used to select, adapt, or create an experiential exercise

Table 2.2   Summary of contextual factors considered by model

Contextual factors	Integrated Design (Fink, 2003a)	Backward Design (Wiggins and McTighe, 2005)	PIE (Newby et al., 2000)	Systematic Planning (Gerlach and Ely, 1980)	ADDIE (Branch and Dousay, 2015; Molenda, 2015)	Effective Experiential Exercise Design (this volume)
Specific context	✓				✓[a]	✓
• Learner characteristics	✓	✓[b]	✓	✓[c]	✓[d]	✓
• Educator characteristics	✓		✓			✓
• Instructional approaches	✓[e]		✓	✓		✓
• Subject characteristics	✓					✓
General context	✓[f]				✓[g]	✓

Notes:
[a] Audit available resources.
[b] Tailor to student needs, interests, and abilities.
[c] Assessment of entering behaviors; typically, a pre-test.
[d] Assess performance, analyze learners.
[e] Special pedagogical challenges.
[f] Expectations of external groups.
[g] Match design model to context.

for use in the classroom. See Figure 2.1, "The Effective Experiential Exercise Design Model" for an overview of the model and Table 2.3, "Effective Experiential Exercise Design Checklist" for a development checklist. This prescriptive procedural model is a guide or roadmap for university educators as they develop and implement effective experiential learning exercises. This is not a model for designing courses or curricula; it is a model for designing experiential exercises for use in the classroom. It incorporates the best thinking of classroom-oriented design models (for example, open systems theoretical foundations, the importance of learning objectives, the critical nature of alignment among learning objectives, assessment and learning activities, and so on) and adds an explicit consideration of both specific and general contextual factors. Further, the model is supported with evidence-based and experience-based best practices for different contexts. After establishing the theoretical and practical foundations for the Effective Experiential Exercise Model, the model is described in detail.

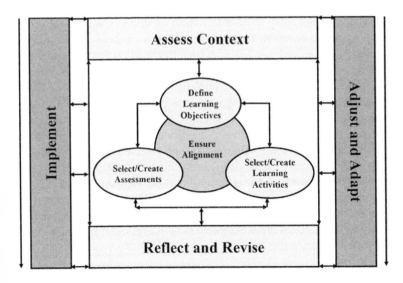

Figure 2.1   *The Effective Experiential Exercise Design Model*

Theoretical and practical foundations

The Effective Experiential Exercise Design Model, like many instructional design models, is based on open systems theory (Scott and Davis, 2007). Open systems theory argues that entities (for example, people, teams, organizations) are influenced by and influence the environment in which they exist. Our model posits that design and implementation of experiential exercises exists in a complex adaptive system. The educator responds and adapts to the context, which includes students. Students respond and adapt to the context, which includes other students, the educator, instructional methods, and assessment approaches. The context can be anything affecting a particular part of the system. The context is typically a multilevel, multidimensional phenomenon. For example, students, student teams, departmental policies/norms, school expectations, university mission/values/strategy/culture, professional norms, and societal influences may all have an impact on the educator (and the educator in turn may have an impact on these contextual factors); they are all part of the context in which an educator designs and implements an experiential exercise. The educator, other students, instructional methods, assessment approaches, departmental policies/norms, school expectations, university mission/values/strategy/culture, professional norms, and societal influences may all have an impact on students, and students may have an impact on them. This complex, adaptive system is the arena for teaching and learning and has important implications for the design and implementation of experiential exercises. Context matters, theoretically and practically. Designing and implementing an experiential exercise means that an educator is engaged in a complicated task with many changing, interdependent parts. There is no single approach or solution. Because there are many evolving, interacting variables, there are many possible solutions. Some solutions may be more efficient and effective than others in terms of achieving learning outcomes, grading burden, and preparation demands, but it is likely that there are many effective, efficient approaches. Given the complex, fluid nature of the situation (that is, a complex adaptive system), the development and implementation of experiential exercises are more likely to be successful if educators adopt the following practices:

- Be open and responsive to feedback. Because there are many, interacting, evolving variables, the educator, who is open to feedback – direct and indirect signals from key players and the environment during design and implementation – is more likely to design and implement an exercise that fits the situation and is effective.

- Maintain agility during design and implementation. If an educator is open to feedback during design and implementation and has the agility to respond to that feedback in real time while designing or implementing an exercise, then the educator is more likely to design and implement an exercise that fits the situation and is effective.

- Routinely reflect and revise. In a complex adaptive environment, change is inevitable, and the educator who routinely pauses to reflect on what is and is not working in an experiential exercise will be more likely to learn and grow as an educator and continuously improve their experiential exercises. Educators should reflect on what is working and not working in relation to the learner, the educator, instructional approaches, and content.

- Integrate evidence-based best practices. Using credible theory and empirical evidence related to the scholarship of teaching and learning to integrate evidence-based best practices into the design and implementation of experiential exercise is likely to increase the odds of effectiveness of the exercise.

The challenge of designing and implementing efficient and effective experiential exercises in the complex adaptive system of teaching and learning may seem overwhelming to novices and experts alike. We offer some tools to make the process more manageable. Figure 2.1 provides a graphic representation of the experiential exercise design and implementation process. No simple figure can capture the complexity, fluidity, and interactivity of an open system; however, this figure does capture the key elements that an educator needs to take into consideration during design and implementation. This figure also reinforces the idea that all elements of the system may have an impact on and be impacted by other elements in the system. This simplified visualization of the process is a touchstone which can help educators effectively navigate a complex and important challenge: creating effective experiential exercises.

Another tool to make complex situations more manageable is a checklist. See Table 2.3 for a checklist which can be used to guide and evaluate the exercise design and implementation process. The checklist may imply a linear or static process, which the exercise design and implementation process is not. This is merely a simplifying tool to facilitate a more systematic approach to a complex task and increase the odds of success. Other tools to support educators in the design process can be found later

Table 2.3　　　　Effective Experiential Exercise Design Checklist

_____Assess Context: Assess your instructional context (see Table 2.17)

    _____ The specific context of the learning situation

        _____ Learner characteristics

        _____ Educator characteristics

        _____ Instructional approaches

            _____ Instructional methods

            _____ Assessment approaches

        _____ Subject/content characteristics

    _____ The general context of the learning situation

_____ Define the learning objectives you want students to achieve

_____ Select or create learning activities which will provide experiences that students need to achieve the learning objectives (see Table 2.6)

_____ Select or create assessments which will help you and the students determine if the learning objectives have been achieved (see Table 2.7)

_____ Ensure Alignment: Compare your learning objectives, learning activities and assessments to ensure they are tightly aligned and appropriate given your context (see Table 2.10)

_____ Adjust and adapt your planned objectives, activities and assessments as needed based on your critical assessment of their alignment and fit with your context

_____ Implement your experiential exercise in the classroom (see Table 2.11)

_____ Adjust and adapt in real time as you implement, responding to the situation as it unfolds

_____ Reflect and Revise: Reflect on your experience and make appropriate revisions (see Table 2.12)

    _____ What worked? (learners, educators, instructional approaches, content)

    _____ What didn't work? (learners, educators, instructional approaches, content)

    _____ Changes you intend to make the next time you implement this activity

in this section and in the next two sections of the chapter, "Considering Context" and "What We Know About What Works," where information about contextual factors and their impact on experiential exercise teaching and learning may be found.

Model description including best practices and evidence for best practices

Assess context

Learning context comprises any variables in a situation which may have an impact on learning. In an open system where people interact with each other and their environment, the educator must understand the learning context to develop an exercise that is appropriate for and likely to be effective in that environment. Assess the context in which you will be teaching. Consider the specific context and the general context. The specific context includes characteristics of the learners, characteristics of the educator, instructional approaches (instructional methods and assessment approaches) and the nature of the subject. The general context includes the department, school, university, and societal/professional influences.

University websites and the Office of Institutional Research webpages are usually good sources of information about student demographics. Once the facts have been assembled about the context, evaluate the context. Is it a good fit with the exercise idea? Can the exercise idea be adapted to better fit the context? To be higher impact?

Consider an educator teaching a digital literacy course at a higher education institution serving primarily minorities, who wants to create an experiential exercise to help students connect the course subject to their lives. This educator might consider the following:

- Specific context:
  - Learner characteristics: students in the course are in their second year of university, most work part-time, about 50 percent are first-generation university students, this is a required course for them, while these students are digital natives – comfortable with technology and social media – most view the course topics (for example, creating an Excel spreadsheet, analyzing data to solve a problem) as boring and hard.
  - Educator characteristics: the educator is an adjunct, he (or she) is teaching two sections of this course, he concurrently teaches two sections of a similar course at another university, he does not have any formal training in the scholarship of teaching and learning, he has been teaching for more than ten years, he is tired of students tuning out and dreading his classes and is looking for a way to better engage his students; a colleague told him that if he implemented at least one experiential exercise in his course, it might make a difference.
  - Instructional approach:
    - Instructional methods: the course has multiple sections, all educators use the same textbook and assignments, there are six quizzes and six projects, the educator usually lectures, answers questions, and works examples in class.

- • Assessment approaches: the quizzes and projects are graded automatically in the learning management system/publisher learning environment providing minimal feedback.
- • Subject characteristics: this is an introductory required course, students are required to take two additional higher-level courses in this subject, the course has a high fail and withdrawal rate, students are generally not enthused about the subject.
- General context:
  - • Department: the department chair is new and trying to improve the quality of teaching in the department, she (or he) is under pressure to find ways to lower the fail/withdrawal rates without sacrificing academic rigor.
  - • School: the school is accredited by the Association to Advance Collegiate Schools of Business (AACSB) and focused on maintaining accreditation, the Dean is concerned that using so many adjuncts may jeopardize accreditation.
  - • University: the university has launched a major campaign to improve graduation rates.
  - • Societal/professional influences: the state legislature is clamoring for more accountability in higher education.

Having assessed the context, now what? In the next section of the chapter, "Considering Context," this example will be revisited to illustrate how to use evidence-based best practices and high-impact contextual factors to improve learning in experiential exercises. See Table 2.4, "Examples of contextual factors" for additional examples of contextual factors.

Define learning objectives
How do you know what success looks like, if you have not defined success? When designing an experiential exercise it is essential that the purpose of the exercise be specified. Defining the purpose of the exercise or the outcomes expected is vital if the educator wants to design an exercise to achieve those objectives. Define the learning objectives you want students to achieve after having completed the exercise. Refer to your course and/or module learning objectives to ensure that you select exercise learning objectives that are important to your course.

Tyler's model (Tyler and Hlebowitsh, 2013; Wraga, 2017) for learning objectives calls for the objective to include the kind of behavior to be developed and the content in which the behavior will operate (for example, construct a business model). According to Anderson et al.

Table 2.4   *Examples of contextual factors*

Contextual factors	Example A	Example B
The specific context of the learning situation	Teaching an undergraduate Business Policy course, a capstone course required of all business majors, with 35 students which meets on Monday nights from 6 to 8.50 pm.	Teaching a graduate strategy course, a capstone course required of all MBA students, with 30 students which meets on Thursday nights from 6.30 to 9.30 pm.
• Learner characteristics	Evening class students tend to be older, non-traditional students who work full-time, most have Grade Point Averages (GPAs) between 2.0 and 2.9, they are focused on passing the course and graduating; this course may be the last hurdle between them and graduation.	The evening MBA courses are taken by students who work full-time and are pursuing their MBA part-time. Most students are in their late twenties/early thirties and hold responsible middle-management jobs. They are generally committed to academic excellence and have high standards for themselves and others.
• Educator characteristics	The educator has extensive business and academic experience, this is her (or his) favorite course to teach, she complies with department guidelines regarding the textbook, simulations, and experiential approach to the course. She is very interested in continuously improving the effectiveness of her teaching. She thinks her job as an educator is to create opportunities for students to learn. She uses active learning methods in all her courses because she is convinced by the evidence that they are more effective.	The educator has just earned her (or his) doctoral degree, she has been engaged as an adjunct, this will be the first time she teaches this course. The department chair tells her what text has been ordered for the course. She is excited to be teaching and to have a chance to put into practice the things she has learned in her doctoral program about teaching and learning.

Contextual factors	Example A	Example B

• Instructional approaches:
  • Instructional methods
  • Assessment approaches
	She (or he) uses a variety of instructional methods (for example, cooperative learning, collaborative learning, team-based learning). In this course students work in teams to run an international business via a simulation, students take three cumulative tests, submit two reflection papers, and participate in weekly debriefs of their firm's performance. She uses formative and summative assessment. All grading is criterion-based.	She (or he) uses a team-based learning strategy. This is her second time implementing this instructional approach in a classroom. Students spend most of class time working in groups solving problems/challenges where they have to apply course content. She uses mini-lectures occasionally when students seem to be struggling with a concept. Students submit a mid-term and final exam paper which are graded using a rubric.

• Content characteristics	This is an advanced course, taken in students' final semester; the course is designed to teach strategy and integrate learning from many of their college courses.	This is an advanced course taken in students' last semester.
The general context of the learning situation • Department characteristics • School/university characteristics • Professional and societal influences	The course is being taught in the United States in the AACSB-accredited business school of a public historically black college and university where 75 percent of the students receive need based financial aid.	This course is being taught in the United States in the AACSB-accredited business school of a private Jesuit Catholic university where most students have a record of high academic achievement.

(2001), "in education, objectives indicate what we want students to learn; they are 'explicit formulations of the ways in which students are expected to be changed by the educative process' " (p. 3). The most commonly used form of a learning objective includes a verb and a noun; the verb describes the cognitive process to be demonstrated or mastered, and the noun describes the knowledge to be acquired or constructed, for example: differentiate (verb) among types of business models (noun) (Anderson et al., 2001). For higher-order learning objectives, such as analyze, evaluate, and create, adding domain-specific concepts, procedures, or metacognitive knowledge helps to clarify and refine the learning objective.

Shingles (2015) recommends that a learning objective be composed of three parts: (1) behavior; (2) criterion; and (3) conditions. The behavior describes what the learner will be able to do. The criterion describes the quality or level of performance that will be considered acceptable. And the conditions describe the conditions under which the student will perform the behavior (for example, critique a firm's business model (behavior), using the business model canvas, given publicly available information about the firm (conditions); see grading rubric for success criteria).

Nilson (2010) also recommends a three-part learning objective, which comprises: (1) a statement of measurable performance; (2) a statement of conditions for the performance; and (3) criteria and standards for assessing performance; for example, critique a firm's business model (1), using the business model canvas and publicly available information (2): accurately critiquing all nine parts of the firm's business model will be a high level of achievement, accurately critiquing less than five parts of the model will be an unacceptable level of achievement (3). Nilson notes that often only the first part is defined in the syllabus; however, the other two parts must be defined before accomplishment of the learning objective can be assessed.

Refer to Noyd's (2001) *Primer on Writing Effective Learning-Centered Course Goals* for more information about the characteristics of effective learning objectives (that is, they describe what students will learn and be able to do; are actionable, visible, and measurable; are clear and understandable to students and educators; have an appropriate level of generality; require high levels of thinking and learning; are developmentally appropriate; and lead to authentic/motivating tasks). Here are some examples of learning objectives:

- After completing this exercise you will be able to:
  - Evaluate (verb) a firm's financial strength (noun) in terms of profitability, liquidity and solvency based upon an analysis of its financial statements (domain-specific procedures).
  - Critique (verb) a firm's marketing plan (noun) using the 'solution, access, value, education' (SAVE) framework (domain-specific concept).
- By completing this exercise students should be able to:
  - Explain (verb) what it takes to succeed (noun) in this course.
  - Analyze (verb) an industry's attractiveness (noun) using the Porter's five forces framework (domain-specific concept).

- You will learn to identify (verb) and assess (verb) sources of financial information (noun) about firms.
- Students should learn to apply (verb) the design thinking process (domain-specific process) to solve (verb) an innovation challenge (noun) (for example, identifying an opportunity, developing a product or service to meet a need, and so on).

When creating learning objectives for an experiential exercise, consider referring to at least one of these three sources of examples: Bloom's Taxonomy, Fink's Taxonomy of Significant Learning Experiences, or Biggs and Collis's Structure of Observed Learning Outcomes (SOLO) Taxonomy (Anderson et al., 2001; Biggs and Collis, 1982; Biggs and Tang, 2011; Fink, 2003a). It is easier to create clear and important learning objectives when you have examples to model.

Bloom's updated taxonomy is widely known and used; it has been criticized for being hard to use, incomplete, not organized appropriately, and hierarchical (Anderson et al., 2001; Krathwohl, 2002). In the 2001 update of the taxonomy by Anderson et al., the taxonomy was revised to address these issues. Fink's taxonomy was developed in response to calls for learning objectives which include "soft" skills, affective and metacognitive dimensions of learning (Fink, 2003a). Biggs and Collis's taxonomy was developed to capture the complexity of learning and to better assess the quality of learning (Biggs and Tang, 2011). See Table 2.5, "Comparison of key learning outcome taxonomies," for a comparison of these three taxonomies of learning outcomes. See recommended resources related to learning objectives in the "Readings/Resources" section at the end of Chapter 3.

Select/create learning activities
Learning or instructional activities are the means by which the learning objectives are achieved. Select or create learning activities which will provide students with the experiences they need to achieve the learning objectives. Examples of learning activities include: reading a chapter in the text, watching a video, solving a problem, working in a small group to solve a problem, analyzing a case, playing a role, observing peers as they solve a problem or apply a concept, debating an issue, creating a concept map, debriefing on an experience, reflecting on an experience, and so on.

Nilson (2010) and Wiggins and McTighe (2005) strongly recommend that the ends (the learning objectives) guide the selection of the means (learning activities): learning activities should be selected because they

Table 2.5 Comparison of key learning outcome taxonomies

Taxonomy	Bloom's	Fink's	Biggs and Collis's SOLO
Levels	Cognitive dimensions: • Remember (e.g., recognize, recall) • Understand (e.g., interpret, exemplify, classify, summarize, infer, compare, explain) • Apply (e.g., execute, implement) • Analyze (e.g., differentiate, organize, attribute) • Evaluate (e.g., check, critique) • Create (e.g., generate, plan, produce)	Significant learning: • Foundational knowledge (e.g., remember, understand, identify, list) • Apply (e.g., use, critique, manage, solve, assess, judge, imagine, analyze, calculate, create, coordinate, solve problems) • Integrate (e.g., connect, identify the interaction between …, identify the similarities between …, relate, compare, integrate) • Human dimension (e.g., come to see themselves as …, interact with others regarding …, understand others in terms of …, decide to become …) • Caring (e.g., get excited about …, be ready to …, be more interested in …, value …) • Learning how to learn (e.g., create a plan for future learning about …, identify important sources of information about …, formulate useful questions about …)	Understanding: • Prestructural (e.g., misses the point) • Unistructural (e.g., a single point: identify, name, follow simple procedure) • Multistructural (e.g., multiple unrelated points, combine, describe, enumerate, perform serial skills, list) • Relational (e.g., logically related or integrated points, analyze, apply, argue, compare/contrast, criticize, explain causes, relate, justify) • Extended abstract (abstract and deep understanding through unexpected extension, create, formulate, generate, hypothesize, reflect, theorize)
Strengths	Well known, widely used, has stood the test of time (originally introduced in 1956)	Developed in response to social, political, and economic demands for learning objectives not easily derived from Bloom's taxonomy: learning how to learn, leadership and interpersonal skills, ethics, communication skills, character, tolerance and ability to adapt to change	Developed to describe different levels of complexity in learning outcomes and to assess the quality of learning (i.e., deep versus surface) Useful description of stages in the growth of thinking

Experiential exercises in the classroom

Taxonomy	Bloom's	Fink's	Biggs and Collis's SOLO
Criticisms	The original taxonomy claimed a cumulative hierarchical nature of learning objectives, implying that mastery of a more complex behavior/cognitive process required mastery of a less complex behavior/cognitive process; this claim has not been supported empirically The order of the cognitive dimensions has been debated Many alternative taxonomies have been developed to respond to perceived weaknesses of this taxonomy: • Lacking important dimensions (knowledge as a separate dimension, affective dimensions) • Hard to use (use verbs instead of nouns to title categories)	Newer, less well-known, introduced in 2003 Some question if the affective and metacognitive objectives are actionable, visible and measurable	Newer, less well-known in the United States (more well-known in Australia and Europe), introduced in 1983 Initial stage is criticized as not being outcome oriented, it is by definition the failure to achieve a learning outcome

Sources: Anderson et al. (2001), Fink (2003a), Biggs and Collis (1982), and Biggs and Tang (2011).

provide students with the experiences they need to learn, practice, and master the learning objectives. See pages 107–111 of Nilson's (2010) *Teaching at its Best* for lists of learning activities useful for accomplishing different types of learning outcomes.

Wick et al. (2006) recommend using "if" (learning objective), "then" (learning activities) statements to select learning activities. For example, if the educator wants students to be able to critique a firm's business model using the business model canvas (learning objective), then they need to do the following activities: learn what a business model is, learn what a business model canvas is, learn what the criteria for evaluating a business model are and how to apply them, practice using the criteria to evaluate a firm's business model, get feedback on their analysis, practice critiquing a firm's business model again, get feedback, and practice critiquing again.

Several experts provide guidance on the types of learning activities that should be included in an experiential exercise. Salas et al. (2012) recommend that learning experiences include getting information, exposure to good and bad examples or demonstrations, having an opportunity to practice, and getting meaningful diagnostic feedback. Ambrose et al. (2010) argue that for students to master a concept or skill they must have an opportunity to acquire component concepts/skills, practice integrating them, and learn when and how to apply what was learned. Fink (2003a) argues that active learning involves: (1) getting information and ideas; (2) experiencing something, by either doing it or observing it; and (3) reflecting on what one is learning and how one is learning.

When creating an experiential exercise, consider including individual, group/team, and class activities. Each type of activity contributes something different to the learning experience (Barkley, 2010; Johnson and Johnson, 2009; Johnson and Johnson, 1999; Nilson, 2010). Individual activities help students focus, think, and be accountable. Group/team activities provide an opportunity for peer-to-peer learning and higher engagement (for example, in group/team discussions, wait time is shorter than in class discussions, so each student has more "airtime"). Whole-class activities provide an opportunity to summarize, share learning and share experiences with the entire class. See Table 2.6, "Worksheet – selecting/creating learning activities" for a worksheet which can be used to select/create learning activities.

If you are looking for existing experiential exercises which you can adopt or adapt, sources to consider include colleagues, conferences, journals, and books. Examples and sources for experiential exercises by discipline may be found at the end of Chapter 3 and in the Resources for Experiential Exercises and Annotated Bibliography of this book. If you intend to design your own experiential exercise, perhaps by combining several learning activities, the resources just mentioned may be useful sources of inspiration.

Select/create assessments

Assessments play two important roles in learning: (1) assessments provide feedback to the educator and students so that they can modify their approaches to teaching and learning, respectively; and (2) assessments help educators and students know whether the learning objectives have been achieved. Select or create assessments that help the educator and students understand how things are going and help the educator understand how the exercise is working.

Formative assessment, feedback (individual, peer, and class), and classroom assessment techniques (for example, minute papers, one-sentence summaries, problem-recognition tasks, directed paraphrasing, chain notes, feedback requests, memory matrices, and concept maps) may be used to help educators and students know whether their approaches are working. Timely, actionable feedback is vital so that both the educator and students have time to adjust their approaches and improve performance. Summative assessments such as quizzes, or presentations made for exhibitions and gallery walks, or reflection papers/discussion boards, may be used to help educators and students know whether the learning objectives have been achieved.

Assessment can take many forms. Assessments may be conducted by individual students (self-assessment), by peers, by teams, by the class, or by the educator. The educator may give feedback to individuals, to groups, or to the whole class. Assessments may be graded or ungraded. Assessments may be used to monitor student learning and provide feedback to the educator and students (formative: for example, feedback on a minute paper or a concept map) or to evaluate student learning at the end of an instructional unit or exercise (summative: for example, a presentation, a debate performance, a reflection paper). Assessments may also be used to assess the experiential exercise itself.

Here are some examples of assessments that one might use in an experiential exercise:

- Pre-exercise:

Table 2.6   *Worksheet – selecting/creating learning activities*

Learning Objectives (write here):

Select/create learning activities (record in table):

What learning activities will help students achieve the learning objectives?

Consider who will do each activity, how each activity will be done, and what each activity accomplishes.

Fill out the worksheet, placing planned learning activities in the appropriate box in the matrix. Determine whether you have all the key components of an effective active learning exercise covered. If not, consider adding activities. Note: Not every box needs to be filled.

Tips:

- People learn best when they are actively engaged in an activity, a life experience; they can't focus for long in a passive state (Nilson, 2010, p. 4).

- People learn best when they receive new material multiple times, in different ways. Use multiple modalities: give students the opportunity to read, hear, talk, write, see, draw, think, act, and feel (Nilson, 2010, p. 5).

	Getting information and ideas	Experiencing doing/observing	Reflecting
Individual			
Team			
Class			

- • Use a quiz before an experiential exercise to assess mastery of the content before application/analysis/evaluation/creation with the content during the exercise.
  - • Use an established scale to assess students' attitudes or perceptions about a relevant topic.
- • During implementation:
  - • Use peer review and feedback during an experiential exercise to give students real-time feedback on their work.
  - • Use classroom assessment techniques, such as a minute paper on lessons learned or a "muddiest points" paper, during or after the exercise, to assess learning and provide feedback.
  - • Use team or class debriefs to reflect on what was learned and how it was learned during the exercise.
- • Post-exercise:
  - • Use a reflection paper assignment or discussion assignment after the exercise to give students an opportunity to reflect on what they learned from the exercise and how they learned it.
  - • Use the actual analysis, problem-solving, or other work product produced during the exercise to assess learning and provide feedback.
  - • Use an established scale to assess students' attitudes or perceptions about a relevant topic; look for changes compared to the pre-exercise assessment.

When developing and implementing a new experiential exercise or adopting/adapting an existing exercise, consider assessing the exercise itself in addition to student learning. The educator may ask for formal or informal feedback from students. An informal approach to student feedback could be having students draw a line horizontally across a blank piece of paper and then writing likes above the line and dislikes below the line. This anonymous feedback is then submitted to the educator for review and consideration. Another informal approach to exercise assessment is to use the Keep–Start–Stop rubric, where students provide feedback on what they think should be kept, added, and/or eliminated from the exercise. A more formal approach to getting feedback on the exercise could be an anonymous online survey. Another approach to assessing a new exercise is to appraise the impact on student learning or changes in students' cognitive, emotional, or behavioral responses via pre–post assessments using standardized scales or customized questions.

Refer to Table 2.7, "Worksheet – select/create assessments" for a worksheet which can be used to define the purpose of your assessment (assess learning and/or assess the exercise), define the target and/or user of the assessment (for example, students, teams, educator), and select assessment approaches. Examples of assessment approaches are also provided in this worksheet. See Tables 2.8, "Exercise assessment – example 1" and Table 2.9, "Exercise assessment – example 2" for examples of exercise assessments.

A learning environment which provides feedback on progress, and where assessment emphasizes understanding, not just memorizing, and is progressive and spaced over time and involves feedback beyond grades, is associated with learning, student satisfaction, and general skill development (Lizzio et al., 2002; Ramsden, 2003). Formative evaluation and criterion-referenced grading are also associated with academic achievement (Hattie, 2009; Lizzio et al., 2002). Therefore, experiential exercises which incorporate formative feedback, an emphasis on deep understanding, and criterion-referenced grading are more likely to be effective.

Whatever the assessment approach, the process and criteria must be explicit and transparent for students (Rust, 2002). Students should be actively engaged in understanding the assessment process and criteria just as they are actively engaged in understanding the content. Having all students use the assessment criteria to assess an example student deliverable, a peer's deliverable, or their own work, will encourage engagement with the assessment process and improve learning directly and indirectly (Rust, 2002).

Several experts provide assessment best practice recommendations. Refer to Nilson's (2010), *Teaching at Its Best*, Ambrose et al.'s (2010) *How Learning Works*, Fink's (2003a) *Creating Significant Learning Experiences*, or Brown et al.'s (2014), *Make it Stick*, for evidence-based best practices for assessment. Walvoord and Anderson's (2010) *Effective Grading* provides a detailed discussion of grading and how to grade in higher education courses. See Angelo and Cross's (1993) *Classroom Assessment Techniques: A Handbook for College Teachers* for examples and detailed explanations of classroom assessment techniques which can be built into experiential exercises or combined to create experiential exercises.

Ensure alignment
Alignment is the degree of correspondence among the objectives, learning activities, and assessment. Lack of alignment can result in:

Table 2.7   *Worksheet – select/create assessments*

1. Define purpose of assessment	2. Define target and/or user for assessment	3. Determine/select assessment approach(es)
Circle all that apply below.	Circle all that apply below. Define target for each purpose, drawing from the list below.	For each purpose, define assessment(s) drawing from the list below.

	• Student
	  • From self
	  • From peers
	  • From group/team
	  • From class
	  • From educator
	• Group/team
	  • From peers
	  • From class
	  • From educator
	• Class
	  • From educator
	• Educator
	  • From self
	  • From peers
	  • From students, individually
	  • From student groups/teams
		Assess learning:
		• Pre–post assessments of knowledge (Before, After)
		• Quizzes/tests (After)
		• Feedback on work (After)
		• Feedback on work using a rubric or checklist (After)
		• In-class assessments (During)
		• Assignments (Before, During, After)
		• Debriefs (During, After)
		• Reflections (After)
		Assess Exercise:
		• Formal or informal requests for feedback on exercise (After)
		• Pre–post assessments of cognitive, emotional, or behavioral changes (using standardized scales or custom surveys) (Before, After)

Assess learning		
Assess exercise		

Note: When is feedback received? Before exercise = (Before); During exercise = (During); After exercise = (After).

Table 2.8   *Exercise assessment – example 1*

Exercise feedback					
Please answer the following questions by circling the number that best captures your feelings about this experiential exercise.					
		Strongly disagree			Strongly agree
1.	The activity was well planned and organized.	1	2	3	4	5
2.	The facilitator made good use of time.	1	2	3	4	5
3.	I learned something useful.	1	2	3	4	5
4.	I had fun.	1	2	3	4	5
5.	The activity was better than I expected.	1	2	3	4	5
6.	I would recommend this experience to a friend.	1	2	3	4	5
7.	What did you like best about this experience?					
8.	What would you suggest to make this a better experience?					

Table 2.9   *Exercise assessment – example 2*

Help to improve this exercise
Please take a few minutes to provide feedback on this exercise. Your feedback will help to improve the exercise. This is an anonymous survey with just a few brief questions. Your feedback is valued, please share it. Thank you.
Using a scale from 0 to 10, where 0 means not at all likely and 10 means extremely likely, how likely is it that you would recommend this experiential exercise experience to a friend or colleague?
Not at all likely   Extremely likely
0   1   2   3   4   5   6   7   8   9   10
What, if anything, did you like about the exercise?
What, if anything, did you dislike about the exercise?
Please share any suggestions for making the exercise better.

Note: This is an adaptation of a satisfaction measure widely used in organizations. See Reichheld's (2003) *Harvard Business Review* article, "The one number you need to grow," for a full discussion of the measure and how to calculate and interpret it.

(1) instruction not helping students accomplish the learning objectives; (2) assessments not measuring achievement of the learning objectives; (3) lack of assurance of learning data to demonstrate compliance with accreditation standards; and (4) student frustration, disengagement, and adoption of surface-level approaches to learning (Anderson et al., 2001; Biggs and Tang, 2011; Nilson, 2010). Integrated design (Fink, 2003a), outcomes-centered design (Nilson, 2010), backward design/understand-

ing by design (Wiggins and McTighe, 2005), and constructive alignment (Biggs and Tang, 2011) all argue that effective, engaging learning environments must have alignment among the learning objectives, learning activities, and assessments.

Biggs and Tang (2011) use the term "constructive alignment" to describe the process or a teaching system in which the learning objectives, learning activities, and assessments are aligned. They recommend that an educator describe the intended learning outcome in the form of a verb (the learning activity), its object (the content), and specify the context and a standard that students are to attain. Then the educator should create a learning environment using learning activities that address the verb (learning activity) and are likely to bring about the intended learning outcome. Finally, the assessment should also contain the verb (learning activity) and should be used to determine whether the learning outcome has been achieved. Essentially, they argue that if the learning objective is to apply a concept, the learning activities should involve applying the concept, and the assessment activities should evaluate application of the concept.

Check for alignment among your learning objectives, learning activities, and assessments. If the learning objective is about creating, the learning activities must give students opportunities to practice creating, and the assessment must assess creating skills. Here is an aligned example:

- If the learning objective is: identify your own leadership strengths; and
- the learning activities include: completing multiple leadership self-assessments and reflecting on the meaning of those assessments; and
- the assessments include: grading the reflections and providing feedback on them; then:
- alignment is strong: the learning objective, learning activities, and assessment all consistently focus on identifying students' leadership skills.

Here is a non-aligned example:

- If the learning objective is: identify your own leadership strengths; and
- the learning activities include: reading a chapter about leadership skills; and

- the assessments include: taking a quiz which measures recall of the chapter content; then:
- alignment is weak: the learning objective focuses on identifying students' leadership skills, but the learning activity and assessment focus on being able to recall the leadership concepts in the chapter; no connection has been made between the learning objective and the activities and assessment.

Use Table 2.10, "Worksheet – ensure alignment" to critically analyze your plans and ensure that the objectives, learning activities, and assessments logically fit together. Also, assess impact. Given the environment in which the exercise will be executed, do the objectives, activities, and assessments make sense? Do they fit? Have high-impact contextual factors been incorporated in the learning activities and assessments?

The next two sections of this chapter ("Considering Context" and "What We Know About What Works") will explore high-impact contextual factors and encourage educators to use evidence-based best practices to accomplish learning objectives. If inconsistencies, a lack of alignment, or lack of fit are discovered among the learning objectives, activities, and assessments, now is the time to adjust plans. If no high-impact factors have been incorporated in the exercise, consider adding at least one. Refine and revise your objectives, activities, and assessments as needed to improve their alignment and their impact. Refer to Chapter 3 for examples which illustrate how this is done.

Implement

Implementation is where the educator and students interact in a classroom. To prepare to implement an experiential exercise, create a lesson plan or plan of action which includes the activities in sequence, estimated timing of each activity, and any notes to guide implementation (for example, questions to ask, summary of key learning points, special instructions for students, and so on). See Table 2.11, "Worksheet – exercise sequence and timing." Once the lesson plan is developed, create any slides, handouts, or other learning aids needed. Identify/source any additional resources needed, such as videos or readings.

The educator may ask students to complete learning activities in advance to prepare for an exercise (for example, read a chapter, complete a pre-assessment, and so on). As in any other higher education learning context, some students will be prepared for the exercise and some will not, for a variety of reasons. As students prepare for and participate in

Table 2.10   Worksheet – ensure alignment

Record learning objectives for the exercise in the first column of the table

Place learning activities and assessments in the appropriate columns next to the learning objective
which they help to achieve. Activities and assessments may be used to accomplish more than one
learning objective. And activities may also be used as assessments.

Assess:

• Does each learning objective have a learning activity?

• Does each learning objective, or at least the most important objective, have an assessment?

• Do the verbs match across a row? That is, are the learning activities and assessments designed to
  do or measure the same thing as the learning objective?

• Have you incorporated high-impact approaches to learning activities and assessment?

If you identified any gaps or inconsistencies, make adjustments to your selections.

Learning objectives (record below)	Learning activities (record below)	Assessments (record below)

an experiential exercise they respond to cues from the educator and cues
from their context or environment. As you implement your experiential
exercise in the classroom, be sure that you have taken into consideration
the contextual factors likely to have an impact on student approaches to
learning (for example, assessment, feedback, expectations, and so on).
For more guidance on evidence-based best practices for doing this, see
the next two sections of this chapter, "Considering Context" and "What
We Know About What Works."

Table 2.11   Worksheet – exercise sequence and timing

Record activities in the order in which they will be completed in the "Sequence of activities" column.

Estimate the time required to complete each activity; remember to include the time for giving instructions, the time for students to get organized and get to work, and the time for the activity itself; record time estimate in the same row as the activity.

Sequence of activities	Timing

Adjust and adapt

Despite the best-laid plans, when in a classroom with students unexpected opportunities and challenges arise. Experiential exercises may evoke strong and unexpected emotional responses in students and educators (Finch et al., 2015; Gilmore and Anderson, 2012; Kisfalvi and Oliver, 2015; Lund Dean and Forray, 2015; Taylor, 2018). Negative emotions in the form of frustration, humiliation, and distress may interfere with learning (Kolb and Kolb, 2009b; Tyson et al., 2009). Some students may fear failure when actively experimenting with phenomena and responding to new situations in the classroom. Students may experience anxiety, feel threatened, or risk rejection if they express minority or unpopular views (Wright et al., 2019). Educators may be unsure how to respond constructively when students express ideas counter to inclusiveness (Kirk and Durant, 2010). Activities may take longer than expected. Students may not interpret instructions as expected. Students may not react as expected. Discussions may take unexpected directions. Students may be more engaged or less engaged than expected. A few students may react differently than most of the students (for example, be more engaged, less engaged, more disruptive, take longer to do tasks, take less time to do tasks, and so on).

Strive to be aware of and open to those opportunities and challenges which may require change. Educators may need to adjust their thoughts, actions, and emotions to successfully respond to the unexpected while facilitating an exercise. Try to anticipate common types of uncertainty and think about how you might respond if they occur (that is, create contingency plans). This mental preparation will increase confidence and the ability to respond effectively when you must make on-the-spot decisions about how to proceed, or as Schön (1983) would characterize it, reflect-in-action.

Reflection-in-action (Schön, 1983) – that is, reflecting on a situation while changes can still be made to affect the outcome, rather than waiting until after the situation to reflect on how things could have been done differently – allows educators to be responsive to students and to the learning context. Adjusting, thinking about the situation differently while in the situation, allows you to consider different options (reframe), take unplanned actions, better navigate the situation, and minimize negative emotions such as anxiety or frustration. Educators who can adjust and adapt are more likely to enjoy their work, and their students are more likely to learn (Collie et al., 2018).

One of the most common types of adjustments needed during experiential exercises is adjustments in timing. Each class, each group of people working together, has its own pace, communication styles, norms, experiences, and interests, so the timing or pacing of activities can vary by class. The educator must decide whether to push the class to meet the planned timing, modify the exercise on the spot, or be flexible and accommodate the rhythm of the class. When things are not going as planned during an exercise, the choices are to:

- Maintain the timing and activities.
- Modify the timing but keep all the activities.
- Maintain the timing but modify the activities.
- Modify the timing and the activities.

If a class is taking longer than expected to complete activities, maintaining timing and activities will make students feel rushed, and they may not achieve the learning objectives. If the class is taking less time than expected to complete activities, maintaining the timing and activities may result in students being bored and losing focus. If the timing is modified but all the activities are kept, the learning objectives may be achieved, but the overall course plan may be negatively affected. If timing is maintained but the activities are modified (drop or add an activity), the learning objectives may be achieved or may be at risk, depending upon the change. If the timing and the activities are modified, the learning objectives may or may not be achieved and the changes may or may not have an impact on the overall course plan. The educator must decide what is best, in the moment, using expertise and knowledge of the class and the learning objectives.

Another type of adjustment or adaptation often needed when implementing an exercise is to determine how long and how far to let discussions go. Discussions can be most effectively facilitated when the facilitator has a clear understanding of the learning objectives for the discussion and key questions are pre-planned to start and guide the discussion.

For all types of changes, keep in mind the learning objectives of the exercise and the contextual factors, then decide when and how to adjust or adapt plans. Use the processes and evidence-based best practices discussed later in this chapter, particularly the high-impact micro contextual factors such as educator beliefs and instructional approaches (for example, building caring and respectful relationships with students, creating clear expectations for learning, establishing relevance, and providing some autonomy and choice) to ensure that exercises are conducted in a manner that builds trust and recognizes and protects the rights of students. Maintaining perspective will help educators to be more effective; if something does not go as planned and it is seen as a minor hurdle as opposed to the end of the world, one is more likely to maintain effectiveness as a facilitator.

Focus on the things you have control over or can influence. Being familiar with best practices for teaching and learning and the effects of contextual factors, provides the facilitator with insights and a tool kit to use when adjusting and adapting to the situation. If something unexpected, beyond your control, occurs (for example, the fire alarm goes off in the middle of an exercise, students get into a fight, or the electricity goes off) stop the activity, regroup, refocus, and tackle the learning objective another day.

Reflect and revise

As soon after implementation as possible, take time to reflect on the experience: reflection-on-action (Schön, 1983). Think about what worked, what did not work, and make notes about what you want to do differently next time or how you want to refine or revise the exercise. Take five to ten minutes immediately after class to sit quietly and reflect on the experience and make notes about things to change. Focus on what you can control and what you can do differently. If you attribute problems or failures to student shortcomings, then you should consider how you can change your approach to elicit a different response from students. Reflection-on-action will be richly rewarded with continuously improving exercises. Waiting until the next time you intend to use the exercise, or until the end of the semester, to reflect on the activity may result in loss of the rich detail and insights of the moment. See Table 2.12, "Worksheet – reflect and revise" for a reflection guide.

In addition to reflection immediately after facilitation of an experiential exercise, there are a number of other ways to reflect on and revise an exercise:

- During implementation: record observations, timing, reactions, ideas for improvement.
- After implementation:
  - Reflect on your implementation experience, immediately after facilitating it (see Table 2.12).
  - Review, analyze and act on student feedback on the exercise (informal or formal), if requested.
  - Review, analyze, and act on any pre–post assessments.
  - Review, analyze, and act on any post assignments (for example, tests, papers, reflections).

• Immediately before next implementation: review all prior reflections and analyses and decide how you will revise the exercise for implementation this time.

It can be very efficient to capture changes to your experiential exercise, implementation plan, and learning aids as you complete your reflections. This ensures that you do not forget or have to recreate your learning and analysis.

Educators who consistently engage in reflection on their teaching and learning approaches are more likely to develop expertise and improve the effectiveness of their teaching practice (Dunn and Shriner, 1999; Porter, 2017). Hattie (2012) argues that critical reflection, considering evidence about teaching, is essential to achieve excellence in teaching. He urges educators to use all available feedback evidence about the success or failure of their instructional approaches to discuss, evaluate, and improve their teaching.

According to Ambrose et al. (2010), to become a self-directed learner, educators must reflect on their practice and adjust if necessary. Typically, reflection involves thinking about a performance episode (for example, facilitating an experiential exercise) and assessing what went well, what did not go so well and needs to be changed, what was learned from the experience, what will be done differently the next time, and plans for change in the future.

Kane (2017) and others (Dunn and Shriner, 1999; Ericsson, 2008; Ericsson et al., 1993) argue that deliberate practice is an effective approach to reflection and improving professional effectiveness. They contend that the educator should actively strive to improve, work towards specific goals, focus intently on practice activities, and get and respond to high-quality feedback. According to Ericsson et al. (1993), "deliberate practice is a highly-structured activity, the explicit goal of which is to improve performance. Specific tasks are invented to overcome weaknesses and performance is carefully monitored to provide cues for ways to improve it further" (p. 368).

Learning is a complex activity; students interact with the educator, each other, and the environment, so if an experiential exercise does not go as well as expected the first time, try it again. With a different group of students, given a different place, time, and environment, it may go differently. Do not give up too soon. Be open to reflecting and revising and trying it again.

Table 2.12   Worksheet – reflect and revise

Reflection questions	Responses
Did I implement the exercise as planned? If not, why? How did I modify the plan? Timing? Activities? Instructions?	
Did I get the outcomes and reactions expected? Note any surprises. What evidence do I have that the learning objectives were achieved (note observations, student comments/reactions, etc.)	
What worked well? Record things I want to be sure to do the same next time.	
What didn't work well? What might I change to make it work better next time? How will I make these changes? Note changes to be made next time.	
Is there anything I can do to be a more effective facilitator of this exercise next time?	
Is there anything I should do to encourage a more effective learning experience for students next time?	

Tools: prescriptive model and checklist

This discussion of the experiential exercise design and implementation process and the checklist may give the impression that creating effective experiential exercises is a linear process. As noted before, this is not true. Creating effective experiential exercises is an iterative process, a complex process embedded in a complex system with many moving parts. An exercise is typically embedded in a course, which is embedded in a curriculum, which is embedded in an organization, which is embedded in an environment, all of which may have personal, institutional, political, economic, social, cultural, technical, and other forces at play. As noted, Figure 2.1 attempts to capture the interactive, iterative nature of experiential exercise design. The figure (2.1) and checklist (see Table 2.3) provide educators with a touchstone and roadmap through the design process; they are tools to simplify a complex process and empower educators to design effective exercises.

CONSIDERING CONTEXT

Learning context comprises any variables in a situation which may have an impact on learning. As discussed in the "Model description including best practices and evidence for best practices" section (see "Assess context"), understanding contextual factors, especially specific contextual factors, is essential to develop and implement effective experiential exercises.

Definitions of Learning Context

Generally, context is the "situation in which something exists and which can help explain it" (*Cambridge Dictionary*, 2019). Context in higher education may be referred to as the setting, environment, situational factors, culture, or climate in which learning takes place. Context in higher education may include the overlapping and interdependent spheres of the academic, learning, classroom, instructional, or social environment (for example, instructional context, classroom setting, learning environment, and so on). Classroom context has been described as the "beliefs, goals, values, perceptions, behaviors, classroom management, social relations, physical space and social-emotional and evaluative climates that contribute to student understanding of the classroom" (Turner and Meyer, 2000, p. 70). Instructional context has been described as "the influences of the teacher, students, content area and instructional activities on learning, teaching and motivation" (Turner and Meyer, 2000, p. 70). According to Biggs and Tang (2011), the United States approach to learning tends to focus on the person, and within the person factors such as intelligence, learning styles, and motivations, while the European approach to learning tends to focus on contextual factors, with teaching being one of the most important contextual factors (p. 21). These various contexts are simultaneous, fluid, often defined implicitly rather than explicitly, and usually defined differently depending on the field. In this book, experiential learning context is defined as the variables in a situation which may have an impact on learning. The experiential learning context includes:

- The specific context:
  - Learner characteristics (beliefs, behaviors, experience).
  - Educator characteristics (beliefs, behaviors, experience, expertise).
  - Instructional approaches:
    - Instructional methods.
    - Assessment approaches.
  - Subject/content characteristics.
- The general context:
  - Departmental characteristics.
  - School/university characteristics.
  - Professional and societal influences.

Theoretical Foundations of Learning Context

Understanding context is essential for a holistic and integrative approach to understanding complex social phenomena such as learning (Egri, 2013; Whetten, 2009). What works in teaching and learning is dependent upon the context (Brophy and Good, 1984). Piaget's theory of constructivism argues that people produce knowledge and form meaning based on their experiences (Wadsworth, 1996). According to Piaget, interactions between the learner and the environment are an essential part of learning, resulting in either assimilation or accommodation: in assimilation, learners respond to the environment by incorporating new experiences into old experiences; in accommodation, learners respond to the environment by modifying or adapting old experiences to fit new experiences. Lewin (1997) also highlighted the importance of people's perceptions of the environment or situation and its effects on people's behaviors.

Bronfenbrenner's (1977) ecological theory of human development posits that there is ongoing interaction and accommodation between an individual and the environment in which they exist. This model suggests that there are four levels of interactions nested or embedded within the system: microsystems, mesosystems, exosystems, and macrosystems. Microsystems are the complex relationships between a person and the environment, where the environment is the immediate context or setting in which the person exists; the setting or context is defined by place, time, physical features, activities, participants, and roles. For example, the complex relationships between a university student and their environment is a microsystem. The environment in which the student is immediately situated during school would be defined by place, time, physical features, activities, participants, and roles (for example, classroom in new business school building: well-lit, clean; Monday afternoon in September; studying accounting; experienced educator; first-generation, minority student/learner).

Mesosystems are interacting collections or systems of microsystems, or the interrelations between the major settings in which an individual is embedded. Settings in which a university student might be embedded include family, social and professional organizations, work, and church/temple/mosque.

Exosystems are other formal and informal social structures related to the mesosystem which an individual might not be part of, but which have an impact on what goes on in settings. These include major societal institutions such as mass media, trade, government, and informal social networks. In a university environment, education policies and accreditation practices are examples of social structure which may affect university student experiences even though students are not part of those structures.

Macrosystems are overarching institutional patterns of culture and subculture, such as economic, social, educational, legal, and political systems which result in, create, or influence micro-, meso- and exo-systems. Macrosystems provide meaning, structure, and information to settings. Economic, social, and political systems are examples of systems which may have an impact on university students (for example, economic systems may impact ability to pay for schooling; social and political systems may create norms or pressures around the desirability of participating in higher education).

The essential properties of the ecological model are: (1) settings are complex social systems; (2) impacts or effects are reciprocal (for example, A may affect B, and B may affect A; or the educator may affect the student, and the student may affect the educator); (3) impacts or effects may be direct or indirect (for example, instructional methods may directly or indirectly influence academic achievement); and (4) impacts or effects may be among settings and across levels.

Important implications for teaching and learning are: (1) learning outcomes are impacted by perceived context; (2) learning outcomes may be directly or indirectly affected by the learning context; and (3) contextual factors may influence or be influenced by people involved in a learning situation. Thus, when developing and implementing experiential exercises, an educator must understand: their own perspectives and influence in the situation; the perceptions and influence of students and the class as a whole; the effects or influence of instructional methods and assessments selected; the interactions among the educator, students, methods, and assessments; and be prepared to adjust and adapt as the exercise unfolds.

Educators, sociologists, psychologists, and scientists have also conceptualized individuals as embedded in complex multilevel systems (Bronfenbrenner, 1977; Katz and Kahn, 1978; Kozlowski and Klein, 2000; Scott, 2003; von Bertalanffy, 1972, 2008). This theoretical conceptualization also supports the importance of context. Like Bronfenbrenner's (1977) ecological theory of human development, an open systems model stresses the complexity and variability of the parts of the system, interdependence of the parts of the system, and interdependence of the system and the environment (Katz and Kahn, 1978; Scott, 2003).

Similar to Bronfenbrenner's (1977) theory, Kozlowski and Klein's multilevel approach to organizational phenomenon argues that micro phenomena, such as student learning, are embedded in macro contexts (Kozlowski and Klein, 2000). For example, a student may be embedded in a team which is embedded in a course, which is embedded in a department, which is embedded in a school, which is embedded in a university, which is embedded in a society. Macro phenomena often emerge through the interaction and dynamics of lower-level elements (for example, university graduation rates evolve in response to many interactions and dynamics between students, faculty, administrators, and campus climate). Neither level alone can adequately account for a phenomenon such as learning; both must be taken into consideration. Further, because context may be perceived differently by different people, it is important to understand micro and macro factors that may influence individual perceptions, attitudes, and behaviors. And because micro and macro factors may have a direct or moderating effect on processes and outcomes, it is important to understand beliefs, affects, behaviors, and characteristics of individuals which may emerge as processes or outcomes at higher levels.

See Figure 2.2, "Basic contextual factors affecting experiential exercises" which illustrates the embedded, interacting, hierarchical nature of the learning context for experiential exercises. In the remaining parts of this section, what is known about the impact of contextual factors on learning, and thus experiential exercises, is summarized.

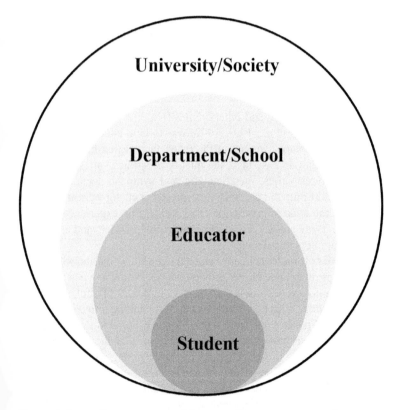

Figure 2.2   Basic contextual factors affecting experiential exercises

Impact of Learning Context: Overview

Now that we understand the theoretical foundations of context, can we make any generalizations about context and its impact on teaching and learning? Given the complexity of teaching and learning, several researchers have attempted to answer this question by systematically reviewing or synthesizing meta-analyses of factors having an impact on academic achievement.

Schneider and Preckel (2017) provide the first international review of meta-analyses of variables associated with achievement in higher education. They identified 38 meta-analyses with 1,920,239 participants and 3,330 effect sizes and used this data to investigate the correlations between 105 variables and achievement in higher education.

Hattie (2009, 2012) synthesized the results of over 800 meta-analyses of variables associated with achievement in education. His synthesis included 52,637 studies with an estimated 236 million participants, and 146,142 effect sizes for variables influencing academic achievement. This synthesis examined the influence of 138 variables on academic achievement.

The purpose of these and other studies (Kulik et al., 1990; Kulik and Kulik, 1989; Wang et al., 1993, 1997) was to help educators and others understand the relative impact of the many factors that influence learning. This was not an easy task; the quality of studies varies, the quality of meta-analyses varies, meta-analytic and synthesis techniques have limitations and must be carefully interpreted. Yet, for educators trying to improve the odds of creating successful learning experiences in their classrooms, these studies are another tool to help understand a complex and challenging phenomenon.

These types of studies help us to understand what works and what works better (that is, may have bigger effects). However, these types of studies do not take into consideration the cost or complexity of implementation. Thus, the findings must be interpreted carefully, taking into consideration other practical matters; not just size of impact, but also the strength of the evidence base, the cost of implementation, and the complexity of implementation. For this book, we focus on discussing contextual factors that have an above-average impact and a strong evidence base. Those interested in digging deeper into a specific contextual dimension should consult the syntheses of meta-analyses or the meta-analyses directly; for a list of meta-analyses see, for example, Tight's (2019) compendium of systematic reviews and meta-analyses in higher education.

All the syntheses of meta-analyses (Hattie, 2009; Kulik and Kulik, 1989; Schneider and Preckel, 2017; Wang et al., 1993) indicate that most contextual factors have a positive effect on academic achievement; however, the effect sizes vary widely, indicating that some contextual factors have a much greater impact on learning than others.

Wang et al. (1993, 1997) used content analysis, expert ratings, and a meta-analysis of 91 studies to assess the relative effects of a wide range of variables on learning in mostly primary and secondary school contexts. They found that distal variables, which we describe as macro factors or general context, have little influence on learning, whereas proximal variables, which we refer to as micro variables or specific context, strongly influence learning. They group contextual factors into six broad categories, presented in order of their impact on learning: (1) student characteristics; (2) classroom instruction and climate; (3) home, peer, and community context; (4) program design; (5) school organization; and (6) state and district characteristics. Direct influences such as instructional approaches were found to have a greater impact on learning than indirect influences such as state educational policies. Based on their multimethod analysis, they concluded that educators who want to increase the odds of learning should focus on proximal contextual variables: (1) psychological variables of the student, particularly metacognition and cognition, (2) classroom instruction and management, (3) educator–student social and academic interactions, and (4) the home environment.

Hattie's (2009) synthesis of meta-analyses in education (primary, secondary, and tertiary levels) supports these conclusions. He identified six contextual factors which influence academic outcomes: the student, the home, the educator, instructional approaches, the school, and the curricula. He concluded that student aptitude and what educators and students do in the classroom are the most important determinants of academic achievement.

Schneider and Preckel's (2017) synthesis of meta-analyses in higher education also supports these conclusions, but indirectly. Like the other syntheses of meta-analyses, they found that what the educator does is strongly related to effective learning. They note that fine-grained differences in instructional approaches, which they call the microstructure of instruction, result in significant differences in learning (for example, asking open-ended questions instead of closed-ended ones; writing a few words instead of half-sentences on presentation slides; and so on). Instructional approaches which incorporate social interaction, stimulate meaningful learning, and incorporate appropriate assessment are strongly associated with achievement in higher education (Schneider and Preckel, 2017).

Thus, there is strong evidence that context matters, particularly the specific context: what students and educators do. The strategies that educators adopt for teaching and the strategies that students adopt for learning are more directly associated with academic success than who they are (Hattie, 2009; Schneider and Preckel, 2017). As a classroom educator designing experiential exercises, it is comforting to know that the variables over which you have the most control – the educator (that is, you) and instructional approaches – have the most impact on learning. See Figure 2.3, "Summary of high-impact contextual factors affecting experiential exercises" for an overview of key processes and the high-impact micro contextual factors at the student and educator levels.

Does this mean that general context does not matter? No. Over the past five decades, researchers from around the world have confirmed that a nation's school system tends to reproduce the inequities that exist within a society (Fenwick and Cooper, 2013). For a number of social, cultural, and economic reasons, schools historically have tended to create environments where higher socioeconomic status students are able to learn more effectively than lower socioeconomic status students. As nations work to develop policies and practices to address these inequities and increase the odds of student success, they are also relying on the growing body of evidence that indicates that educators – what they think, know, and do in the classroom – are essential to improving student academic achievement.

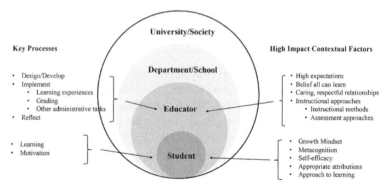

Figure 2.3   Summary of high-impact contextual factors affecting experiential exercises

In Figure 2.8 at the end of this section the micro contextual factors which interact to influence learning are summarized. Some readers may prefer to refer to this figure now, for an overview; others may prefer to proceed directly to the findings and discussions that follow.

Impact of Specific Learning Context

Student perceptions of the specific learning context influence learning outcomes directly and indirectly. That is, perceptions about context directly affect outcomes, and perceptions about context also indirectly affect outcomes via adoption of different learning approaches. See Figure 2.4, "Illustration of direct and indirect impact of context on learning outcomes" which illustrates these relationships.

Positive perceptions of the specific learning context directly, positively influence academic achievement, satisfaction, and generic skills development (that is competency development, or transferable skill development relevant to employability and lifelong learning such as written communication, problem-solving, teamwork and other skills). See Table 2.13, "Summary of relationships between context and outcomes" for a summary of the relationship between the specific learning context and learning outcomes. The specific learning context accounts for a significant amount of the variance in learning outcomes: 28 percent, 49 percent, and 25 percent, respectively, for academic achievement, satisfaction, and generic skills development (Lizzio et al., 2002).

Clear patterns of relationships have been established over time and across disciplines between university students' perceptions of their academic context, their approaches to study, and their academic outcomes: learning, course satisfaction, and generic skills development (Biggs and Tang, 2011; Hattie, 2009, 2012; Lizzio et al., 2002; Ramsden, 2003). Elements of the learning environment which are under the control of

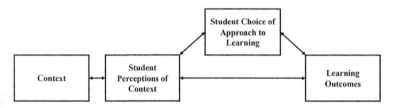

Figure 2.4   *Illustration of direct and indirect impact of context on learning outcomes*

the educator can and do positively influence the ways students approach their studies and their learning outcomes (Biggs and Tang, 2011; Hattie, 2009; Lizzio et al., 2002; Ramsden, 2003). Using the Course Experience Questionnaire, which assesses students' perceptions of their learning context (that is, good teaching, clear goals, appropriate assessment, appropriate workload, independence in learning, and generic skills development), studies have established relationships between the specific learning context, student approaches to studying, and learning outcomes (Wilson et al., 1997).

When designing and implementing experiential exercises, the specific learning context matters. At a micro level, student perceptions of the learning context directly influence learning outcomes (that is, academic achievement, student satisfaction, and general skills development). Student perceptions of the context also indirectly influence learning outcomes, by influencing student choice of approach to learning (that is, surface or deep), which in turn influences learning outcomes. Thus, educators developing an experiential exercise should select instructional approaches and assessments which are more likely to result in a deep approach to learning and positive learning outcomes. Instructional approaches and assessment methods are two of the most influential specific contextual factors for learning. Good teaching (that is, caring, respectful relationships, high expectations, clear and useful explanations, making the subject interesting, and feedback on progress), clear goals, appropriate workloads, and some independence or choice in learning are other specific contextual factors which have a high impact on learning outcomes. Figure 2.5, "Specific contextual factors to increase learning in experiential exercises" illustrates how an educator's choices during the design and development of an experiential exercise affects learning outcomes. These findings underscore the importance of clear learning objectives and tight alignment of learning objectives, learning activities, and assessments when creating experiential exercises. These findings also highlight the importance of using experiential exercises in the class-room, particularly if they make the subject more relevant to students.

Impact of learner characteristics
Students bring their experiences, expectations, intentions, and beliefs to the learning environment. Students may be burdened with extra-curricular activities, work responsibilities, or family commitments. Furthermore, students may be accustomed to and comfortable with the banking model of education (Freire et al., 2012); they may resist the shift from passive

Table 2.13   Summary of relationships between context and outcomes

Context	Outcomes (strongest predictors)
Good teaching: An academic environment that is involving for students because educators ...	Academic achievement (clear goals, good teaching, appropriate assessment)
• Show an interest in students' opinions and attempt to understand difficulties students may be having	Overall satisfaction (good teaching, clear goals, independence)
• Express positive expectations and seek to motivate students to do their "best work"	Generic skills development or competency or transferable skill development, for example written communication, problem-solving, analysis, teamwork, and planning one's own work (good teaching and independence)
• Provide clear and useful explanations of ideas	
• Work to make subjects interesting	
• Provide feedback on progress	
Clear goals: An academic environment where students know what is expected of them because educators ...	Academic achievement (clear goals, good teaching, appropriate assessment)
• Explain "right from the start" the learning objectives	Overall satisfaction (good teaching, clear goals, independence)
• Provide progressive markers of "where we are going"	Generic skills development
• Explain the standard of work expected	

Context	Outcomes (strongest predictors)
Appropriate assessment: An academic environment that enhances learning by using assessments that ….	Academic achievement (clear goals, good teaching, appropriate assessment)
	Overall satisfaction
• Emphasize understanding, not just memorization of facts	Generic skills development
• Are progressive and spaced over time	
• Involve feedback beyond grades	
Appropriate workload: An academic environment that effectively manages students' workloads and stress by ….	Overall satisfaction
	Generic skills development
• Setting a feasible amount of material to be covered	
• Focusing the range of topic areas covered	
• Allowing adequate time frames for work to be completed	

Context	Outcomes (strongest predictors)
Independence in learning: An academic environment that, within the limits of practicality, offers students a degree of choice in … • Developing areas of academic interest • How they learn material • The forms or modes of assessment	Overall satisfaction (good teaching, clear goals, independence) Generic skills development (good teaching and independence)
Generic skills: An academic environment that provides opportunities for students to develop generic meta competencies through … • Using analytical skills • Developing problem-solving capabilities • Developing written communication skills • Using problem-solving to tackle unfamiliar problems • Working as a team member • Planning their own work	Overall satisfaction

Notes:
28% of the variance in academic achievement is accounted for by context.
49% of the variance in satisfaction is accounted for by context.
25% of the variance in generic skills development is accounted for by context.
Source: Lizzio et al. (2002).

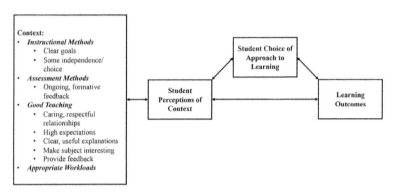

Figure 2.5   *Specific contextual factors to increase learning in experiential exercises*

to active learning methodologies (Breunig, 2005). Students may not actively participate in exercises, use higher-order thinking skills, or learn sufficient content (Snyder, 2003). Students may differ in their ability to reflect upon experiences and engage in constructive dialogue (Cajiao and Burke, 2016). For students to successfully engage in experiential learning activities, educators must help students discover the benefits of the activity and how it relates to solving real-life problems (Silberman, 2007). In addition, the educator must carefully manage student expectations (Ungaretti et al., 2015) and provide support and guidance when it comes to processing the experiential learning activity.

Meta-analyses indicate that as much as 28 percent of the variance in student behavior in learning environments is associated with their intentions about learning (for example, their aims, resolve, decisions, and so on), especially if they have some control over learning (Hattie, 2009). When students and educators have and share challenging goals and strong learning intentions, they have established major conditions for academic success (Hattie, 2009; Schneider and Preckel, 2017).

Intelligence and prior achievement

Of all the person-related variables for students in higher education, intelligence and prior achievement show the strongest relationship to achievement (Schneider and Preckel, 2017). This is true for education in general (Hattie, 2009). Intelligence and prior achievement variables tend to have moderate to large effects. Prior achievement is typically related to prior effort and intelligence, and the virtuous cycle of effort leading to achievement leading to rewards (for example, self-concept, social identity, self-efficacy, grades, recognition, and so on) which leads to engagement and further effort.

Learning strategies, mindsets, and motivation
Students may adopt self-regulation strategies and approaches to learning which have an impact on their academic achievement. When students regulate their affective, cognitive, and behavioral processes to learn successfully, they are engaging in self-regulated learning (de Bruijn-Smolders et al., 2016; Dent and Koenka, 2016; Jansen et al., 2019; Sitzmann and Ely, 2011). When students are active participants in their own learning (that is, self-regulated learners), they set goals for their learning, choose from a variety of strategies to achieve their goals, recognize when alternative strategies would be more effective, adapt their approaches, and evaluate their performance (Ambrose et al., 2010; Dent and Koenka, 2016; Jansen et al., 2019; Sitzmann and Ely, 2011). Self-regulated learning is positively related to success in higher education, specifically to better grades and faster completion rates (de Bruijn-Smolders et al., 2016). Self-regulated learning processes can be taught, and there is strong evidence that interventions to teach these processes increase student achievement and engagement in self-regulatory processes (Jansen et al., 2019). Self-regulated learning processes are highly interrelated, and most have a positive impact on learning (Sitzmann and Ely, 2011). According to the syntheses of meta-analyses (Hattie, 2009; Schneider and Preckel, 2017), growth mindset, metacognitive learning skills, self-efficacy, appropriate attributions, and approach to learning are high-impact micro contextual factors related to self-regulated learning which have an above-average impact on student success.

The more students engage in self-regulated learning strategies, particularly the management of effort and time, the more they are likely to achieve academically (Schneider and Preckel, 2017). The more students adopt a strategic approach to learning – using learning strategies in an appropriate task-dependent manner and being motivated to achieve – the more they are likely to learn (Schneider and Preckel, 2017). Learning how to learn – learning not just how to solve a problem, but how to select an effective and appropriate strategy to solve the problem, and how to monitor the use of that strategy as it is applied (that is, metacognitive learning skills) – increases academic success if integrated in the course or subject being learned (Hattie, 2009).

Growth mindset
Students may have beliefs about their ability to learn: mindsets or
implicit theories. Students with growth mindsets, who believe they
can learn with effort, are more likely to engage in effort regulation, to
pursue learning goals, persist when faced with adversity, be engaged,
and achieve higher academic outcomes (Ambrose et al., 2010; Dweck,
2008; Dweck and Yeager, 2019). But can a growth mindset be taught?
Recent meta-analyses suggest that growth mindset interventions can
increase academic achievement, especially for students from lower
socioeconomic backgrounds (Sisk et al., 2018). "Mindset interventions
are relatively low cost and take little time, so there may be a net benefit
for students' academic achievement" (Sisk et al., 2018, p. 568). Further,
higher-achieving students, who may already have a growth mindset, tend
to have an increase in willingness to take on challenges after participating
in a growth mindset intervention (Dweck and Yeager, 2019; Yeager et
al., 2016a; Yeager et al., 2016b). In Chapter 3, one of the implementation
examples shows how a growth mindset experiential exercise was developed for students in a business school.

Metacognition
Teaching students to think about their thinking, or teaching metacognitive learning skills – the processes used to plan, monitor, and assess one's
understanding and performance – is an effective approach to instruction
(Bransford et al., 2000; Chick, 2020; de Boer et al., 2018; Donker et al.,
2014; Hattie et al., 1996). However, metacognitive learning skills are not
generic, they must be adapted to the specific learning context of a course
or discipline, and they must be integrated into a course over time so that
students have an opportunity to learn about and apply the appropriate
skills as needed within the course (Bransford et al., 2000; Hattie, 2009;
Pintrich, 2002; Zohar and Ben David, 2009). This just-in-time approach
to acquiring metacognitive skills makes the learning more relevant and
results in an above-average impact on learning. See page 190 in Hattie's
(2009) *Visible Learning* for a description of high-impact metacognitive
learning strategies. See McGuire and McGuire's (2015) *Teach Students
How to Learn* for practical advice on how to integrate effective metacognitive strategies into any course or learning activity.

Self-efficacy
Self-efficacy, the belief in one's capabilities to achieve a goal or an
outcome (Ackerman, 2018; Bandura, 1999), is associated with many per-

sonal and professional benefits; for example, better performance, more effective personal adjustment, coping better with stress, and better health (Chemers et al., 2001; Richardson et al., 2012; Stajkovic and Luthans, 1998). Self-efficacy has a positive causal effect on achievement, which in turn causally affects self-efficacy (Schneider and Preckel, 2017). Performance self-efficacy – self-efficacy about a specific performance goal – is strongly positively associated with academic performance (Schneider and Preckel, 2017).

Self-efficacy is derived from mastery experiences, vicarious experiences, verbal persuasion, and emotional states (Bandura, 1997, 1999; Margolis and McCabe, 2006). Mastery experiences are the experience of working hard to achieve success and overcoming obstacles through effort (Ackerman, 2018; Bandura, 1999). For example, role plays, case analyses, simulations, and experiential exercises can provide opportunities for students to tackle a challenging situation and through hard work and sustained effort respond successfully to the challenge.

Vicarious experiences are the experience of seeing people like you succeed through sustained effort (Ackerman, 2018; Bandura, 1999). For example, a peer may model or demonstrate an approach to problem-solving, explaining what they are doing and thinking at each step. Other examples include a fishbowl exercise, or any classroom exercise where students observe others like themselves working hard to achieve mastery, such as in a debate, a role play, or a simulation.

Verbal persuasion provides learners with information which they interpret and evaluate, which in turn affects their self-efficacy. For example, peer and/or educator feedback and encouragement can influence a student's self-efficacy.

Emotional states are how students feel. For example, a positive mood can boost self-efficacy, and anxiety or stress can reduce it.

The type of learning environment created and instructional methods selected by an educator can influence students' self-efficacy (Bandura, 1997, 1999; Fencl and Scheel, 2005; Schunk and Pajares, 2002). Bandura (1997, 1999) concludes that cooperative learning strategies improve both self-efficacy and academic achievement. Margolis and McCabe (2006) recommend eight approaches to improve self-efficacy and ultimately academic achievement among struggling students: (1) assign moderately difficult tasks; (2) use peer models; (3) teach specific learning strategies; (4) capitalize on students' interests; (5) allow students some autonomy; (6) encourage students to try; (7) give frequent, focused feedback; and (8) encourage accurate attributions.

Appropriate attribution

Kelley's (1973) attribution theory posits that people attribute behavior to either internal factors such as ability and effort, or external factors such as the task difficulty or bad luck. Further, people tend to have biases in their attributions. They tend to attribute other's behavior to personal (that is, internal) characteristics rather than situational (that is, external) factors; this is the fundamental attribution error (Ross, 1977). And people tend to take more responsibility for their successes than their failures: the self-serving bias (Harvey et al., 2018). In the context of self-regulated learning, some students have a tendency to habitually attribute negative academic outcomes to uncontrollable factors rather than controllable factors; this can result in a downward spiral of negative emotions and poor academic performance (Haynes et al., 2009; Lazowski and Hulleman, 2016; Reivich and Shatté, 2002). There is significant evidence that attributional retraining, even as a brief intervention, can help students to change this pattern. Interventions that help students see academic struggles as being due to lack of effort (controllable) versus being due to a lack of ability (uncontrollable) result in higher grades and lower dropout rates (Haynes et al., 2009; Lazowski and Hulleman, 2016).

Approach to learning

Several approaches to studying have been identified: a surface approach, a deep approach, and a strategic or achieving approach (Biggs, 1979; Marton and Saljo, 1976; Ramsden, 1979). A surface approach means that students intend to do just what they must do to get by in the course. A surface approach involves reproducing or regurgitating content, accepting content passively, doing only what is required for assessment (for example, to pass the test), memorizing to recall, and failing to see guiding principles or patterns (Entwistle, 1998; Ramsden, 2003). A deep approach to learning means that students intend to understand ideas. A deep approach involves vigorous and critical interaction with content, relating content to one's previous knowledge and experiences, discovering and using organizing principles, relating evidence to conclusions, and examining the logic of arguments (Entwistle, 1998; Ramsden, 2003). A strategic or achievement approach to learning means that students intend to achieve by selecting the learning strategies that best fit the situation. A strategic or achievement approach involves both surface and deep learning, with learning approaches selected to fit the learning context (Biggs, 1979; Entwistle, 1998; Ramsden, 1979).

Learning approaches are not individual traits or styles, they are approaches to learning that students adopt in response to perceptions about the learning context and prior experiences. Learning approaches are not fixed and may change with changes in context. Biggs and Tang (2011) argue that the focus of effective teaching should be on getting more students to adopt the learning approaches needed to achieve the learning outcomes. There is substantial evidence that student choice of learning approach is substantially influenced by the learning context; specifically, by the instructional methods and assessment approaches adopted by educators (Biggs and Tang, 2011; Lizzio et al., 2002; Ramsden, 2003).

Positive perceptions of the specific learning context indirectly influence academic outcomes by influencing study approaches (Lizzio et al., 2002). Generally, favorable perceptions of context, as outlined in Table 2.13, influence students to adopt a deep approach to learning (Lizzio et al., 2002). The most significant predictors of students adopting a deep approach to learning are student perceptions about: (1) teaching and assessment methods that foster active and long-term engagement with learning tasks; (2) stimulating and considerate teaching, especially teaching which demonstrates commitment to the subject matter and stresses its meaning and importance to students; (3) clearly stated academic expectations; and (4) opportunities to exercise responsible choice in the method and content of study (Lizzio et al., 2002; Ramsden, 2003).

Generally, unfavorable perceptions of the specific learning context (as outlined in Table 2.13) influence students toward surface approaches to studying (Lizzio et al., 2002). Specifically, perceptions of heavy workload and inappropriate assessment influence students towards surface approaches to studying (Lizzio et al., 2002; Ramsden, 2003). See Table 2.14, "Summary of relationships between context, learning approach, and learning outcomes" for a summary of contextual factors which influence student choice of learning approach (that is, deep or surface), which in turn influences learning outcomes.

Personality
Personality variables tend to have weak relationships with academic achievement (Schneider and Preckel, 2017). None of the 16 personality variables (694 effect sizes based on over 1 million students) in Schneider and Preckel's (2017) synthesis of meta-analyses had a strong effect on college students' learning. Conscientiousness – the tendency to be organized, take purposeful action, be achievement-oriented, and

have self-discipline – is moderately related to academic achievement. In higher education, the association between conscientiousness and academic achievement is about as strong as the relationship between intelligence and academic achievement (with an effect size of $d = .047$).

Summary of the impact of learner characteristics
Student beliefs and approaches to learning are significant determinants of their success in learning. Educators who understand how these beliefs are formed and how/why students adopt certain approaches to learning have a better chance of creating effective experiential exercises. See Figure 2.6, "Learner characteristics – high-impact micro contextual student factors" for a summary of learner characteristics, or student-centered micro contextual factors, which have a high impact on student learning. Educators who find ways to encourage, reinforce, or cue these micro contextual factors in experiential exercises will increase the odds of student learning; that is, encourage, reinforce, or cue: growth mindset, metacognitive learning skills, self-efficacy (mastery experiences, vicarious experiences, verbal persuasion, and positive emotional states), appropriate attributions, and a deep approach to learning.

Impact of educator characteristics

Biggs and Tang (2011) assert that teaching is the most important contextual factor for learning. Teaching includes both the educator and the instructional methods used. Hattie's (2009) synthesis of meta-analyses found that educators are a very influential contextual factor for learning. As noted, the quality of teaching as perceived by students is a critical contextual factor affecting learning outcomes. It is what educators get students to do in the classroom that most strongly influences student academic achievement (Hattie, 2009). Students must be actively involved in their learning, with multiple opportunities to learn. Educators who use particular teaching methods, have high expectations for all students, and build positive student–teacher relationships are more likely to have above-average effects on student achievement (Hattie, 2009, p. 126). From an educator perspective, the beliefs and interpersonal behaviors that lead to better student learning outcomes are: (1) high expectations for all students; (2) a belief that all students can learn; and (3) a willingness to develop positive relationships with students, using listening, empathy, caring, and respect for others (Hattie, 2009). In addition to their personal beliefs and interpersonal behaviors, educators can use specific instructional methods which get students actively engaged and encourage them

Table 2.14   Summary of relationships between context, learning approach, and learning outcomes

Context	Approach	Outcomes
Deep approaches are encouraged by: Educator providing:	*Deep approach (transforming)* Intention: To understand ideas Characteristics:	*Positively related to outcomes:* • Academic achievement • Course satisfaction
• Teaching and assessment methods that foster active and long-term engagement with learning tasks[a]	• An intention to understand material for oneself	• Generic skills development or competency or transferable skill development, for example written communication, problem-solving, analysis, teamwork, and planning one's own work
• Stimulating and considerate teaching especially teaching which demonstrates educator's commitment to the subject matter and stresses its meaning and importance to students[a]	• Vigorous and critical interaction with knowledge content	
	• Relating ideas to one's previous knowledge and experience	
• Clearly stated academic expectations[a]	• Discovering and using organizing principles to integrate ideas	
• Opportunities to exercise responsible choice in the method and content of study[a]	• Relating evidence to conclusions	
Student having:	• Examining the logic of argument	
• Interest in and background knowledge of the subject matter		
• Previous experiences of education settings that encourage deep approaches		

Context	Approach	Outcomes
Surface approaches are encouraged by: Educator providing: • Assessment methods emphasizing recall or the application of trivial procedural knowledge[a] • Assessment methods that create anxiety • Cynical or conflicting messages about rewards • An excessive amount of material in the curriculum[a] • Poor or absent feedback on progress • Lack of independence in studying Student having: • Lack of interest in and background knowledge of the subject matter • Previous experience of educational settings that encourage surface approaches	*Surface approach (reproducing)* Intention: To cope with course requirements Characteristics: • An intention simply to reproduce part of the content • Ideas and information accepted passively • Concentrating only on what is required for assessment • Not reflecting on purpose or strategies • Memorizing facts and procedures routinely • Failing to distinguish guiding principles or patterns	*Negatively related to outcomes:* • Academic achievement • Course satisfaction • Generic skills development

Notes:
[a] Most significant predictors of approach
Deep and surface approaches are not individual traits or styles; they are approaches which students adopt in response to context and experience. Approach is an intention that a student has in a particular context; this intention is not fixed and may change as the context changes. Memorization plays a role in both approaches; it plays a different role in each approach (deep: memorize and make sense; surface: memorize to recall).
Sources: Entwistle (1998), Institute for the Advancement of University Learning (2019), Ramsden (2003).

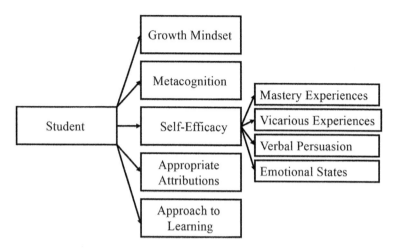

Figure 2.6   *Learner characteristics – high-impact micro contextual student factors*

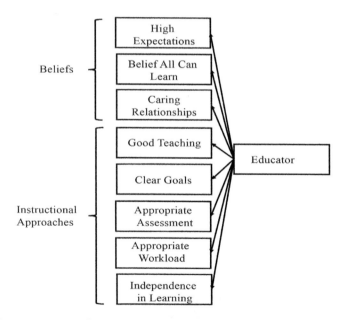

Figure 2.7   *Educator characteristics and teaching practices – high-impact micro contextual educator factors*

to adopt a deep approach to learning, to increase the odds of students achieving learning outcomes. See Figure 2.7, "Educator characteristics and teaching practices – high-impact micro contextual educator factors" for a summary of educator characteristics and instructional methods or educator-centered micro contextual factors, which have a high impact on student learning. Educators who find ways to communicate these beliefs to students and who select high-impact instructional strategies for their experiential exercises will increase the odds of student learning.

The lack of skills needed to facilitate experiential learning may be a significant hurdle for educators interested in developing or adopting experiential learning activities (Brown et al., 2013). Experiential learning methods require a considerable amount of time and effort to implement (Austin and Rust, 2015; Gentry, 1990; Kolb and Kolb, 2009b), and integrating experiential exercises into a course may require more, new, or different skills relative to the skills required for teaching textbook knowledge (Katula and Threnhauser, 1999). The tools in this book, training in evidence-based best practices and ongoing reflection and revision within one's teaching practice, can help to build the skills and experiences needed to successfully integrate experiential exercises in the classroom.

Impact of instructional approaches
Which instructional methods are more likely to lead to above-average academic achievement? There are many instructional approaches which have a positive impact on learning. However, the magnitude of the educational impact varies widely by instructional approach. Approaches may also vary in cost and complexity of implementation. Further, "it is not only what teachers do on the microlevel but also exactly how they do it that critically affects achievement" (Schneider and Preckel, 2017, p. 593). So how should an educator select an instructional approach? High-impact, low-cost, easy-to-implement (with high fidelity) instructional methods seem ideal for classroom educators.

Schneider and Preckel (2017) argue that in higher education and education in general, we know that academic achievement is strongly related to social interaction, student-directed activity, assessment practices, and students' learning strategies (Biggs and Tang, 2011; Perry and Smart, 2007; Richardson et al., 2012; Schwartz and Gurung, 2012). Based on their synthesis of meta-analyses, they conclude that instructional methods which encourage social interaction and stimulate meaningful learning, and assessment methods which provide educators and students with timely and actionable feedback about progress, tend to have a bigger impact on academic achievement than student variables or other instructional approaches.

Effective instructional methods which encourage social interaction include: encouraging questions and discussion, use of open-ended questions, and use of small group learning (where students must work interdependently to accomplish a goal, and have individual accountability).

Instructional approaches which stimulate meaningful learning include: thoughtful preparation and organization of learning experiences, clear learning objectives and success criteria, helping students to see the relevance of the material, providing intellectually challenging learning opportunities, and encouraging independent thinking.

Both formative and summative assessment are valuable, and high-impact assessment practices include: quality and fairness of exams; nature, quality, and frequency of feedback from educator to students; mastery learning; and more frequent testing. Schneider and Preckel (2017) argue that any educator can improve the quality of learning in their classroom [or experiential exercises] by making these small, easy-to-implement changes:

- Encourage frequent class attendance.
- Stimulate questions and discussion, asking open-ended questions.
- Provide clear learning goals.
- Relate content to students.
- Provide detailed task-focused and improvement-oriented feedback.
- Be friendly and respectful with students.
- Complement spoken words with visualizations and written words.
- Use a few key words rather than half- or full sentences on slides.
- Have students construct concept maps of central ideas only, not details.
- Begin each instructional unit [or experiential exercise] with an advance organizer. This is a tool provided by the educator that helps students to bridge between current knowledge and knowledge to be acquired; for example an overview, a framework, an illustration, an exemplar, and so on. See Stone (1983) or Ylvisaker et al. (2006) for more information about advance organizers.
- Avoid distracting or seductive details in presentations (Schneider and Preckel, 2017, p. 593).

Hattie (2009) argues that educators with high expectations of all students who have created positive educator–student relationships are more likely to have an above-average impact on student achievement. In his synthesis of meta-analyses, he identifies several high-impact instructional approaches:

good teaching, clear goals, appropriate assessment, and appropriate work-load. Educators who challenge students to think, have high expectations for students, give and receive timely and actionable feedback, and develop warm and empathetic relationships with students, are more likely to have a positive impact on student learning. Educators who organize learning experiences, provide clear goals, give clear explanations, share examples, and provide opportunities for guided practice, are also more likely to positively influence student learning.

In Hattie's (2009) synthesis, the use of formative evaluation is the assessment method with the highest positive impact on student learning. Formative assessment means collecting and sharing information during the learning process which can be used to adjust educator and student approaches and improve learning outcomes (for example, classroom assessment techniques, self-assessments, feedback on work in progress, and so on). Formative evaluation affects students' perceptions of the micro learning context; specifically, formative assessment increases students' perceptions that teaching is good and assessment is appropriate. Thus, formative assessment directly and indirectly affects learning and is one of the instructional approaches that educators can use to increase the effectiveness of experiential exercises.

Hattie (2009) summarizes the instructional approaches which are associated with student learning as:

- Paying deliberate attention to learning intentions and success criteria.
- Setting challenging tasks.
- Providing multiple opportunities for deliberative practice.
- Knowing when one (teacher/student) is successful in attaining these goals.
- Understanding the critical role of teaching appropriate learning strategies (that is, metacognitive learning skills).
- Planning and talking about teaching.
- Ensuring the teacher constantly seeks feedback information as to the success of their teaching for the students. (Hattie, 2009, p. 36)

In Table 2.15, "Practices/conditions related to context and their effect sizes" the instructional approaches that have an above-average impact on learning from Hattie's (2009) and Schneider and Preckel's (2017) syntheses of meta-analyses are organized by aspect of the specific learning context they have the potential to affect (as perceived by students). Additionally, there are a few other high-impact instructional methods from each of the two syntheses, not directly related to specific contextual factors, which can increase the effectiveness of experiential exercises: reciprocal teaching (peers teaching each other), metacognitive learning strategies, and concept mapping.

Impact of subject/content characteristics

Although a number of authors have asserted that the subject matter context determines which instructional methods are appropriate, there is little empirical evidence to support these claims. A study by Murray and Renaud (1995) found that low-inference instructional approaches (for example, use concrete examples, stress most important points) did vary by field (arts and humanities versus social sciences versus natural sciences and mathematics); however, the relationships between instructional methods and academic outcomes did not change by field. If these findings are replicated, it would suggest that educator use of effective instructional methods may vary by field, but effective instructional approaches are similar across academic disciplines (Murray, 2007).

Impact of General Learning Context

As discussed previously, syntheses of meta-analyses and multimethod studies indicate that specific, micro contextual factors have a bigger impact on student academic outcomes than general or macro contextual factors (Hattie, 2009; Schneider and Preckel, 2017; Wang et al., 1993, 1997). These findings are further reinforced by a Gallup-Purdue (2014) study of over 30,000 graduates that found where graduates went to university hardly matters at all to their current well-being and their work lives in comparison to their experiences at university. "Feeling supported and having deep learning experiences means everything when it comes to long-term outcomes for college graduates" (Gallup-Purdue, 2014, p. 6). According to the research, students who had a professor who cared about them as a person, one who made them excited about learning, and had a mentor who encouraged them to pursue their dreams, are more than twice as likely to be engaged in their work and thriving in terms of well-being. If graduates have any of these six undergraduate experiences, they are almost twice as likely to be engaged at work: (1) I had at least one professor who made me excited about learning; (2) My professor cared about me as a person; (3) I had a mentor who encouraged me to pursue my goals and dreams; (4) I worked on a project that took a semester or more to complete; (5) I had an internship or job that allowed me to apply what I was learning in the classroom; or (6) I was extremely active in extracurricular activities and organizations while attending college.

Table 2.15   Practices/conditions related to context and their effect sizes

Context	Meta-analytic effects (effect size; key descriptors)
Good teaching: An academic environment that is involving for students because educators …	*Hattie:*
	Educator clarity (0.75; organize, explain, provide examples, guided practice and assessment)
• Show an interest in students' opinions and attempt to understand difficulties students may be having	Feedback (0.73; must be received and acted upon, from educator to student and from student to educator)
• Express positive expectations and seek to motivate students to do their "best work"	Educator–student relationship (0.72; empathy, warmth)
	Quality of teaching (0.44; challenge students to think through and solve problems, have high expectations for students)
• Provide clear and useful explanations of ideas	Educator expectation (0.43)
• Work to make subjects interesting	*Schneider and Preckel:*
• Provide feedback on progress	Teacher clarity and understandableness (1.35; interprets abstract ideas and theories clearly, makes good use of examples and illustrations to get across difficult points)
	Teacher's stimulation of interest in the course and its subject matter (0.82)
	Teacher's encouragement of questions and discussion (0.77)
	Use of open-ended questions (0.73)
	Teacher availability and helpfulness (0.77)
	Teacher's elocution skills (0.75)
	Teacher relates content to student (0.65)
	Teacher enthusiasm for subject or teaching (0.56)
	Intellectual challenge and encouragement of independent thought (0.52)
	Teacher concern and respect for students (0.47)

Context	Meta-analytic effects (effect size; key descriptors)
Clear goals: An academic environment where students know what is expected of them because educators …	*Schneider and Preckel*: Teacher preparation and organization of course (1.39)
• Explain "right from the start" the learning objectives	Clarity of course objectives and requirements (0.75)
	Hattie:
• Provide progressive markers of "where we are going"	Goals (0.56; challenging goals)
• Explain the standard of work expected	
Appropriate assessment: An academic environment that enhances learning by using assessments that …	*Hattie*: Provides formative evaluation (0.9)
	Schneider and Preckel:
• Emphasize understanding, not just memorization of facts	Student self-assessment (0.85)
• Are progressive and spaced over time	Quality and fairness of exams (0.54)
• Involve feedback beyond grades	Nature, quality, and frequency of feedback from educator to student (0.47)
Appropriate workload: An academic environment that effectively manages students' workloads and stress by …	*Hattie*: Spaced vs. massed practice (0.71; three to four exposures over time)
• Setting a feasible amount of material to be covered	
• Focusing the range of topic areas covered	
• Allowing adequate time frames for work to be completed	

Context	Meta-analytic effects (effect size; key descriptors)
Independence in learning: An academic environment that, within the limits of practicality, offers students a degree of choice in ...	
• Developing areas of academic interest	
• How they learn material	
• The forms or modes of assessment	
Generic skills: An academic environment that provides opportunities for students to develop generic metacompetencies through ...	*Hattie:* Problem-solving teaching (0.61; defining or determining the cause of the problem; identifying, prioritizing, and selecting alternatives for a solution; using multiple perspectives to uncover issues; designing an intervention plan; evaluating outcomes)
• Using analytical skills	
• Developing problem-solving capabilities	
• Developing written communication skills	
• Using problem-solving to tackle unfamiliar problems	
• Working as a team member	
• Planning their own work	

Notes:
Findings from the two most recent syntheses of meta-analyses are reported in the table: Hattie (2009) and Schneider and Preckel (2017). Effect sizes may not be comparable due to differences in study populations, study characteristics, meta-analytic techniques, and synthesis techniques.
Sources: Hattie (2009), Lizzio et al. (2002), Schneider and Preckel (2017).

A research review by the Stanford Graduate School of Education found similar results: a university's selectivity is not a reliable predictor of student learning, job satisfaction, or well-being (Challenge Success, 2018). Active engagement in learning processes is more important than the university you attend. That is, "What students do at college seems to matter much more than where they go" (Pope, 2019). As noted previously, this does not mean that general context is unimportant; as researchers from around the world have confirmed, a nation's school system tends to reproduce the inequities that exist within a society (Fenwick and Cooper, 2013).

Impact of department characteristics

Few studies have examined the effects of departmental contextual factors on academic outcomes, and to date the findings are inconclusive (Hartnett and Centra, 1977; Umbach and Porter, 2002). This does not mean that departmental factors do not have an impact on context: they appear to do so, but what exactly it is about departments that results in differences in academic outcomes has not yet been clearly established. Wright et al. (2004) posit that departmental histories, traditions, norms, and composition may have a significant impact on perceived standards for effective teaching, and thus teaching. They propose that faculty who take advantage of cross-departmental instructional development (for example, a center for teaching excellence), who are in a department which encourages conversations and collaboration around teaching, and who participate in professional organizations with a commitment to teaching scholarship, are more likely to be effective educators.

Educators in departments with competing priorities, pressure to cover course content, administrative demands for research productivity, large class sizes, uncertainty regarding how to assess learning from experiential exercises, and lack of faculty training, may find it more challenging to adopt and successful implement experiential exercises (Austin and Rust, 2015).

Impact of school/university characteristics

Wright et al. (2004) note that not much is known about the impact of institutional structure and context on teaching and learning. They argue that higher education institutions place high demands on employees; specifically, high demands to spend time on research and teaching. They contend that increased pressure for accountability in higher education has resulted in increasing demands for productivity in research and teaching, which creates conflicting and perhaps unreasonable demands on educators. They posit that teaching-oriented institutions, research-oriented institutions, and comprehensive institutions (master's colleges and universities) are all placing increased demands on faculty to produce more research, and spend more time preparing for teaching and teaching. They suggest that teaching-oriented organizations are demanding more research, while maintaining high demands related to teaching and offering few resources or support for faculty to attain these goals. They suggest that research-oriented institutions which demand very high research results often provide very limited support for faculty to accomplish their teaching responsibilities. They suggest that comprehensive institutions with growing student populations, especially from academically underprepared groups, place the most demands on faculty, demanding increased research performance while requiring more hours of instruction per week than other institutions, except for community colleges. Wright et al. (2004) call for more research on the impact of institutional structure and context on teaching and learning. Even without more research, one can imagine that increasing demands for higher levels of research deliverables and higher teaching workloads might have unintended negative consequences for student learning. As educators, being one of the most important contextual variables affecting student learning, juggle the competing demands of research, teaching, and service, they may fall short in teaching.

At the institutional level, the absence of a widely recognized model for incorporating experiential learning into the university curriculum, a lack of strategic coordination and oversight of experiential learning activities, and a scarcity of institutional support (Johnston and Sator, 2017), mean that faculty may take a fragmented approach to incorporating experiential exercises in their courses (Hodge et al., 2014; Ungaretti et al., 2015). A sound institutional approach requires "a holistic program of institutional development that includes curriculum development, faculty development, student development, administrative and staff development and resource development" (Kolb and Kolb, 2005, p. 209).

Impact of professional and societal influences
The society and culture in which teaching and learning occurs has a significant impact on teaching and learning, primarily through cultural influences on the beliefs, motivations, and behaviors of educators and students (Hofstede, 1986; Munro, 2012). Culture may determine or influence what is learned, the purpose or importance of learning, ways of thinking and learning, and what is socially and culturally accepted. Thus, a nation's school system tends to reproduce the inequities that exist within a society (Fenwick and Cooper, 2013), because the norms of society are built into and reinforced through the school system, including educators and students. Meertens (2018) claims that cultures with a preference for authority tend to have teacher-centered

educational systems, while cultures with a preference for egalitarianism tend to have student-centered educational systems.

Hofstede (1986) notes that differences in culture between the educator and student can lead to challenges regarding perceptions about the social status of educators, relevance of the content, ways of thinking, and expectations regarding educator–student and student–educator interactions. See pages 312–314 of Hofstede's (1986) "Cultural differences in teaching and learning" for detailed descriptions of how educator–student interactions and expectations might vary by dimension of country culture. He argues that the best way to address challenges related to different cultural backgrounds is through educator training, although teaching students how to learn may also be a viable approach.

Summary of Impact of Context on Learning

Context is essential to understand a complex social phenomenon such as learning. What works in teaching and learning is dependent upon the context, the micro and macro factors that have an influence on and are influenced by each other. All the syntheses of meta-analyses of contextual factors in education affirm that context matters; particularly, the micro context, the student, and the educator. The educator is a micro contextual factor both as an individual (beliefs and behaviors) and in terms of what they can get students to do in the classroom via instructional methods and assessment approaches. In Figure 2.8, "Micro contextual factors which interact to influence learning," the key micro contextual factors that interact to have an impact on academic outcomes are visualized. This figure provides a simplified depiction of the interactions among key micro contextual factors which, based on the evidence, have a higher than average impact on academic outcomes, specifically learning, satisfaction, and skill development.

Students with a growth mindset are more likely to persist in the face of adversity and take on challenges. Students who know how to learn and become self-directed learners are more likely to learn. Self-efficacy and appropriate attributions about failures lead to higher academic performance. Students' perceptions of the quality of teaching, clarity of goals, appropriateness of assessments, appropriateness of workload, and degree of autonomy in learning influence their choice of learning approach (that is, surface or deep), which in turn affects their learning achievement.

Educators who have high expectations for all students, believe all students can learn, and work to establish appropriate educator–student relationships based on respect and caring are more likely to have a significant positive impact on student learning. Further, educators who use evidence-based best practices (for example, encouraging questions and discussion, using open-ended questions, use of collaborative or team-based learning) to create an environment where students feel involved because the educator shows an interest in their opinions, has high expectations for them, provides clear explanations, makes subjects relevant, and provides feedback on their progress, are more likely to improve the quality of learning in their classrooms. Educators who provide clear learning goals and performance expectations, formative feedback, assessments which emphasize understanding, appropriate workloads, and some degree of choice in learning, are more likely to have higher learning among their students.

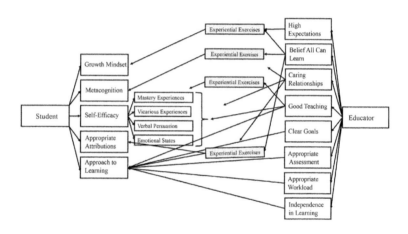

Figure 2.8   Micro contextual factors which interact to influence learning

Students may not come into the classroom with the beliefs or skills needed to succeed (for example, growth mindset, metacognitive learning skills, self-efficacy, appropriate attributions, and/or a deep approach to learning). In these situations there is considerable evidence that if educators implement appropriate and effective experiential exercises related to these beliefs/skills, students can develop these vital beliefs and skills and subsequently improve their academic performance. Educators who are able to form appropriate, caring, respectful relationships with students will be even more effective if they incorporate high-impact instructional approaches into their experiential exercises (that is, good teaching, clear goals, appropriate assessment, appropriate workload, and some choice in learning).

An Example: Applying What We Know About Context

With a deeper understanding of context and its impact on learning, let us re-examine the experiential exercise example from the "Assess Context" section. In this example, an educator teaching a digital literacy course at a university with mostly minority students wants to create an experiential exercise to help students connect the course subject to their lives (that is, to help students discover the relevance of the subject/course). So, how can an educator use what we have learned about context to design a better experiential exercise? In Table 2.16, "Assessing the impact of context: an example (creating an experiential exercise to help students connect the content to their lives)," a worksheet is used to assess the context of a digital literacy educator while considering evidence-based high-impact contextual factors to develop design/implementation action plans for the experiential exercise.

First, the educator's specific and general context is organized in the "My context" column. The evidence-based high-impact contextual factors are organized in the next column: "High-impact contextual factors to be considered." Then the existing contextual factors and high-impact contextual factors are compared to determine whether there are opportunities to leverage any high-impact contextual factors to help achieve the learning objectives.

According to the learner characteristics, there are many first-generation college students taking a required course that they perceive as boring and hard. From the syntheses of meta-analyses, we know that when educators work to make topics relevant to students, they perceive this as good teaching and are more likely to adopt deep approaches to learning and have better academic outcomes. The evidence indicates that the educator's decision to create an experiential exercise to help students connect the course content to their lives is likely to increase the odds of learning in the course. The educator may also want to look for ways to incorporate mastery learning or vicarious learning into the experiential exercise, since this will build student self-efficacy and likely increase student engagement. Further, given the university student population (for example, minority) and student characteristics (working, first-generation), these students would likely benefit from interventions or experiential exercises related to growth mindset, metacognitive learning skills, and appropriate attributions. These topics are clearly outside of the scope of the specific exercise the educator is working on; but this analysis has brought these opportunities to create other experiential exercises to the educator's attention.

According to the educator characteristics, this educator has a high work-load, limited expertise in pedagogy, some frustration about lack of student engagement, and some willingness to try something new to increase student engagement. The evidence indicates that an educator's belief that all students can learn, and having high expectations for all students, are strongly related to above-average academic performance. How can the educator ensure that these beliefs and expectations are incorporated into the exercise? It may be as simple as a statement of intention when introducing the exercise. The educator should also look for ways to structure the exercise so that students and the educator get to know each other better. Simply by doing the exercise, assuming there is an opportunity for discussion and sharing at some point, this should happen.

According to the instructional approaches context, this is a multisection course with large classes, where most assignments are standardized and automatically graded, providing minimal feedback. The lack of regular developmental feedback is likely to negatively affect student perceptions about the course, and cue students to use a surface approach to learning. To address this negative contextual factor, the educator should build some form of feedback into the exercise. An easy way to do this is to build a think–pair–share activity with a debrief into the exercise.

The findings about instructional context reinforce the importance of creating and implementing this experiential exercise to help students see the importance and relevance of the course. The educator probably cannot change the basic set-up of the course, but they can make sure that the learning objectives for the exercise are clear and relevant, allow enough time for the exercise, provide some choice in the exercise, encourage discussion, and encourage small group work. Incorporating any or all of these instructional approaches into the exercise is likely to increase student learning.

Because most grading in the course is summative, with little other feed-back, the educator might use a classroom assessment technique such as a minute paper after the exercise to get feedback and/or determine what students learned. The educator could then use this feedback to modify/improve the exercise and/or clarify any student misunderstandings. Providing form-ative feedback like this to both the educator and students will increase learning.

The general context is quite challenging, with departmental, school, university, and societal pressures for improved performance and accountability. These macro factors may affect demands on the educator and the educator's

Table 2.16   Assessing the impact of context: an example (creating an experiential exercise to help students connect the content to their lives)

Contextual factors	My context	High-impact contextual factors to be considered	Action plan
Specific context			
Learners	Students in the course are in their second year of school, most work part-time, about 50% are first-generation university students, this is a required course for them, while these students are digital natives – comfortable with technology and social media – most view the course topics (e.g., creating an Excel spreadsheet, analyzing data to solve a problem) as boring and hard	Growth mindset Metacognition Self-efficacy Appropriate attributions Approach to learning	Creating an experiential exercise to help students connect the course content to their lives is appropriate and likely to help students learn Incorporate mastery and/or vicarious experiences into the exercise Consider implementing growth mindset, how to study and/or appropriate attribution experiential exercises during the course to help first-generation college student succeed in the course (out of scope for this exercise)

Experiential exercises in the classroom

Contextual factors	My context	High-impact contextual factors to be considered	Action plan
Educator	The educator is an adjunct, he (or she) is teaching two sections of this course, he concurrently teaches two sections of a similar course at another university, he does not have any formal training in the scholarship of teaching and learning, he has been teaching for more than ten years, he is tired of students tuning out and dreading his classes and is looking for a way to better engage his students, a colleague told him if he implemented at least one experiential exercise in his course, it might make a difference	High expectations for all Belief all students can learn Establishes caring and respectful relationships with students	Can the exercise be designed in a way that reinforces high expectations for all; belief all students can learn? Can the exercise help students and the educator get to know and respect each other? Consider revising syllabus and/or course polices to be clear about expectations and beliefs (out of scope for this exercise)
Instructional approaches			
Instructional methods	The course has multiple sections, all educators use the same textbook and assignments, there are six quizzes and six projects The educator usually lectures, answers questions and works examples in class	Good teaching[a] Clear goals[b] Appropriate assessment[c] Appropriate workload[d] Independence in learning[e]	Make sure the learning objectives for the exercise are clear Allow enough time for the activity Provide students with some choice in the exercise Encourage discussion Encourage small group work

Contextual factors	My context	High-impact contextual factors to be considered	Action plan
Assessment methods	The quizzes and projects are graded automatically in the learning management system/publisher learning environment providing minimal feedback	Normative assessment	Use an ungraded minute paper after the exercise to assess what students learned; share feedback on what students write at the next class
Subject	This is an introductory required course, students are required to take two additional higher-level courses in this subject, the course has a high fail and withdrawal rate, students are generally not enthused about the subject		Focus on high-impact micro contextual factors
General context			
Department	The department chair is new and trying to improve the quality of teaching in the department, she (or he) is under pressure to find ways to lower the fail/withdrawal rates without sacrificing academic rigor. The state legislature is clamoring for more accountability in higher education		Focus on high-impact micro contextual factors

Contextual factors	My context	High-impact contextual factors to be considered	Action plan
School/university	The school is accredited and focused on maintaining accreditation, the Dean is concerned that using so many adjuncts may jeopardize accreditation The university has launched a major campaign to improve graduation rates		Focus on high-impact micro contextual factors
Profession/society	The state legislature is clamoring for more accountability in higher education		Focus on high-impact micro contextual factors

Notes:

[a] Show an interest in students' opinions and attempt to understand difficulties students may be having; express positive expectations and seek to motivate students; provide clear and useful explanations; work to make subjects interesting; provide feedback on progress.

[b] Explain right from the start the learning objectives; provide markers of where we are going; explain the standard of work expected.

[c] Emphasizes understanding, not just memorizing; assessment is progressive and spaced over time; involves feedback beyond grades.

[d] Setting a feasible amount of material to cover; focus the range of topics to be covered; allow adequate time for work to be completed.

[e] Offers a degree of choice in: developing areas of interest; how material is learned; the forms or modes of assessment

resilience and priorities. However, at this time, the evidence suggests that the best path for the educator is to rely on high-impact, easy-to-implement, evidence-based approaches as they create this exercise, which means focusing on the specific context (students, educator, and instructional approaches) and high-impact micro contextual factors (see Figure 2.8). See Table 2.17, "Worksheet – assessing the impact of context" for a worksheet that educators can use to assess their context, consider high-impact contextual factors, and develop action plans when designing experiential exercises.

WHAT WE KNOW ABOUT WHAT WORKS

Given a better understanding of contextual factors, their impact on learning and their implications for the creation, adaptation, adoption, and implementation of experiential exercises, we now share: (1) essential insights; and (2) recommendations. For each step in the Effective Experiential Exercise Design Model, theory, evidence, best practices, and practical experience about context and process are synthesized to define essential insights about experiential exercises, whether creating an original exercise or adapting or adopting an existing exercise. For each step in the process, practical advice and prescriptive actions are shared. Finally an Experiential Exercise Implementation Checklist is provided (see Table 2.18), so that educators can assess the extent to which an exercise complies with best practices and recommendations. The nature of the subject and the macro contextual factors are not discussed here because of the limited evidence of their direct or high impact on learning.

It is vital to remember that the effectiveness or impact of any micro contextual factor, particularly instructional approaches such as experiential exercises, is dependent on appropriate use and proper implementation. For example, a highly engaging game may be used in the classroom, but if there is no clear learning objective and no opportunity to debrief or reflect on learning, there may be little learning. Or, if a debate is used in a course, but the instructions are not clear, no feedback is provided for questions, and personal attacks are allowed, there may be little learning and student motivation may suffer. For educators implementing experiential exercises in the classroom, both what you do and how you do it matters.

Assess Context

Essential insights
Specific context is more important than general context. Specific context has a higher impact on learning and is more influenceable by educators. The characteristics of the learner, the characteristics of the educator and instructional methods (instructional approaches and assessment) are the highest-impact specific contextual factors and therefore the key levers for consideration when creating, adapting, or implementing experiential exercises.

Recommendations (practical advice)
When creating or modifying an experiential exercise, focus on incorporating activities and cues that are most likely to encourage student motivation and a deep approach to learning (that is, clear learning goals; some independence or choice in the exercise; clear, useful explanations and directions; adequate time for the exercise; ensure relevance to students is clear; and listen/be engaged so that you can provide feedback and make adjustments as needed during the exercise).

Remember, the educator's beliefs and behaviors, as perceived by students, are high-impact contextual factors. So make sure that before, during, and after the exercise you continue to communicate and send cues to students that you have high expectations for all of them related to the exercise, that you believe they are all capable of successfully doing the exercise, and that you respect each student and care about them and their learning.

Define Learning Objectives

Essential insights
Clear learning objectives are a high-impact contextual factor and a crucial element of an effective experiential exercise. Clear, aligned learning objectives increase the likelihood of learning during an experiential exercise. Clear learning objectives influence students' approach to learning during an exercise and their perceptions about the quality of teaching during an exercise.

Recommendations (practical advice)
Invest the time required to create strong, clear learning objectives for your exercise. Familiarize yourself with the best practices for creating learning objectives as reviewed earlier in the "Model description including best practices and evidence for best practices" section and use them. When developing the objectives for an exercise, refer to examples which can be modeled (see

Table 2.17   Worksheet – assessing the impact of context

Use this worksheet to assess your context:
• In the "My context" column, describe the context for your experiential exercise.
• Review the "High-impact factors to be considered."
• In the "Action plan" column, describe the actions you will take to increase the odds of student learning after considering the high-impact factors; it is not necessary to adopt every high-impact factor: select only those appropriate for your exercise.

Contextual factors	My context	High-impact factors to be considered	Action plan
Specific context			
Learners		Growth mindset Metacognition Self-efficacy Appropriate attributions Approach to learning	
Educator		High expectations for all Belief all students can learn Establishes caring and respectful relationships with students	
Instructional approaches			
Instructional methods		Good teaching[a] Clear goals[b] Appropriate assessment[c] Appropriate workload[d] Independence in learning[e]	
Assessment Methods		Normative assessment	
Subject			
General context			
Department			
School/university			
Profession/society			

Notes:
[a] Show an interest in students' opinions and attempt to understand difficulties students may be having; express positive expectations and seek to motivate students; provide clear and useful explanations; work to make subjects interesting; provide feedback on progress.
[b] Explain right from the start the learning objectives; provide markers of where the course is going; explain the standard of work expected.
[c] Emphasizes understanding, not just memorizing; assessment is progressive and spaced over time; involves feedback beyond grades.
[d] Setting a feasible amount of material to cover; focus the range of topics to be covered; allow adequate time for work to be completed.
[e] Offers a degree of choice in: developing areas of interest; how material is learned; the forms or modes of assessment.

examples in Chapter 3). Avoid overuse of lower-level learning objectives such as know and understand; experiential exercises are ideal for accomplishing higher-order learning objectives such as apply, analyze, evaluate, integrate, and create. Focus on creating a few, important learning objectives for the exercise; too many learning objectives may muddle the purpose of the exercise.

Clearly and effectively communicate learning objectives. Use multiple modes of communication to convey objectives (that is, verbal, visual, written; say it, show it, recap it/reinforce it).

Help students see the relevance or importance of the exercise learning objectives to their lives. Creating situations/activities within an exercise where students discover the relevance of the objective or tell each other why the learning objective is relevant (peer-to-peer teaching) are more effective than educator telling approaches.

Given the importance of clear learning objectives to learning, educators should proactively check for student understanding of the objectives. Confirm that students understand the purpose of the exercise by asking them to restate it in their own words, write it in their own words, or explain it to a peer; this can be done before, during, and/or after an exercise.

Select/Create Learning Activities

Essential insights
Instructional methods are a high-impact contextual factor. Choice of instructional methods/learning activities is one of the most powerful tools an educator has to create effective experiential exercises and influence student learning and motivation during an exercise and throughout a course. Experiential exercises which incorporate mastery experiences, vicarious experiences, verbal persuasion, and emotional engagement will increase student self-efficacy and learning. Experiential exercises can be used by educators to influence students to adopt high-impact beliefs and behaviors (that is, growth mindset, metacognitive learning skills, and appropriate attributions) that increase the efficiency, effectiveness, persistence, and depth of their learning.

Recommendations (practical advice)
Whenever possible, look for opportunities to incorporate mastery learning, vicarious learning, verbal persuasion, and emotional engagement into experiential exercises. Include challenging tasks/activities in exercises that students have to work hard to master. Give them the time and support needed

to achieve mastery; this may require feedback and guidance during the exercise, and flexibility around the timing of the exercise. Include opportunities for students to learn from each other, in pairs, in small groups, or as a class. Before and during an exercise, express confidence in students' ability to successfully complete the exercise. Some students may need individual encouragement during the exercise. If possible, give students some opportunities for autonomy or choice within the exercise (for example, students select the firm they will analyze; students select the format for their deliverable – written or video, slide deck or paper; students have a choice of roles, and so on). Encourage emotional engagement by selecting or letting students select activities that are meaningful, relevant, and/or involve peer interaction.

Incorporate other high-impact, effective learning activities into experiential exercises, such as advance organizers, worked examples (that is, a step-by-step demonstration of how to do a task or solve a problem), small group and/or class discussions based on open-ended questions, concept mapping, multiple opportunities for practice (with feedback between practices), peer teaching, and cooperative learning.

Consider incorporating a variety of types of learning activities (that is, getting information, doing/observing, and reflecting) into exercises; this can increase engagement and effectiveness. Also consider engaging students at multiple levels within an exercise (that is, individual, team, and class levels) to ensure individual accountability and achieve the social, emotional, and learning benefits of peer interactions. Use Table 2.6 to design and/or assess the learning activities in an exercise. A word of caution: do not overdo it; do not cram too many activities into the time allotted. Each activity should contribute to accomplishment of the learning objective in a unique way.

Consider creating or adopting/adapting experiential exercises which increase student motivation and learning; that is, exercises which teach growth mindset, metacognitive learning skills, and appropriate attributions. Although these types of exercises do not directly support course content learning objectives, they do help students develop the capacity to achieve course content learning objectives. Thus, they indirectly support achievement of course learning objectives, and they support resilience and persistence in learning. These benefits can be especially important when teaching minority and/or underprepared students.

Select/Create Assessments

Essential insights
Appropriate assessment is a high-impact contextual factor. Appropriate assessment emphasizes understanding, not memorization, is progressive and spaced over time, and includes feedback beyond grades. Timely, developmental formative feedback with opportunities to try again/make revisions positively affects student perceptions of teaching and student approaches to learning.

Recommendations (practical advice)
Include assessment in your experiential exercises, even brief exercises. Assessment ensures that both the educator and the students know whether the learning objectives for the exercise have been achieved. Be upfront and specific about how learning from the exercise will be assessed. Share expectations about what "good" looks like for any deliverables or work products. Communicate assessment specifics before the exercise, check for student understanding of the assessment approach, and clarify if needed.

Learning activities can also be assessments. For example, if an exercise includes creation of a deliverable (for example, a solution/decision/plan, a presentation, a poster, a reflection, a concept map, a role play performance, or a debate), the creation of that deliverable is a learning activity and the learning activity may be assessed and/or graded (for example, using self-assessment, peer feedback, class feedback, a grading rubric, or grading checklist). Take advantage of this dual functionality to make more efficient experiential exercises.

Use formative and criterion-referenced assessments in experiential exercises. Formative feedback and criterion-referenced grading encourage students to take a deep approach to learning. Pair formative assessments with opportunities to revise and/or re-do; this gives students opportunities to learn and grow: to master the concepts being taught.

Use rubrics. Rubrics help clearly communicate expectations. Rubrics save time and increase objectivity in assessment. Invest in creating rubrics or adapt/adopt existing rubrics for your experiential exercises; rubrics will help you to grade faster and more accurately, plus students will receive feedback via the rubric. If educators want to create their own rubrics, consider using one of the free online platforms that allow you to create custom rubrics: RubiStar, iRubric, Rubric Maker, or Annenberg Learner. If educators want to adopt established rubrics, consider the Association of American Colleges and Universities' (AACU) Valid Assessment of Learning in Undergraduate

Education (VALUE) rubrics, free online rubrics for 16 essential learning outcomes (that is, from critical thinking to teamwork, to written communication, to ethical reasoning, to intercultural knowledge and competence).

Assess both the exercise and student learning from the exercise. As noted above, assessments of learning help both students and the educator understand whether the learning objectives have been accomplished. Assessments of exercises help the educator know if the exercise is working, and how to adjust or adapt it. Use Table 2.7 to develop an assessment plan for your exercise.

Ensure Alignment

Essential insights
Alignment of learning objectives, learning activities, and assessments is required for learning; lack of alignment encourages a surface approach to learning.

Recommendations (practical advice)
Use Table 2.10 to assess the alignment of the learning objectives, learning activities, and assessments for your experiential exercises. Use the diagnostic questions to check for both fit and impact.

Implement

Essential insights
Planning and preparation pay off. The educator will be more confident, and the exercise will be delivered more effectively, if exercises are well planned, contingency plans have been developed, and appropriate preparations have been made.

Recommendations (practical advice)
Create and use an exercise sequence and timing table to plan, guide, and monitor implementation. Use Table 2.11 to create an exercise activity sequence and timing plan. During the exercise, note how long each part of the exercise actually took; this information will be valuable when reflecting and revising.

Assemble, in advance, any props, supplies, materials, and/or learning aids needed during the exercise. After the exercise, store any leftover materials and consider replenishing any depleted materials, so you are ready for the next implementation.

Remember, what the educator says and does – how they act – during an exercise are some of the most important cues for students. Students are more likely to engage, focus, and learn if the educator has high expectations, those expectations are clear, the educator shows through words and actions that they believe all students are capable of succeeding in the exercise, the educator treats students with respect and demonstrates that they care about them (that is, answers their questions, is responsive to their concerns and feedback, makes adjustments based on their feedback, provides support and guidance as needed).

Use pre-prepared questions, which are tightly aligned with the exercise learning objectives, to guide discussions during an exercise (for example, during small group discussions, during whole class discussions, during a debrief). These questions ensure that the discussion is aligned with the learning objectives. During the exercise the educator can refer to these questions to keep the discussion on track, know when the discussion is getting off-topic, and know when the discussion's purposes have been accomplished.

Adjust and Adapt

Essential insights
As clichéd as it sounds, expect the unexpected. Be prepared, emotionally and mentally, to make adjustments/adaptations during exercises; consider this part of the process, not an anomaly.

Recommendations (practical advice)
Use the experiential exercise learning objectives and knowledge of high-impact micro contextual factors to guide decision-making during implementation. Do not let commitment to the plan, time pressure, or frustration lead to poor decision-making during the exercise. Adjust and adapt based on what will best help to achieve the learning objectives, taking advantage of your knowledge of what works and what is high impact.

Be caring and respectful regarding student needs during the exercise. If students need more time to complete a learning activity, give it to them. If the discussion is taking much longer than anticipated, students seem deeply engaged, and the discussion is productive, allow the discussion to continue.

Do not be afraid to admit that an exercise is not going as planned. Consider, in the moment, brainstorming with students about possible adjustments or inviting them to vote/express their opinions about adjustment options you are considering.

Reflect and Revise

Essential insights
Reflection is a crucial part of continuous improvement. Reflecting sooner is better for capturing rich detail and recollections; reflecting later is better for perspective; so do both. Evidence helps to make better, more informed revisions.

Recommendations (practical advice)
Reflect; do it. Think of it as an investment in your professional development, an investment in developing expertise. Educators face many demands on their time and talents and therefore have a tendency to put off important but less urgent tasks such as reflection. Make reflection a priority and you will realize the benefits in the classroom with more efficient and effective learning experiences.

Build reflection and revision of experiential exercises into your routine. If reflection is integrated into teaching routines, it is more likely to be done. For example, educators may have routines for recording attendance, grading, or recording grades after class. Build time for reflection into these routine processes. Educators also have routines for weekly class preparation, end-of-semester course clean-up, and beginning-of-semester course preparation. Integration of reflection on experiential exercises into these processes increases the probability of doing reflection and increases the odds of the educator achieving continuous improvement in their teaching practice.

Consider partnering with a trusted colleague for periodic reflection reviews, class observations, and troubleshooting/problem-solving sessions. Having an accountability partner who shares an interest in refining and improving experiential exercises can be a source of support, perspective, and ideas.

Tools: implementation checklist
See Table 2.18, "Experiential Exercise Implementation Checklist" for a checklist which can be used to assess the extent that an exercise complies with best practices and recommendations.

RECAP

In this chapter, we have reviewed classroom-oriented instructional design models and introduced a model specifically developed for creating and implementing effective experiential exercises in the classroom. This model more explicitly addresses contextual factors than other models. The pre-

Table 2.18   *Experiential Exercise Implementation Checklist*

Use this checklist to prepare for and/or assess implementation of an experiential exercise. The goal is not to be able to check every item on the list, but to remind yourself of best practices and to consider how you might incorporate some or more high-impact practices into an exercise.

_____ Assess context (see Table 2.17)

    _____ Include cues, actions, and activities likely to encourage motivation and a deep approach to learning

        _____ Have clear learning goals

        _____ Communicate/demonstrate high expectations for all students

        _____ Communicate/demonstrate a belief that all students can learn

        _____ Communicate/demonstrate respect and caring for students

            _____ Know and use their names

            _____ Listen to their opinions

                _____ Polls

                _____ Votes

            _____ Be responsive to their questions and feedback

        _____ Offer some autonomy or choice for students

        _____ Provide clear, useful explanations and directions

        _____ Allow adequate time for activities

        _____ Have opportunities for students to discover or learn about the relevance/importance of the exercise

        _____ Listen and watch for feedback

        _____ Be responsive to feedback

        _____ Make adjustments as needed/able

_____ Define the learning objectives you want students to achieve

        _____ Focus on a few, important, clear objectives

        _____ Focus on appropriate level of objectives (not too low; not too high)

        _____ Use multiple modes to clearly and effectively communicate objectives

            _____ Verbal

            _____ Visual

            _____ Written

        _____ Ensure relevance is discovered/learned versus told

        _____ Confirm student understanding of objectives

_____ Select or create learning activities which will provide experiences that students need to achieve the learning objectives (see Table 2.6)

    _____ Include opportunities for mastery learning

    _____ Include opportunities for vicarious learning

    _____ Use verbal persuasion/encouragement from educator and peers

    _____ Include opportunities for emotional engagement with activities, content, peers, and educator

    _____ Include opportunities for peer learning in pairs or small groups

    _____ Use high-impact instructional methods

        _____ Advance organizer

        _____ Worked examples

        _____ Small group discussion using open-ended questions

        _____ Whole-class discussion using open-ended questions

        _____ Concept mapping

        _____ Multiple opportunities to practice (with feedback between practices)

        _____ Peer-to-peer teaching

        _____ Teamwork/cooperative learning

    _____ Include a variety of types of activities

    _____ Engage students at more than one level

        _____ Individual

        _____ Pairs

        _____ Small groups

_____ Class
_____ Find ways to incorporate cues, actions, activities related to:
    _____ Growth mindset
    _____ Metacognitive learning skills
    _____ Appropriate attributions
_____ Select or create assessments which will help you and the students determine if the learning objectives have been achieved (see Table 2.7)
    _____ Include some assessment activity
        _____ Formative
        _____ Criterion-referenced
        _____ Opportunities to revise/redo
        _____ Assess student learning
        _____ Assess the exercise
    _____ Use rubrics
    _____ Share expectations/review examples about what good looks like before exercise and/or assessment
    _____ Check for student understanding of assessment criteria
_____ Ensure alignment: compare your learning objectives, learning activities, and assessments to ensure they are tightly aligned and appropriate given your context (see Table 2.10)
_____ Adjust and adapt your planned objectives, activities, and assessments as needed based on your critical assessment of their alignment and fit with your context
_____ Implement your experiential exercise in the classroom (see Table 2.11)
    _____ Assemble props, supplies, and learning aids in advance
    _____ Use words and actions to cue and reinforce
        _____ High expectations for all students
        _____ Belief all students can learn (with effort, new strategies, and feedback)
        _____ Respect and care for students
    _____ Use pre-prepared discussion questions aligned with learning objectives to guide and manage discussion
_____ Adjust and adapt in real time as you implement, responding to the situation as it unfolds
    _____ Use learning objectives and expertise to guide decision-making
    _____ Demonstrate respect and care for student needs
_____ Reflect and revise: reflect on your experience and make appropriate revisions (see Table 2.12)
    _____ Complete reflection worksheet immediately after exercise
    _____ Revise exercise and supporting materials as needed before next use of exercise

scriptive model was described and the theory, evidence and best practices associated with each part of the model were summarized.

Contextual factors, micro and macro, were examined in detail and the evidence of their impact on teaching and learning was assessed and summarized. Micro contextual factors – specifically, the student, the educator, and instructional methods, that is, instructional approaches and assessments – are high-impact contextual factors. These micro factors have more impact on learning and are more influenceable by educators than macro factors.

Finally, for each step in the model, theory, evidence, best practices, and experience were synthesized to define essential insights and recommendations for practitioners. And an implementation checklist was introduced.

In Chapter 3, three examples of experiential exercise development and implementation in action are shared, and resources for implementing experiential exercises are provided.

3. How to prepare and implement

Designing and implementing an experiential exercise can be complex and intimidating, yet the rewards for tackling this challenge are enormous in terms of the educator's ability to deliver significant, engaging, authentic learning experiences. In the first chapter, the theory underpinning experiential exercises was reviewed, and evidence about the effectiveness of experiential exercises was summarized. In the second chapter, a process for creating, adapting, and adopting experiential exercises was defined, best practices for creating and implementing exercises were summarized, high-impact contextual factors which influence learning were discussed, and the evidence about what works when designing, creating, and implementing experiential exercises was summarized. In this third chapter, development and implementation of experiential exercises are illustrated via three specific examples: a graduate exercise to develop mindset and learning skills, a professional training exercise to develop cross-cultural and cross-functional communication skills, and an undergraduate exercise to develop leadership skills. This chapter also includes recommended readings and resources related to implementation of experiential exercises, and examples of experiential exercises available by discipline.

Each of the authors shares an example of how they approached the design and implementation of an experiential exercise using the model or process described in Chapter 2 (see Figure 3.1 for reference). These examples illustrate how different people with different backgrounds, experiences, and beliefs create and use experiential exercises. The first exercise, Embracing a Growth Mindset, requires graduate-level students to critically reflect on their beliefs and openness to learning. The exercise combines video content, individual reflection, and small group discussions to foster growth mindset development. The second exercise, Global Strategy Meeting, immerses professionals in an interactive game. During the game, students play specific functional and cultural roles while collaborating as an executive team to determine organizational priorities. The last exercise, Creating a Leadership Brand, provides undergraduate students with the opportunity to identify and articulate their personal leadership brand. This semester-long exercise allows students to learn about themselves via self-assessments and regular reflection on their learning; the exercise culminates with a gallery walk where students share their work with the class and interact with each other and their projects. These examples provide insights into each educator's design and implementation choices. Our hope is that these examples will be useful to you in thinking through and planning your own experiential exercises in the classroom.

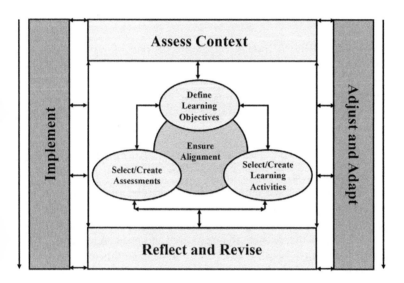

Figure 3.1   The Effective Experiential Exercise Design Model

IMPLEMENTATION IN ACTION: EMBRACING A GROWTH MINDSET – MARY K. FOSTER

Embracing a Growth Mindset (Foster, 2020) is an experiential exercise designed to introduce students to a foundational concept related to learning: mindsets or implicit theories – people's beliefs about the nature of human attributes (Dweck, 1999, 2008). This exercise introduces and explores growth mindset: the idea that skills can be learned, that you can learn and grow, and that to do so you must focus on getting better through sustained effort (tackling challenges, making mistakes, getting feedback, changing your approach, and so on). This exercise engages students cognitively and emotionally at the individual, team, and class levels. A detailed explanation of this exercise and all the associated implementation materials for it may be found in Foster (2020).

BOX 3.1 EDUCATOR'S PERSPECTIVE – MOTIVATION

In August of 2015, I came across the concept of growth mindset in *How Learning Works: 7 Research-Based Principles for Smart Teaching* (Ambrose et al., 2010). As I learned more about the research related to growth mindset, I was struck by three things: (1) a growth mindset can be learned; (2) many positive outcomes are associated with a growth mindset (for example, persistence in the face of adversity, higher levels of engagement, and higher academic performance); and (3) growth mindset interventions yield larger benefits for disadvantaged or underprepared students.

Because I teach at a university with many underprepared minority students, I decided to create a way to teach growth mindset in all my courses. I wanted to design an effective, easy-to-implement experiential exercise that was based on research and pedagogical best practices. In addition, because I wanted to implement this exercise in all my courses, it had to be relatively short; I did not think I could justify devoting more than 50 to 90 minutes of a course to this activity.

Assess Context

Educators designing an experiential exercise should first assess the context. Educators who think they already have a general understanding of their context should still formally assess it. Having the discipline to formally research and evaluate context pays off with useful insights. See the "Getting Started" and "Considering Context" sections in Chapter 2 for more insights on contextual factors to be considered, the impact of contextual factors, and how process and contextual factors may interact. See Table 2.4 for examples of contextual factors; see Table 2.16 for examples of how assessment of contextual factors can influence exercise development and execution.

BOX 3.2 EDUCATOR'S PERSPECTIVE – ASSESS CONTEXT

General Context

I teach at Morgan State University, a public historically black university in Baltimore, Maryland, USA. The university has about 7,000 students (about 6,000 undergraduate and 1,000 graduate). Seventy-nine percent of students are African American, 10 percent are international, and 3 percent are Hispanic. The international students mostly come from Saudi Arabia, Kuwait, and Nigeria (3 percent, 3 percent, and 1 percent, respectively). Fifty-five percent of students are federal Pell Grant recipients and 75 percent receive federal need-based loans. Twenty-eight percent of students are non-traditional (that is, older). According to the university's strategic plan, student success as measured by retention and graduation rates is one of five key goals for the institution.

Specific Context

Within the university, I teach in the Earl G. Graves School of Business and Management, an Association to Advance Collegiate Schools of Business (AACSB)-accredited institution. I teach a variety of courses: strategy, a capstone course all undergraduate business students must take in their last semester; innovation and entrepreneurship, a capstone course for MBA students; and instructional methods and case research and writing, required courses for doctoral students. I love teaching; I believe in active learning; and I am committed to continuous improvement in my practice of teaching and learning.

Assess the Context

My general context is an environment where my idea (that is, implementing a growth mindset experiential activity) might be useful because students are more likely to be underprepared and may be more likely to benefit from this intervention. Plus, this exercise is consistent with the university's goal of enhancing student success and will likely be appreciated by my school's administration (that is, it could be a teaching innovation to highlight in accreditation reports).

Because I wanted to implement the exercise in a variety of courses serving various levels of students (that is, my specific context), I needed to be sure that the exercise would be widely perceived as useful and engaging by students, otherwise I would risk losing credibility and student attention. Because I believe in active learning and continuous improvement, I was comfortable tackling this project and committed to revising and refining the exercise until it was efficient and effective.

My evaluation of the context suggested that this idea was a good fit with my general context, specific context, characteristics of the learners, and characteristics of the educator. Researching and evaluating my context helped me to see that this idea was generally a good fit with the context; and I discovered some insights about special considerations that I needed to address, given my context.

Define Learning Objectives

When thinking about learning objectives or learning outcomes, focus on the two to three things that students should learn, remember, or take away. Ideally, the learning objectives should be what a student would recall if you ran into them a year or two later and asked them: what did you learn from that activity? Focusing on student takeaways a year or two later helps to focus on only the most important learning objectives. Refer to the discussion in Chapter 2 about how to define learning objectives. See Table 2.5 for a comparison of key learning outcome taxonomies.

Upon completion of the Embracing a Growth Mindset exercise, students will be able to:

- Define growth and fixed mindsets (so students and the educator have a shared understanding and can use the terms in class and conversations going forward).
- Explain the benefits of a growth mindset versus a fixed mindset (if students can compare and contrast the concepts, it indicates a higher level of learning; they are discriminating between the concepts and evaluating the differences).
- Explain how to develop a growth mindset (if students can explain how to develop a growth mindset, they may be able to develop one

themselves, they may be able to act and/or to teach others how to develop a growth mindset).

Select/Create Learning Activities

When designing learning experiences, try to include three different types of learning activities in an exercise: getting information and ideas, experiencing (for example, doing or observing), and reflecting. See Table 3.1 for the worksheet used to select/create learning activities for this exercise. Refer to Table 2.6 in Chapter 2 for a worksheet template for your own use.

BOX 3.3 EDUCATOR'S PERSPECTIVE – SELECT/ CREATE LEARNING ACTIVITIES

As I learned about growth mindset, I learned about various interventions that had been developed and proven effective via research. I was looking for an effective, easy-to-implement, low-burden (in time, cost, effort) exercise, when I came across an article by Aronson et al. (2002) which described approaches to attitude change likely to be effective based on research:

* "Saying is believing": advocate a position in your own words, and you are more likely to believe it.
* Make a public commitment to a position, and you are more likely to accept the position.
* Consider how past behaviors are consistent with a belief; you are more likely to maintain the belief if your behaviors are consistent with the belief.

I integrated these findings with best practices for experiential exercises and created Table 3.1.

Based on this plan, the exercise was developed. A summary of the learning activities incorporated into this exercise follows:

* Part A: Getting in Touch with Beliefs. Students are asked to reflect on their work and life experiences and create a list of attitudes and beliefs they associate with success. Using peer recorders and a class

Table 3.1   *Select/create learning activities for the Embracing*
               a Growth Mindset exercise

Types of learning activities	Getting information and ideas	Experiencing (doing or observing)	Reflecting
Individual	Watch video (Part B)	Recall beliefs (Part A) Recall past actions/ behaviors (consider past behaviors) (Part A) Capture learning from video (Part B)	Reflection assignment (Part E)
Group/Team		Share past actions/ behaviors ("saying is believing") (Part C)	Summarize lessons learned (public commitment; "saying is believing") (Part C)
Class	Watch video (Part B)	Share learning from video Share beliefs (public commitment) (Part D)	Share impactful story (public commitment; "saying is believing") Share lessons learned (public commitment; "saying is believing") (Part D)

discussion, all the ideas generated by students are captured on the board.

- Part B: Learning New Ideas. Students are asked to watch a brief video about mindsets; they are asked to look for several things in the video and to be prepared to discuss these matters after viewing the video.
- Part C: Learning From Each Other. Students are asked to think about a specific time they faced adversity and how they overcame it. Students are given a few minutes to collect their thoughts, then they share their stories with each other in small groups and discuss lessons they can learn from their experiences. A few stories are shared with the class, and then teams share the lessons they have learned from their stories.
- Part D: Debrief. Students are asked to summarize lessons learned, explain the advantages of a growth mindset, and explain how a growth mindset can be developed or invoked. Depending upon the class length, deliberate practice (that is, a purposeful and systematic approach to improving or learning) may be briefly discussed.

- Part E: Reflecting on learning. The objective of the reflection assignment is to give students an opportunity to think about their experiences overcoming adversity, what they have learned from their experiences, and how what they believe and know is connected to what they have learned about mindsets.

BOX 3.4 EDUCATOR'S PERSPECTIVE – SELECT/ CREATE LEARNING ACTIVITIES

I decided to start the exercise with an individual learning activity to focus students and get them on task and engaged. To bring the class together and give students an opportunity to learn from each other, student volunteer scribes record all the ideas on the board (public declaration).

Then I introduced the concept of growth mindset. I used a video to introduce this new information, since I did not have a reading to assign. Before showing the video, I gave students a few questions that I expected them to be able to answer after watching the video. This increased individual focus and engagement with the video. After the video, I used a class discussion to confirm comprehension and depth of understanding.

Next, I asked students to think about a time when they faced adversity and used a growth mindset to overcome it. To lower the perceived social risk for students and to increase engagement, I had students work in small groups/teams so that each student could share their story in a smaller group setting. Using peer-to-peer learning and within-group/team public declaration helps to solidify acceptance of learning and reinforces learning.

Next, I asked students to share the most impactful stories they have heard, because this peer selection and support has more emotional impact than people self-selecting and telling their own stories. This approach also ensured that the class does not just hear from the extroverts or strong egos.

Finally, the debrief allows students to publicly explain what they have learned or now believe; it also allows students to reflect on their past beliefs and behaviors and see how they are or are not connected to what they have learned about growth mindset. They also discuss actions which they can take to invoke a growth mindset.

Select/Create Assessments

When designing an experiential exercise, consider a variety of assessment approaches. As noted in Chapter 2, assessments can be used to assess both the experiential exercise and student learning. See Table 2.7 for the assessment worksheet, and Tables 2.8 and 2.9 for example exercise assessments.

In this exercise, originally the assessment focus was on assessing the exercise versus assessing student learning. First, an informal student survey was used to elicit feedback; this evolved into use of a formal anonymous feedback survey on the exercise itself. Ultimately, the assessment focus shifted to assessment of student learning via the introduction of a formal reflection assignment and a pre–post assessment using the growth mindset scale.

BOX 3.5 EDUCATOR'S PERSPECTIVE – SELECT/ CREATE ASSESSMENTS

When assessing an exercise, I almost always start with student feedback on the exercise itself, because this type of assessment is easy to implement, and if done properly often yields significant insights. I summarize the feedback and share results with students, explaining how I will use the feedback to improve the activity; closing the feedback loop ensures that students know their feedback was heard and is being used.

When focused on developing and/or refining an experiential exercise, it is easy to lose focus on assessment of the learning objectives, which I did. After facilitating this exercise several times, I realized that this was a weakness of my implementation. So, I created a written reflection assignment. I have since translated this assignment into a discussion board assignment and a video assignment. In some classes this is a graded assignment, in other classes it is an extra credit opportunity.

Ensure Alignment

Are the learning objectives, learning activities, and student assessments aligned? Are they consistent, do they fit, do they make sense? It is easy to assume that they are, because you have selected or created them. However, it is valuable to self-assess: to double-check to ensure alignment, whether you are creating a new exercise or adopting/adapting an existing exercise. See Table 2.10 for a worksheet to assess alignment. See Table 3.2 for such a table for this exercise.

Table 3.2   Assessing alignment – consistency of learning objectives, activities, and assessments for the Embracing a Growth Mindset exercise

Learning objectives	Learning activities	Assessments
Define growth and fixed mindsets	Watch video (Part B)	Answer questions about video (class discussion, Part B)
Explain the benefits of a growth mindset versus a fixed mindset	Watch video (Part B) Recall how overcame adversity (Parts C and D) Share stories about overcoming adversity (Parts C and D) Define and explain lessons learned (Parts C and D) Share lessons learned (Part D)	Answer questions about benefits of a growth versus a fixed mindset (class discussion, Parts B and D)
Explain how to develop a growth mindset	Share stories about overcoming adversity (Part C) Define and explain lessons learned (Parts C and D) Share lessons learned (Part D) Connect lessons learned to beliefs (Part D)	Written reflection assessment (Part E)

BOX 3.6   EDUCATOR'S PERSPECTIVE – ENSURE ALIGNMENT

As I created the table, I tested each learning activity and assessment: where do they fit, will they really help students achieve the learning objective? If not, I needed to rethink my activities and assessments. From my original analysis, I saw that the exercise was light on formal, individual assessment, which is why I created a written reflection assignment.

Implement

To prepare to implement an experiential exercise, create a lesson plan or plan of action which includes the activities in sequence, estimated timing of each activity, and any notes. See Table 2.11 for an exercise sequence and timing worksheet. See Table 3.3 for the sequence of activities for this exercise.

BOX 3.7   EDUCATOR'S PERSPECTIVE – IMPLEMENTATION

Creating the plan helped me to think through every step of implementation in class, which helped me to think through what props/resources I needed to make the exercise flow. I often use student worksheets when implementing an exercise, because having the written instructions/expectations can help students focus and stay on track, especially if they are distracted during my verbal explanation. My best practice is to communicate important ideas/directions in three ways: via displayed slides, verbally, and in writing (for example, individual worksheets). In a distracted, short attention span world, I am trying to ensure that if a student misses the message in one format, they may get it in another format.

If an experiential exercise involves a number of activities, I often use the "what, why, how" format to describe each activity in my lesson plan and in slides and worksheets):

- What – an overview of what students will be doing (for example, work individually to brainstorm behaviors and beliefs you associate with success).
- Why – explain the rationale for why you are asking students to do this (for example, to draw upon your experience and learn from it).

Table 3.3   *Sequence and timing of activities for the Embracing a Growth Mindset exercise*

Sequence of activities	90 min. class	80 min. class	50 min. class over 2 days[a]
			Day 1
Part A: Getting in Touch With Beliefs	*17*	*14*	*14*
Introduction	2	1	1
Individually create list of attitudes and behaviors you associate with success; distribute worksheets; use worksheet A	3	3	3
Share items on lists (whole class)	12	10	10
Part B: Learning New Ideas	*22*	*20*	*20*
Watch video (share focus questions before viewing): https://www.youtube.com/watch?v=pN34FNbOKXc	12	12	12
Answer focus questions (whole class discussion)	10	8	8
Part C: Learning from Each Other	*18*	*16*	*16*
Form teams	5	3	3
Individually reflect on a time you faced adversity and overcame it (refer to worksheet B; record notes/thoughts on worksheet)	3	3	3
Within team share stories	5	5	5
Within team reflect on what you have learned from these experiences	5	5	5
			Day 2
Part D: Consolidating Learning	*33*	*29*	*25*
Debrief (whole class discussion)			
Share stories and lessons learned	10	10	7
Recap lessons learned (i.e., changes in thinking, changes in strategies, asking for help, etc.)	5	5	5
Explore connections between experiences and mindsets/deliberate practice	5	5	5
Review deliberate practice	3	3	2
Explore connections between growth mindset and beliefs about success (Part A)	5	3	2
Summarize learning, changes in thinking, plans to change	4	3	3
Wrap-up Explain reflection assignment and grading rubric Distribute and collect feedback form, if using	1	1	1
Total class time	90	80	75
Part E: Reflection Assignment (completed outside of class)			

Note:
[a] In this sequence, the exercise is implemented over two days or two class sessions. The reflection assignment (Part E) is completed after the first class session.

- How – provide detailed instructions about what students will be doing (for example, working individually, use this worksheet to list behaviors and beliefs you associate with success; list as many as you can; you have three minutes to create your list).

Finally, I assemble any props, copies of handouts, or other materials I need to implement the exercise. Then, I am off to class to implement the exercise: the plan.

Adjust and Adapt

Each class, each group of people working together, has their own pace and culture, so adjustments will vary by class. You must decide what is best in the moment, using your expertise and knowledge of the class and the learning objectives.

A particular type of adjustment or adaptation often needed when implementing an exercise is how long and how far to let discussions go. For example, in Part B of this exercise, learning objectives are for students to be able to define growth and fixed mindsets and explain the benefits of a growth versus a fixed mindset after watching a video. Therefore, pre-planned discussion prompts include:

- In your own words define a growth mindset. Share an example.
- In your own words define a fixed mindset. Share an example.
- In your own words, explain the benefits of a growth mindset versus a fixed mindset.

Having a clear understanding of the learning objectives and pre-planned discussion questions allows the facilitator to quickly rein in and/or refocus a discussion that may be getting off track. These resources also help an educator know when to end a discussion and move on to the next activity.

BOX 3.8 EDUCATOR'S PERSPECTIVE – ADJUST AND ADAPT

On one occasion when implementing this exercise, I had a few very verbal, vocal, debate-oriented students in the class. When students were sharing their ideas about behaviors and beliefs associated with success, they wanted to debate every idea. As soon as I realized what was happening, I clarified the purpose of the activity (the 'why') and redirected their focus to sharing, not debating. This allowed us to accomplish the learning objectives and keep on schedule.

Another time, I had a graduate class that moved slowly. The pace at which students engaged and completed activities was just slower than other sections of the course (for example, they talked a lot among themselves, were not great listeners, engaged in side chatter). When I implemented the growth mindset exercise early in the semester, part of the exercise which I expected to take 50–60 minutes was on pace to take 80 minutes. I decided to give students more time to finish the activities and moved the debrief for the exercise to the start of the next class. I proceeded with the reflection activity and asked them to complete it before the next class and the debrief. During the next class session, we had one of the best debriefs of this exercise (that is, highly engaged class discussion, high emotional connection to the content, and deep understanding of the benefits and drivers of a growth mindset), and I made an important discovery. This exercise could be successfully implemented over two class sessions, and the reflection could be placed between the two sessions. I now had another effective way to implement this exercise.

Reflect and Revise

After implementing an experiential exercise in the classroom, take a few minutes immediately after class to think about what worked and what didn't work. See Table 2.12 for a list of reflection questions.

BOX 3.9 EDUCATOR'S PERSPECTIVE – REFLECT AND REVISE

During Implementation

The first time I implemented the growth mindset exercise, I did not use worksheets. I noticed that a few students did not have paper or writing instruments; they borrowed paper and a pen or pencil from other students. On reflection, I decided to add pens and pencils to my supply list for the exercise, and I decided to follow my own best practices and provide worksheets, because I wanted students to be totally focused on the exercise and learning, and not distracted by looking for or sharing basic supplies.

After Implementation

During one of my latest post-implementation reflections, I realized that I was inserting/allowing a wide-ranging discussion after each part of the exercise. This was distracting students from the learning objectives, and making the exercise too long and unfocused. I revisited my original learning objectives and lesson plan and was reminded that the exercise only needed a class discussion after two parts of the exercise: after watching the video and during the debrief. I subsequently implemented these changes and the exercise is now more focused and effective.

Immediately Before Implementation

As I approached a new semester, where I would be teaching undergraduate and graduate courses, I reviewed my prior reflections and feedback to see whether I needed to make any changes to respond to the specific context in each course and the level of students. Based on this review, I selected the appropriate time for the exercise in each course. I also realized that, based on past experience and feedback, no special adjustments were needed to accommodate graduate or undergraduate students for this particular exercise.

Exercise Resources

See Appendix 3.1 for additional resources related to growth mindset, and how to integrate growth mindset ideas into your teaching practice.

IMPLEMENTATION IN ACTION: GLOBAL STRATEGY MEETING – JENNIE L. WALKER

This cross-cultural strategic meeting game is a two-hour or four-hour activity that is particularly valuable at the graduate and professional levels. In the exercise, each participant represents a unique culture and functional role within a senior executive team in the same organization. The group must work through differences in both culture and the priorities of their respective business functions to agree upon operational strategies for the coming year. Ultimately, they must agree on the top three priorities for the year and then present them to their organization's chief executive officer (CEO). Since students and professionals alike may not have first-hand experience with truly diverse team interactions, this exercise allows them to immerse themselves in a situation where they need to recognize different cultural behaviors and respond accordingly to achieve the objectives of the team. This places students in a complex learning situation that requires them to use both cognitive and affective skills.

The principal game elements were designed by one of the co-authors of this text, Jennie Walker, including the scenario, roles, supporting business briefs for each role, and the game protocol.

BOX 3.10 EDUCATOR'S PERSPECTIVE – MOTIVATION

In 2014, after several years working at Thunderbird School of Global Management, it became apparent to me that there were few available exercises designed specifically for developing professional expertise in global leadership. Since my specific area of expertise is in dynamic learning in global leadership development, I decided to use this expertise to create an exercise that would address the learning needs of our professional students. Since many of our students worked in cross-cultural teams, and many of them were in senior roles in their organizations, I decided that it would be most impactful to create a scenario where they had to work with multiple cultures in senior-level roles to make critical business decisions.

Assess Context

This exercise was originally created for MBA and executive education students at a highly diverse institution in the United States with students from more than 70 different nations. Since these learners have mid- to senior-level professional experience, it was important to design the exercise to reflect the real-world interaction of leaders across business disciplines in an organization. Strategy-level decisions were incorporated, as the students were on either a capstone or an executive education course that had strategic thinking as a learning objective.

Another important contextual factor was that the exercise was being used in a program with a specific global business emphasis. This meant that collaboration across cultures was a key consideration in the overall curriculum. A diverse mix of cultures was chosen to maximize the diversity component of the exercise.

BOX 3.11 EDUCATOR'S PERSPECTIVE – ASSESS CONTEXT

When I developed this exercise, I was working at a school that was a graduate-level only institution which granted globally focused MBA degrees and executive education certificates in global leadership and management. The students were highly diverse, with representation from many different countries. For these reasons, this experiential exercise needed to have a global focus.

While I could have chosen to focus on any industry, I decided to focus on wine production and distribution. In my research, I found that there was a strong sense of national pride about wine production, and distinct cultural preferences and laws about the sale and consumption of wine. I believed that these cultural tensions would enhance the potential for cross-cultural debate and negotiations within the exercise. It would require students to consider the complexities of production and distribution of a regulated product in different regions of the world, while also navigating the immediacy of cross-cultural communications with their senior team members. Since global leadership is inherently complex, this exercise needed to mirror that for the benefit of student learning. However, if I were to use this exercise in a culture where wine consumption was not condoned or illegal, then I would change the organizational context of the scenario.

Define Learning Objectives

This exercise was designed to increase the cross-cultural leadership skills of mid- to senior-level managers from many different countries. Upon completion of this exercise participants will be able to:

• Identify unique communication norms in several different cultures.
• Evaluate a cross-cultural context and adapt communication appropriately.
• Analyze data, figures, and processes to make informed business decisions.
• Assess the real-world impact of implementation tactics across business disciplines, such as marketing and finance.
• Demonstrate culturally appropriate negotiation and influencing skills in a multicultural context.

BOX 3.12 EDUCATOR'S PERSPECTIVE – DEFINE LEARNING OBJECTIVES

In designing the scenario, I placed students in roles that did not match their own native culture. This allowed them to learn about another culture's unique communication norms and use them throughout the exercise. These aims are captured in the first two learning objectives: identify unique communication norms in several different cultures; and evaluate a cross-cultural context and adapt communication appropriately.

In order to make an informed decision on team priorities, students have to identify communication barriers and modify their own communication behaviors to receive the information needed from all team members. For example, some roles are given cues to wait until they are called upon to share information, while others are given direction to be very assertive in the meeting.

Culture is the first consideration that students reflect on in preparation for the exercise. However, they also need to become familiar with their functional roles and business priorities. The third and fourth learning objectives relate to these roles: analyze data, figures, and processes in making informed business decisions; and assess real-world impact of implementation tactics across business disciplines, such as marketing and finance. I curated a series of industry news articles and resources for each role to help students quickly understand trends, concerns, and key information within their functions. In a traditional class that lasts several weeks, students may curate their own resources. However, in executive education sessions, pre-work tends to be minimal, so I felt that curating the resources was better to ensure the success of the activity. I designed the learning objectives to be flexible enough to accommodate a range of resources that may be brought into the exercise.

To succeed in the exercise, a team must work together to discuss and agree upon the top business priorities and then present them to the CEO. Therefore, the final learning objective is to demonstrate culturally appropriate negotiation and influencing skills in a multicultural context. In my experience, having run this exercise several times with different groups of professionals, meeting the final learning objective is often the greatest source of discussion in the small group and class debriefs. Working through the cultural and functional differences in the groups is both frustrating and exhilarating for students, making this a highly memorable exercise for them.

Select/Create Learning Activities

In this exercise, participants receive a briefing on their firm and their functional roles and culture, then they are asked to work in a small group as an executive team to make important business decisions. Each team presents their recommendations to the firm CEO. Each team debriefs their process, reports lessons learned to the class, and finally, the class debriefs the entire exercise. See Table 3.4 for the worksheet used to define the learning activities for this exercise.

Step 1: Introduction to the activity and learning objectives

During the session introduction, the educator passes a handout to all students that provides an overview of the activity, learning objectives, and firm scenario. The scenario includes a description of the company, including its history, overview of operations around the world, current goals, and the challenges it faces in current market conditions. Students are given time to read the scenario. The educator discusses the instruc-

Table 3.4   *Select/create learning activities for the Global Strategy Meeting exercise*

Types of learning activities	Getting information and ideas	Experiencing (doing or observing)	Reflecting
Individual	Read exercise overview, firm scenario, functional roles, and individual functional and cultural information.	Observe individual behaviors and team interactions during team meeting. Present individual arguments and ideas related to your functional responsibilities throughout the team meeting. Actively solicit information and ideas from colleagues during the team meeting.	Individually reflect on the experience during the small group debrief. Share reflections during the class debrief.
Group/team		Negotiate organizational priorities with colleagues during team meeting to produce a top three list of priorities. Create an executive presentation with colleagues to present to the CEO.	Discuss debrief questions in small group. Summarize insights to share with class.
Class		Observe group presentations to the CEO. Identify differences in group priorities and rationales.	Discuss insights from small group debrief sessions with class. Discuss similarities and differences in approaches across groups.

tions and answers any questions students may have before they are placed in groups.

Step 2: Formation of small groups

Students are divided into small groups, ideally in a break-out room or separate small table areas. Because there are multiple roles and cultures represented, each team member has a name tent with their role and national culture. Since learning to observe and respond to others' cultural cues is a part of the exercise, it is helpful to create diverse student groups where possible. Other materials needed include flip-chart paper or a whiteboard, markers, and a handout with cultural norms for meetings.

Step 3: Assignment of individual roles

To capture the interdisciplinary nature of an organizational setting, each person represents a different functional area: marketing and communications, finance, supply chain, production, merchandising, and sales. Each function has its own concerns and priorities. Therefore, the scripts indicate what these are for each role. The global meeting's objective is for this diverse, cross-functional team to agree upon the top three priorities and then to present these to the CEO of the organization. This creates a high-stakes challenge for each function to promote its interests while also negotiating for a list of consensual team priorities. The presentation to the CEO is included to simulate the real pressure functional leaders face to create deliverables, and then explain and defend their rationale to organizational stakeholders.

The educator assigns individual roles within the groups. Every student receives a handout with a brief overview of each team member's role and a more extensive overview of their own role, which includes supplemental information specific to their function. The handout that provides an overview of each team member's role includes: (1) role title and responsibilities, (2) tenure in the role and organization, (3) direct reports by location for each role, (4) headquarters or office location for each role, and (5) nationality of the person in each role. So everyone knows the composition of the team in terms of diversity, functions and authority/ experience. The roles include Senior Vice President Global Production from the United States, Vice President Global Imports and Exports from China, Vice President Global Merchandising from Italy, Vice President Global Sales and Inventory from France, Vice President Global Financial Operations and Assets from the United States, and Vice President Global Marketing and Communications from the United Kingdom.

The more extensive overview of each role is provided only to the person playing that role. Everyone receives three important pieces of information about their role: (1) detailed information about the person's perspective and personality; (2) specific functional priorities; and (3) one big idea. The big idea is an innovative idea that the person wants to be a top strategic priority for the firm, such as an acquisition, moving the business to an emerging market, direct sales via the internet, changes to business partnerships, and target marketing. Since the big idea is innovative, it may be perceived as risky but also potentially more rewarding for the organization. The role overview provides guidance about how the person prefers to share their idea with the group (for example, boldly, upon request). The overview also includes a few resources that will provide the person with evidence and metrics to support their position.

Time is provided for the students to review the role/culture materials. Participants are asked not to share the details of their roles with others, as there are behavioral cues in the instructions that allow them to introduce culturally specific behaviors and expectations into the discussion. These behaviors should be identified by others independently during the activity. In the event that the exercise is divided over multiple classes, students may be asked to review their briefing materials on their own.

Step 4: Implementation of the cross-cultural Global Strategy Meeting exercise

Once the exercise begins, the educator quietly rotates around groups to observe the students in action. It is important that the educator does not interfere by either answering questions that are not related to the activity protocol or offering coaching. The exercise is meant to challenge students to identify issues and attempt to resolve them themselves. As the time for the exercise comes to an end, it is helpful to give students a 10 to 15 minute warning so that they can finalize their list of priorities and prepare their presentation.

Step 5: Small group presentations of top strategic priorities to the CEO

When the specified time for the exercise is over, each group will select a representative to present the strategic priorities to the CEO of the company. The CEO is played by the educator. The brief presentation is made in front of the class. Each group should have a minimum of 5–7 minutes, assuming four teams in a two-hour session. Longer or distributed sessions could allow 10–12 minutes per team, which provides ample time for sharing the results of the team meetings.

The focus of the presentation should be on the rationale for the strategies chosen and their respective priority ranking. There is no formal presentation preparation time, as the discussion of the priorities and their rationale is generally straightforward, leveraging information already in the exercise resources. However, teams may use part of their allotted discussion time to prepare their presentations.

The educator should make notes during the priority presentations, for reference during the debrief sessions, as there will be several group presentations. This is also helpful if the exercise is distributed over multiple sessions. The presentations are not being evaluated for any particular answer. The purpose of the presentations is for the entire class and the educator to clearly hear the priorities selected by each team and their respective rationales. This provides important information for the debrief discussions as students identify how differences in priorities resulted from the same information. Differences usually are found to have some relationship with the communication and cultural dynamics in the teams.

Step 6: Debrief experience in small groups

At the end of the exercise, there are three planned discussions. The first discussion in a small group allows students to share their personal experiences and observations from the exercise. This is valuable to each person on the team, as they will discover cultural or functional information that they may not have picked up during the exercise. It will help those who encountered challenges to better understand why they occurred. Ultimately, the discussion will help each student to understand strategies which they could have taken to enhance their success.

The educator asks each group to debrief their experiences as a small group (Table 3.5) and identify key observations to share in a class debrief. Each group will need to identify a spokesperson to discuss the points they would like to share with the class.

Step 7: Debrief key observations as a class

The second discussion brings all of the small groups together as a class to discuss their key learnings. This helps students across groups to identify unique issues, concerns, and experiences that may not have surfaced in their own groups but could occur in a similar setting. It also opens issues to the larger class for additional ideas and success strategies.

The educator brings the groups together for a class debrief, asking each small group to share their key observations (Table 3.6). The educator should note these observations on the board or have group members do so.

Table 3.5   *Small group debrief questions for the Global Strategy Meeting exercise*

Activity	Discussion questions
Small group debrief	What challenges did you encounter?
	Did you feel included by the team? Why or why not?
	Do you feel others were equally included in the team discussions? Why or why not?
	Do you feel the team was successful? Why or why not?
	What did you learn?

Table 3.6   *Class debrief discussion questions for the Global Strategy Meeting exercise*

Activity	Discussion questions
Class debrief	How would you characterize the experience of your team overall during the simulation?
	What were the main challenges you encountered?
	What did your team discover in your small group discussion about inclusion on your team?
	Did your team agree that the negotiation was a success? Why or why not?
	What were key learnings you had as a team?

Step 8: Reinforcement of learning

The final discussion, the review of learning, is an opportunity for the educator to summarize and synthesize key observations and learnings from the exercise. This is also a good opportunity to link learnings back to the overall curriculum of the course.

The educator may decide to enrich this exercise by adding subsequent related assignments that involve deeper exploration of some aspect of the activity, such as collaboration with a specific culture or how to effectively implement their proposed organizational priorities.

Select/Create Assessments

The principal method of assessment in this exercise is reflection through small group and class debrief sessions. At the end of the activity, students are asked to self-assess their performance against the learning objectives. This self-assessment may be formalized in a written assessment, if desired. This could include both a self-assessment and a group assessment.

Ensure Alignment

See Table 3.7 for a comparison of the exercise objectives, activities, and assessments to ensure alignment. The first learning objective, to identify unique communication norms in several different cultures, is achieved through the cross-cultural design of the team roles in the exercise. Since the scenario involves as many as six different cultures, students must demonstrate the ability to identify cross-cultural cues in communication. By identifying them, they will be able to draw on their knowledge of other cultures to adapt communication accordingly. This skill is particularly important for students who are currently working in or preparing to work in diverse, global organizations.

After identifying cross-cultural cues in communication, the students then must adapt communication appropriately to maintain a productive and collegial collaboration with peers. This helps them to achieve the second learning objective, to evaluate a cross-cultural context and adapt communication appropriately. Students are not expected to have detailed knowledge of every culture, but their cross-cultural training in their program of study should at least provide them with high-level differences in cultures (for example, cultural dimensions) and communication strategies to bridge these. Students who are not already prepared have an immersive opportunity in this exercise to recognize opportunities for further development.

The third learning objective, to analyze data, figures, and processes in making informed business decisions, is achieved within the context of a specific role in the exercise. Because each role is specific to a function, students must become familiar with the concerns of their function in the context of the specific organization in the scenario. A business brief is provided to each student which arms them with information to understand the role and priorities within the respective function. Participants are not provided with briefs for the other roles, as the team meeting serves as a forum for presenting and discussing the priorities of each function. This mirrors organizational reality, where employees are principally focused on their own functions. However, the exercise could be re-engineered to focus on a senior leader meeting within a specific functional area if needed. This would require assigning roles within the function and curating resources to describe those positions.

Table 3.7   *Assessing alignment – consistency of learning objectives, activities, and assessments for the Global Strategy Meeting exercise*

Learning objective	Learning activity	Assessment of learning
Identify unique communication norms in several different cultures	Review of personal role that includes normative cultural behaviors Observation during team meeting Group discussions	Self-assessment in small group debrief Group assessment in class debrief
Evaluate a cross-cultural context and adapt communication appropriately	Review of personal role that includes normative cultural behaviors Observation during team meeting Group discussions	Self-assessment in small group debrief Group assessment in class debrief
Analyze data, figures, and processes in making informed business decisions	Review of personal role Observation and discussion during team meeting Group discussions	Self-assessment in small group debrief Group assessment in class debrief
Assess real-world impact of implementation tactics across business disciplines, such as marketing and finance	Observation during team meeting Presentation to the CEO Group discussions	Self-assessment in small group debrief Group assessment in class debrief
Demonstrate culturally appropriate negotiation and influencing skills in a multicultural context	Observation and discussion during team meeting Presentation to the CEO	Self-assessment in small group debrief Group assessment in class debrief

In setting organizational priorities, the executive team in this exercise must understand and assess how the prioritization impacts the success of the overall organization and the health of individual functions. This helps participants to achieve learning objective four, to assess the real-world impact of implementation tactics across business disciplines, such as marketing and finance. Each participant plays a critical role in sharing metrics and trends related to their functional priorities. This opens the dialogue for real-world impact in the scenario. Ultimately, teams have to present and rationalize their priorities to the CEO in the scenario using sound data.

Because each executive represents a different function, the priorities being promoted are biased toward the respective functions. In order to set organizational strategy, the executive team must negotiate each of their priorities and influence other team members to consider adopting them. Given the diversity of cultures involved in the scenario, they must do this through culturally responsive communication. The exercise mirrors the multiple layers of complexity in a global organization in the context of strategy setting, and helps participants achieve the final learning objective, to demonstrate culturally appropriate negotiation and influencing skills in a multicultural context.

Implement

This activity can be completed in two hours or in a longer four-hour session. If the scheduled class time is less than two hours, it could be completed over multiple sessions. If the activity is conducted over multiple one-hour sessions, the first session could be used for providing an overview of the activity, assigning roles, and allowing time to review the briefing materials. A second session could be dedicated to implementation of the team meeting portion of the exercise. The presentation to the CEO could take place in session three, while the fourth session could be focused on the debrief discussions and reinforcement of learning. The flow of the exercise given different time constraints is outlined in Table 3.8.

This experience could be situated early in a course to provide exposure to the concepts that will be taught in a course, or near the end of a course as a cumulative demonstration of learning. Situating the exercise early in the course is an instructional strategy that can pique student interest, and help to illuminate strengths and areas of opportunity that students may want to enhance or build throughout the course. When using this strategy, it is helpful to provide students with a second opportunity later in the course to apply their new knowledge and skills from the course, so that achievement of learning objectives may be properly assessed. This also provides students with an opportunity to appreciate their skill building during the course. Because time is often limited, end-of-course placement may be necessary to streamline learning and provide a robust assessment of learning for students.

Regardless of the time allotment or placement in the course flow, the exercise should be introduced in the course syllabus with a description of the learning objectives. This may provide a sense of positive anticipation

Table 3.8   *Sequence and timing of activities for the Global Strategy Meeting exercise*

Sequence of activities	Timing for 2-hour version	Timing for 4-hour version	Suggested distribution over multiple 60-minute sessions
Introduction to the activity and learning objectives	10 minutes – includes reading scenario	15 minutes – includes reading scenario	*Session 1* 15 minutes – includes reading scenario
Formation of small groups	5 minutes	5 minutes	*Session 1* 5 minutes
Assignment of individual roles	10 minutes – includes reading role-specific information	20 minutes – includes reading role-specific information	*Session 1* 20 minutes – includes reading role-specific information
Implementation of the cross-cultural global strategy meeting exercise	45 minutes	90 minutes	*Session 2* 60 minutes
Small group presentations of top strategic priorities to the CEO	20 minutes total for all groups (approximately 5–7 minutes each, assuming 4 groups)	60 minutes total for all groups (approximately 10–12 minutes each, assuming 4 groups)	*Session 3* 60 minutes total for all groups (approximately 10–12 minutes each, assuming 4 groups)
Debrief experience in small groups	10 minutes	20 minutes	*Session 4* 20 minutes
Debrief key observations as a class	10 minutes	20 minutes	*Session 4* 20 minutes
Reinforcement of learning	10 minutes	10 minutes	*Session 4* 20 minutes
Total time	120 minutes	240 minutes	220 minutes

for some students, while also allowing time for those who are nervous about the activity to learn more and ask questions. The educator should read through the scenario, all roles, and the flow of the activity well before the course starts. This allows time for any modifications that may be needed. There is also some preparation of materials for each student and for the teams that needs to be completed by the educator well before the session.

BOX 3.13 EDUCATOR'S PERSPECTIVE – IMPLEMENTATION, TIMING, AND BREAKS

When there are only 45–60 minutes allotted for the team meeting, the groups often ask for more time. This is because engagement in the activity has been very high. Students are actively presenting their business cases, working to understand other perspectives and the cultural challenges they encounter, and also struggling to come to consensus on the top priorities. They tend to be very serious and intently focused on the negotiation among colleagues. A natural tension is built into the exercise, where two of the most senior team members from the same culture are aggressively pushing for the same idea. So it is not uncommon to hear frustration and disagreement among the teams, or sometimes uncomfortable silence, as individuals figure out how to present their perspectives.

When there are 90 minutes, students are more likely to finish the exercise comfortably. I do always encourage a short break after one hour, though, as the negotiations can be emotionally and intellectually intense for students. When any additional time is unused in the exercise, it can be used for a break, or to add to the time for small group and class debriefs. Since no breaks are built into the exercise, I encourage students to step out briefly as needed. Depending upon the culture of the institution or organization where this is being used, breaks may need to be more formalized.

Educator Perspective – Implementation: Debrief Discussions

The debrief discussions are usually very active, because students are eager to hear others' experiences. They often ask directly about cultural norms for others' roles to better understand why communication dynamics occurred in the way they did during the exercise. They also will clarify functional priorities to see more directly what may have driven the priority setting. There is much learning through sharing and processing of experiences in the small group debrief. So it is important not to rush this. Because of the intense discussion, students usually ask for more time.

The class discussions provide rich insights about how different approaches among groups led to different outcomes even with the same functional priorities and information within groups. In this discussion, students will often shift off their individual experiences to their past and current organizational experiences, as they apply them to this exercise. This is a great opportunity to pull in other course concepts and learnings as they relate to working across cultures, team dynamics, and organizational strategy. What I have most enjoyed about this activity is the high level of engagement among students, and the many connections they find to their real-life experiences.

Adjust and Adapt

This exercise can elicit a great deal of emotion, as students encounter behaviors that they either do not understand or cannot seem to negotiate during the activity. Students may find their attempts to communicate being suppressed or not well received, while others have a more positive reception. The dynamics of the exercise build quickly, so it is important that the educator is circulating and observing in the event that emotions escalate. Should emotions become high, it is helpful to encourage students to remember that this is just a simulated exercise, and to refocus them on the learning objectives. While this degree of emotion is not always a concern, it is helpful to be prepared for it, as the demands of the activity and time compression can heighten student emotions.

A common issue that may need to be addressed is when students have in-depth discussions of functional issues or strategies that may not relate to the exercise, or place an exclusive focus on one particular function. Should this occur, it is helpful to remind students that the goal of the activity is to collaboratively identify and rank the strategic priorities for the meeting with the CEO. This means that excessive time should not be spent on a single function.

As with many experiential exercises, students will likely want more time for the exercise, presentation, and discussions. You may find sufficient value in the exercise that you decide to extend the activity into the next class or break the activity out over multiple class sessions. You may also decide to extend the timing in the moment, should your class schedule allow for it.

Reflect and Revise

This exercise incorporates disciplinary-specific considerations for marketing, finance, and supply chain; participants are required to analyze data, figures, and processes to make informed decisions. The discussion of organizational metrics during the activity captures real-world considerations for implementation across business disciplines. The activity also provides awareness of cross-cultural cues, reinforces cross-cultural communication skills, and provides an opportunity to practice negotiation and influencing skills in a multicultural context. It is ideal as a capstone experience in a graduate business degree program, or as a professional development experience for a team in an organization. However, it can be modified for use in a single-discipline course such as marketing or finance. This exercise could also be modified for more specific treatment of certain disciplines, trending business issues, or industries.

In facilitating this exercise multiple times with different groups, it has been found that when students in the class have experience with the industry used for the exercise, it can be problematic. Students may introduce their personal experiences and focus on particular organizations or industry issues at the expense of participating in the exercise. This could diminish achievement of the learning objectives. So it can be helpful to use an industry in which students do not have an affiliation. Students should also be encouraged to focus on the information they have for the scenario and their roles. Should there be a compelling reason to match industry to student experience, the exercise would likely require more time to allow for the extended discussions that may arise.

Exercise Resources

In creating this exercise I compiled normative cultural behavior and cross-cultural meeting etiquette through research. Supplementary industry information for each role was drawn from digital news sources and industry publications. Thus, the exercise incorporates authentic industry information and can be continually updated to reflect market conditions and industry trends. See Appendix 3.2 for resources useful for students during the exercise itself to inform their roles. They are divided into cultural resources and wine industry resources, as students will need both to enact their roles. These are not all inclusive, but do provide a range of examples. These are not meant to be scholarly in nature, as the practical nature of this exercise is best supported by publications aimed at practitioners, such as trade publications, industry news, industry reports, and web-based cultural dimension tools.

Do note that each student would only need the cultural and industry resources specific to their own roles. This could be as streamlined as one cultural resource and one or two industry resources. However, all students at the conclusion of the exercise should receive a master list of resources provided to all students, for further research and reflection. To be mindful of copyright requirements, consider presenting students with a list of suggested resources and links that they may access on their own.

Educators may also choose to create follow-up assignments, such as cultural research papers or industry analyses, to build on the learning from this exercise.

IMPLEMENTATION IN ACTION: CREATING A LEADERSHIP BRAND – VICKI FAIRBANKS TAYLOR

This exercise was adapted from *Building Your Leadership Brand* (Miller, 2014) and incorporates numerous self-assessments, reflective writing assignments, small group discussions, and a gallery walk poster presentation. The goal of this exercise is to help students clarify and articulate their "leadership brand." Through self-assessments and reflective writing, students identify their strengths, challenges, and behavioral intentions (or philosophy) relative to leadership. They work in small groups and receive feedback on their behavioral examples of strengths in action and a plan for addressing their leadership challenges. At the end of the semester, students create a poster board presentation of their leadership brand using Google images or clip art, and share their final project in a gallery walk. See Gooding and Metz (2011) for instructions on a gallery walk process.

BOX 3.14 EDUCATOR'S PERSPECTIVE – MOTIVATION

A leadership brand results when a leader understands what they want to accomplish, develops consistent means of pursuing their goals, and works to build attributes that align with the achievement of these goals (Intagliata et al., 2000). According to Ulrich and Smallwood (2007), a leadership brand conveys one's identity and distinctiveness as a leader. A leadership brand reflects one's priorities, values, behavioral intentions, and what one hopes to consistently deliver to one's constituents (Horth et al., 2016). Helping undergraduate management students to identify their values, intentions, strengths, and challenges relative to leadership is a learning outcome embedded in my undergraduate leadership courses. Therefore, I searched for an existing leadership brand exercise to adopt or adapt, and came across the Building Your Leadership Brand exercise (Miller, 2014) using the search term "leadership brand exercise" in Google. From this initial exercise, I created a series of activities that I facilitated over the semester to help students identify and articulate their leadership brand. I also wanted to give students practice in sharing behavioral examples of their strengths in preparation for future employment interviews.

Assess Context

Leadership and Decision-Making is a third-year required course for students majoring in management and an elective for other business majors. The purpose of the course is to introduce students to the theory and practice of leadership and decision-making in organizations; to apply leadership theory and concepts to organizational, team, and individual situations; and to develop students' understanding of their leadership competencies, challenges, and personal philosophy of leadership. The course is offered twice a year, face-to-face, during a 14-week semester. Enrollment in the course ranges from 30 to 36 students. Most of the students have limited leadership experience and are unfamiliar with the concept of a leadership brand. Finally, most of the students are third- or fourth-year college students actively interviewing for internships and entry-level managerial positions.

BOX 3.15 EDUCATOR'S PERSPECTIVE – ASSESSING CONTEXT

A review of these contextual factors helped to guide me in revising the exercise. I recognized that introductory material and examples would be needed to introduce students to the concept of a leadership brand. I also had 14 weeks of instructional time over which numerous self-assessments could be conducted. My class size influenced my use of activities. I decided to use end-of-semester presentations and in-class, small group discussions. Small-group discussions would help students to refine their leadership examples and develop action plans for addressing leadership challenges. Additionally, developing examples of the leadership strengths in action would help prepare students entering the job market in the near future to respond to behavioral-based interview questions. Behavioral-based questions are frequently used during employment interviewing to assess an applicant's qualifications for a job (Levashina et al., 2014).

Define Learning Objectives

The exercise was designed to increase student self-awareness of their strengths, weaknesses, and behavioral intentions relative to leadership, and provide students with an opportunity to practice their verbal communication skills. Upon completion of the exercise, students would be able to do the following:

1. Identify their leadership strengths and challenges.
2. Provide at least one behavioral example of five leadership strengths in action.
3. Formulate a specific, measurable, attainable, realistic, time-based (SMART) action plan for addressing at least three personal challenges.
4. Articulate their philosophy of leadership by identifying their values, beliefs, and behavioral intentions.

Table 3.9   Select/create learning activities for the Creating a Leadership Brand exercise

Types of learning activities	Getting information and ideas	Experiencing (doing and observing)	Reflecting
Individual	Lectures Reading assignments	Self-assessments (ten; one per week)	Self-assessment reflection papers (ten; one per week) Final paper Poster board
Group/team		Small group discussions	Small group discussions
Class		Poster board presentation and gallery walk	Poster board presentation and gallery walk

Select/Create Learning Activities

The activities associated with this exercise include self-assessments, written self-assessment reflections, small group discussions, a final paper, and a poster board presentation with a gallery walk. See Table 3.9 for the worksheet used to select/create the learning activities for this exercise.

To develop a leadership brand, students need to be aware of their values, goals, strengths, and challenges. To build self-awareness, students will complete at least ten self-assessments throughout the semester. The self-assessments correspond with the leadership topic being covered in the course. Examples of self-assessment that align with the undergraduate leadership course include motivation to lead, emotional intelligence, Big 5 personality, preferred leadership styles, decision-making style, conflict management style, value clarification, listening skills, and resistance to change. Leadership texts often come replete with self-assessments. In addition, self-assessments can be found by searching online (educators should be sure to select validated measures). By completing self-assessments, students build an awareness of their values, preferences, behavioral tendencies, strengths, and challenges relative to influencing and leading others.

The process of creating a leadership brand also entails reflection, an essential part of experiential learning (as discussed in Chapters 1 and 2). Therefore, students complete a reflective writing assignment after taking a self-assessment. The reflective writing assignment asks students to do the following: (1) interpret their self-assessment results; (2) identify their strengths relative to the self-assessment results; (3) provide a behavioral example of a strength in action; (4) identify a weakness or challenge relative to the self-assessment results; and (5) identify an action to take to address the challenge or weakness. After writing their self-assessment reflections, students work cooperatively in groups of two or three to refine their example of a strength in action and plan for addressing identified challenges.

At the end of the semester, students write a final paper and create a poster board presentation using computer clip art or Google images representing their leadership philosophy, leadership strengths, and leadership challenges (see Figure 3.2 for an example of a student's poster board). Student presentations are conducted over two days using a gallery walk activity. A gallery walk is a discussion technique where students

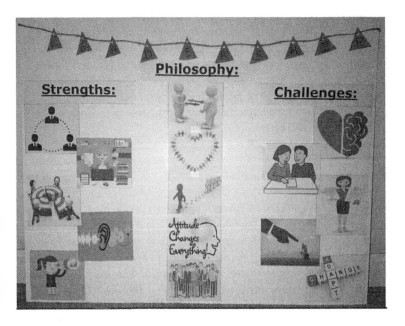

Figure 3.2   *Sample student poster board for the Creating a*
                Leadership Brand Exercise

visit each of the presenters, listen to a brief presentation, and ask questions about the content of the presenter's posters.

BOX 3.16 EDUCATOR'S PERSPECTIVE – SELECT/ CREATE LEARNING ACTIVITIES

The original leadership brand exercise suggested the use of one self-assessment to help identify weaknesses. However, I wanted students to take a variety of self-assessments to gain a broader knowledge about their strengths, challenges, and how they might operate as leaders. The textbook I used offered a selection of 37 different self-assessments. I had students complete at least ten self-assessments from the textbook, to get a broader understanding of their strengths, challenges, and behavioral tendencies.

I also added additional activities designed to strengthen the learning experience. The reflective writing activity enabled individuals to create meaning from the self-assessments. Small group discussions provided students with feedback on their leadership example and action plan for addressing a weakness. The final paper had students articulate their leadership brand. Having students present their leadership brand using images capitalizes on their creativity (Fuller, 2000). The gallery walk also encouraged participation, interaction, and increased the likelihood of collaboration among students as they exchanged feedback on the posters (Chin et al., 2015).

Select/Create Assessments

Learning is assessed through the educator's evaluation of the work created by students. For the learning outcome to identify strengths and challenges, students' written reflections, final paper, and poster board presentation are evaluated by the educator to ensure that students have identified leadership strengths and challenges. The learning outcomes to provide at least one behavioral example of five leadership strengths in action, and to formulate an action plan for addressing at least three personal challenges, are assessed using students' written reflections and the final paper. The final learning outcome, to articulate their philosophy of leadership by identifying their values, beliefs, and behavioral intentions, is assessed using the final paper and poster board presentation. In column three of Table 3.10 the assessment of learning for this exercise is outlined.

Ensure Alignment

Table 3.10 shows the alignment among learning objectives, learning activities, and learning assessments.

Table 3.10   *Alignment of learning objectives, activities, and assessments for the Creating a Leadership Brand exercise*

Learning objective	Learning activity	Assessment of learning
Identify leadership strengths and challenges	Self-assessments Self-assessment reflection papers Small group discussions Final paper Poster/poster presentation	Each of the self-assessment reflection papers contain at least one strength and one weakness/challenge The final paper includes at least five leadership strengths and five leadership challenges The poster board contains at least five images representing the student's leadership strengths and five images representing their leadership challenges
Provide at least one behavioral example of five leadership strengths in action	Self-assessment reflection papers Small group discussions Final paper Poster/poster presentation	Each of the ten self-assessment reflection papers contain at least one example of a strength in action The final paper includes at least one behavioral example for each of the five leadership strengths
Formulate a specific, measurable, attainable, realistic, time-based (SMART) action plan for addressing at least three personal challenges	Self-assessment reflection papers Small group discussions Final paper	Each of the self-assessment reflection papers contain at least one action for addressing an identified weakness The final paper includes a SMART action plan for addressing at least three personal challenges
Articulate their philosophy of leadership by identifying their values, beliefs, and behavioral intentions	Poster board presentation Final paper	The student verbally articulates a leadership philosophy during the poster presentation The final paper includes an explanation of the student's priorities, values, and behavioral intentions for leading others

BOX 3.17 EDUCATOR'S PERSPECTIVE – ENSURE ALIGNMENT

After I created Table 3.10, I realized that the small group discussion activity was not used for learning assessment. That's okay. Not all learning activities result in an evaluative assessment. The important thing to figure out is how an activity will reinforce the learning objectives and prepare students for assessment. Still, I needed to ask myself: does the discussion activity reinforce learning and prepare students for assessment? The answer was, yes. The small group discussions provide students with feedback from their peers on how well they described their behavioral example of a strength in action, and helps students to clarify their action plan for addressing a challenge.

Implement

Implementation takes place throughout the semester and during the final full week of instruction (two 75-minute classes, three 50-minute classes, or one 150-minute class). During the first or second week of the semester, take one class (50–75 minutes) to discuss the exercise in detail. Provide introductory information on the concept of a leadership brand. Ask students to describe the brand of one of their past or present leaders. Describe the rationale for creating a leadership brand, the benefits of knowing one's leadership brand, how the leadership brand exercise ties into the learning goals of the course, and how students will be working on the leadership brand assignment throughout the semester. Describe the assignment requirements. Elucidate how the various activities (self-assessments, self-assessment reflections, and small group discussions) will prepare students to write their final paper and present their leadership brand. Finally, provide examples of leadership brand posters from past courses.

At the end of the second week of class, students complete their first self-assessment, write their first reflection paper, and participate in a small group discussion. The 30-minute small group discussion is repeated after every assigned self-assessment throughout the semester, and consists of the following steps:

• Students bring their written reflections to class and share their examples of a strength in action in small groups.

- Educator asks for volunteers from the groups to share their example with the entire class.
- Educator provides feedback as needed to help ensure examples reflect students' strengths relative to the assessment.
- Students share the challenges identified from the self-assessment within the small group.
- Students work in their groups to develop an action plan for addressing a challenge.
- Educator asks for student volunteers to share their action plan.
- Educator provides feedback as needed to help ensure action plan is specific, measurable, attainable, and time-based.
- Educator answers any questions students have concerning their reflection assignment.

Based on a minimum of ten self-assessments, the educator will need to schedule ten 30-minute small group discussions throughout the semester. In a 14-week semester, with breaks, an exam, and one week set aside for final presentations, the educator should plan on covering self-assessment reflections approximately once a week throughout the semester. In this course example, a leadership topic is introduced in one class and the self-assessment reflection is discussed in small groups during the following class.

Approximately four weeks before the assignment is due, the educator should review the final paper and presentation requirements with the students in detail. Using Google, demonstrate how to find clip art and images. The educator may want to have students use their cell phones to find an image representing a leadership strength, challenge, and philosophy. Ask students to share their images in small groups and explain why they selected the image. Once again, provide at least one sample poster. If this is your first time using the exercise, create your leadership brand poster and share it with students. Finally, explain the logistics of the gallery walk.

- Students will be divided into two groups.
- Individuals in group one (presenter) will hang their posters on the classroom walls (using blue painter's tape) and stand next to their posters.
- Individuals from group two (gallery walker) will pair with one presenter to hear them briefly describe their leadership brand.

Table 3.11   Sample sequencing and timing of activities for the Creating a Leadership Brand exercise

Week	Activity	Timing
Week 1	Introduction to the exercise	50–75 minutes
Weeks 2–12	Small group discussion based on self-assessments 1–10[a]	30 minutes
Week 13	Work on poster board presentation outside of class	
Week 14	Poster board presentation/gallery walk Final paper due	150 minutes

Note:
[a] Self-assessments and self-assessment reflection papers are completed by students outside of class.

- Presenter will describe their leadership strengths, challenges, and philosophy of leadership (approximately three minutes).
- Gallery walker will ask at least one follow-up question (approximately one minute).
- Assign a timekeeper, who calls time every four minutes; when time is called, the gallery walkers move to their right to the next presenter. Then presenters and walkers repeat the process of presenting and providing feedback, respectively, in four minutes.
- Once all presenters have presented, the students switch roles: walkers become presenters and presenters become walkers. The process is repeated until all students have presented.
- The educator also visits each presenter, listens to the presenter describe their leadership brand, and asks at least one follow-up question.

Presenters are asked to share their leadership brand by referring to their poster board rather than to notes. Table 3.11 shows the sequencing and timing of the activities across the semester.

BOX 3.18 EDUCATOR'S PERSPECTIVE – IMPLEMENTATION

The biggest challenge I face when implementing this exercise is making sure to devote enough time to the small group discussions. At times, the material I want to cover takes more time than I planned, and I find myself with 15 minutes for small group discussions rather than the full 30 minutes. The extra instructional time cuts into the time students have to get feedback on their behavioral examples and action plans. It limits the amount of time students have to ask me questions about their self-assessment results. Finally, it limits the amount of time I have to review student examples in class. The small group discussions are a valuable and formative part of the exercise and should not be rushed or neglected.

Adjust and Adapt

The leadership brand exercise consists of separate but related activities. Educators may need to make adjustments to each of the activities contained in the exercise. For example, educators may want to add or delete self-assessments as course content changes. Writing prompts may need to be adjusted to enhance student reflection. When facilitating the small group discussions, educators may need to modify the composition of the small groups to adjust for unprepared or absent students. Make sure that at least two students in the group are prepared and can exchange examples and discuss action plans. Educators may want to consider penalizing students who are unprepared for small group discussions, or rewarding prepared students. Throughout the activity, monitor the groups' discussions, answer questions, and provide discussion prompts and suggestions where needed.

Adjustments to presentations may be required, based on the number of students in your class. A minimum of four minutes per presentation is needed in order for the students to share their leadership brand (strengths, challenges, and philosophy) and answer one question. The use of a timekeeper is strongly encouraged. In addition, some students are nervous during their presentations. Educators should be prepared to accommodate students experiencing severe anxiety. However, students may find that being able to refer to their poster during the gallery walk decreases the stress of giving a presentation.

BOX 3.19 EDUCATOR'S PERSPECTIVE – ADJUST AND ADAPT

Students typically do not encounter problems when completing self-assessments; however, students sometimes disagree with their results. It is important to listen to students' concerns and help them to figure out how they arrived at a particular score or interpretation. While general explanations for confounding results can be addressed in class, it is best to discuss specific scores with students privately.

Concerning students coming to class unprepared, I ask them to listen to their fellow students and provide feedback on the quality of the examples given. They can also participate during the action planning process. Unprepared students lose class participation points.

For the class presentations, I have had to accommodate a few students with public speaking anxiety by allowing them to present their leadership brand in my office. These students are still required to attend the presentation sessions and participate in the gallery walk as a walker.

Reflect and Revise

Because this exercise spans the entire semester, educators will have numerous opportunities to reflect and revise. Each self-assessment is followed by a written reflection and a small group discussion. Because the written reflections are submitted and graded throughout the semester, educators receive ongoing assessment data that helps to determine whether or not learning objectives are being achieved. If a pattern emerges (such as students not providing enough detail in their behavioral examples), further instruction with exemplars should be provided. Educators should also reflect after each small group discussion. Are students receiving valuable feedback from their peers? Do students need training on how to provide effective peer coaching?

While the poster presentation and gallery walk tend to take on a celebratory tone, educators should consider how well poster presentations worked in achieving their intended objectives. Did the students present comprehensive leadership brands? Were questions being asked that were on-topic? Was useful feedback provided? Finally, educators may want to consider conducting a brief survey of students at the end of the semester to solicit their feedback on the exercise and its various components (self-assessments, reflective writing assignments, small group discussions, and poster presentation).

BOX 3.20 EDUCATOR'S PERSPECTIVE – REFLECT AND REVISE

What started as a relatively simple, end-the-year reflective writing assignment has grown into an integrated, semester-long project. Through reflection, I discovered many things that caused me to revise the exercise. First, many of my students' self-assessment reflections contained weak examples of their strengths, and limited or superficial actions to address weaknesses. So, I provided exemplars of self-assessment reflections and introduced peer feedback through small group discussions. After using the small group discussions following the first two assigned self-assessments, I noticed an improvement in the overall quality of reflections. I also noticed that student feedback at the end of the year indicated that students enjoyed talking about their self-assessment reflections in small groups, and wanted small group discussions following every self-assessment reflection. The feedback caused me to reflect upon my teaching priorities and philosophy of teaching. I decided to adopt a more student-centered teaching approach and adjust my syllabus so that students could work on their self-assessment reflections in small groups after every assessment. In the following semester, I revised my syllabus. When assessing learning at the end of the semester, I observed that not only were the self-assessments better, but the quality of the final papers improved.

The next revisions to the assignment concerned the final presentation. During the first four semesters (two years) using the exercise, I found that I dreaded the final presentations. They were tedious and repetitive, and some students were visibly uncomfortable when presenting in front of their peers. I wanted to find a way to transform the boring presentations into engaging learning experiences. I decided to have students create leadership collages using clip art and images found on the internet to reflect their creativity and individuality. The collages were an improvement;

however, students still presented their collages one by one in front of the entire class, limiting feedback and interaction. When I read about using a galley walk for presentations (Gooding and Metz, 2011), I decided to try it. The gallery walk got every student out of their seat and interacting with other students. Students received feedback from their peers, and not just from their educator. The feedback I collected from the students indicated that they enjoyed sharing their leadership brand using the gallery walk technique.

I continue to reflect on this exercise and solicit student feedback every semester. During the Fall of 2018, a student mentioned that we were wasting a lot of paper and poster board doing the presentations, and wondered whether I should have students present their leadership brands on computers. In the future, I plan on giving students the option of using their computers to share their images, rather than having them use poster boards.

IMPLEMENTATION IN YOUR TEACHING PRACTICE

We hope these experiential exercise examples help you see that there are many ways to design and implement experiential exercises in the classroom. Consider using these resources as inspiration and guidance for incorporating more effective exercises into your teaching practice.

READINGS/RESOURCES RELATED TO STEPS IN THE EXERCISE DESIGN PROCESS

For those interested in delving more deeply into readings or resources related to each step in the design and implementation process, a brief set of resources is highlighted below (including specific pages or sections of some documents).

Assess Context

University websites
Office of Institutional Research webpages and reports
Aronson, J., Fried, C.B., and Good, C. (2002). Reducing the effects of stereotype threat on African American college students by shaping theories of

intelligence. *Journal of Experimental Social Psychology*, *38*(2), 113–125. doi:10.1006/jesp.2001.1491.

Fink, L.D. (2003a). *Creating Significant Learning Experiences: An Integrated Approach to Designing College Courses*. Jossey-Bass, pp. 68–74.

Define Learning Objectives

Anderson, L.W., Krathwohl, D.R., Airasian, P.W., Cruikshank, K.A., Mayer, R.E., et al. (2001). *A Taxonomy for Learning, Teaching, and Assessing: A Revision of Bloom's Taxonomy of Educational Objectives* (complete edn). Longman.

Biggs, J.B., and Collis, K.F. (1982). *Evaluating the Quality of Learning: The SOLO Taxonomy (Structure of the Observed Learning Outcome)*. Academic Press.

Biggs, J.B., and Tang, C. (2011). *Teaching for Quality Learning at University* (4th edn). Open University Press, McGraw Hill Education, pp. 113–131.

Fink, L.D. (2003a). *Creating Significant Learning Experiences: An Integrated Approach to Designing College Courses*. Jossey-Bass, pp. 74–81.

Fink, L.D. (2003b). *A Self-Directed Guide to Designing Courses for Significant Learning*. https://www.deefinkandassociates.com/GuidetoCourseDesignAug05.pdf.

Noyd, R.K. (2001). *A Primer on Writing Effective Learning-Centered Course Goals*. https://www.utm.edu/departments/rgc/_pdfs/Noyd%20-%20Writing%20Good%20Learning%20Goals.pdf.

Select/Create Learning Activities

Ambrose, S.A., Bridges, M.W., DiPietro, M., Lovett, M.C., and Norman, M.K. (2010). *How Learning Works: 7 Research-Based Principles for Smart Teaching*. Jossey-Bass, pp. 91–151.

Nilson, L.B. (2010). *Teaching at Its Best: A Research-Based Resource for College Instructors*. John Wiley & Sons, pp. 103–112.

Schneider, M., and Preckel, F. (2017). Variables associated with achievement in higher education: A systematic review of meta-analyses. *Psychological Bulletin*, *143*(6), 565–600. doi:10.1037/bul0000098, p. 593.

Select/Create Assessments

Angelo, T.A., and Cross, K.P. (1993). *Classroom Assessment Techniques: A Handbook for College Teachers* (2nd edn). Jossey-Bass.

Brown, P.C., Roediger, H.L., and McDaniel, M.A. (2014). *Make it Stick: The Science of Successful Learning*. Belknap Press.

Fink, L.D. (2003a). *Creating Significant Learning Experiences: An Integrated Approach to Designing College Courses*. Jossey-Bass, pp. 82–99.

Nilson, L.B. (2010). *Teaching at Its Best: A Research-Based Resource for College Instructors*. John Wiley & Sons, pp. 271–328.

Walvoord, B.E., and Anderson, V.J. (2010). *Effective Grading: A Tool for Learning and Assessment in College* (2nd edn). Jossey-Bass.

Ensure Alignment

Biggs, J.B., and Collis, K.F. (1982). *Evaluating the Quality of Learning: The SOLO Taxonomy (Structure of the Observed Learning Outcome)*. Academic Press.
Biggs, J.B., and Tang, C. (2011). *Teaching for Quality Learning at University* (4th edn). Open University Press, McGraw Hill Education, pp. 279–365.

Implement

Ambrose, S.A., Bridges, M.W., DiPietro, M., Lovett, M.C., and Norman, M.K. (2010). *How Learning Works: 7 Research-Based Principles for Smart Teaching*. Jossey-Bass, pp. 91–152.

Adjust and Adapt

Ambrose, S.A., Bridges, M.W., DiPietro, M., Lovett, M.C., and Norman, M.K. (2010). *How Learning Works: 7 Research-Based Principles for Smart Teaching*. Jossey-Bass, pp. 188–216.
Schön, D.A. (1983). *The Reflective Practitioner*. Basic Books.

Reflect and Revise

Dunn, T.G., and Shriner, C. (1999). Deliberate practice in teaching: What teachers do for self-improvement. *Teaching and Teacher Education*, 15(6), 631–651. https://doi.org/10.1016/S0742-051X(98)00068-7.
Kane, D. (2017). A focus on self-improvement: Five principles of deliberate practice can help teachers consistently improve their teaching. *edutopia*. https://www.edutopia.org/blog/focus-self-improvement-dylan-kane.
Schön, D.A. (1983). *The Reflective Practitioner*. Basic Books.

EXPERIENTIAL EXERCISES BY DISCIPLINE

For those interested in finding proven experiential exercises in their field, a list of experiential exercises by discipline is presented; see Table 3.12, "Example experiential exercises by business discipline." The exercises are drawn from publications in the disciplines of accounting, business ethics, entrepreneurship, human resources management, international business, management, operations management, marketing, strategic management, finance, supply chain

Table 3.12   Example experiential exercises by business discipline

Discipline / key learning objective	Example 1	Example 2	Example 3	Example 4	Example 5
Accounting	Stefaniak, C.M. (2016). Using "the wave" to facilitate participants' understanding of the implicit pressures associated with the auditing profession. *Current Issues in Auditing, 10*(1), 11–117.	Dunn, C.L. (2016). A portable factory: Experiential learning of manufacturing concepts. *Journal of Emerging Technologies in Accounting, 13*(1), 141–159.	Mastilak, C. (2012). First-day strategies for millennial students in introductory accounting courses: It's all fun and games until something gets learned. *Journal of Education For Business, 87*, 48–51.	Greenberg, R.K. and Schneider, A. (2010). Job order costing: A simulation and vehicle for conceptual discussion. *Academy of Educational Leadership Journal, 14*, 39–57.	Lafond, C.A., Vinciguerra, B., and Malhotra, D.K. (2009). Integrating personal finance concepts into the financial accounting course. *Business Education Forum, 64*, 17–22.
Key learning objective	Decide how to handle social complexities resultant from identifying errors in an accounting system.	Analyze applications for cost/ managerial accounting and to a lesser extent operations management or human resources management.	Discover the demand for accounting information and basic cost concepts through games.	Simulate manufacture of a table from purchase of raw materials through sale of finished product to illustrate actual and normal costing systems.	Combine knowledge of personal finance concepts with introductory accounting concepts through a series of unique exercises.
Business ethics	Tromley, C., Giapponi, C., and McDevitt, R. (2014). Cultural identity and ethical decision making: an experiential exercise. *Organization Management Journal, 11*(1), 17–30.	Baker, S.D., and Comer, D.R. (2012). Business ethics everywhere: An experiential exercise to develop students' ability to identify and respond to ethical issues in business. *Journal of Management Education, 36*, 95–125.	Oldfield, J., and Slessor, A. (2009). Shades of grey: The business ethics game. In *Proceedings of the 2009 Ascilite Conference*, 714–716.	Comer, D., and Vega, G. (2005). An experiential exercise that introduces the concept of the personal ethical threshold to develop moral courage. *Journal of Business Ethics Education, 2*, 171–197.	Nelson, K. (1992). The work ethic game. *Moral Education Forum, 17*(3), 1–19.

Discipline / key learning objective	Example 1	Example 2	Example 3	Example 4	Example 5
Key learning objective	Explore an ethical decision and the relationship between cultural identity and ethical decision making.	Identify ethical issues and to respond to them in ways that consider relationship between organizational factors and ethical action.	Evaluate ethical dilemmas to apply ethical codes of conduct.	Assess one's personal ethical threshold for behavior through an exercise that develops awareness of moral courage.	Evaluate legal, judgment, and policy issues in the workplace to make decisions that uphold integrity.
Entrepreneurship	Allegra, M., La Guardia, D., Ottaviano, S., Dal Grande, V., and Gentile, M. (2013). A serious game to promote and facilitate entrepreneurship education for young students. In *Proceedings of the 2013 International Conference on Education and Educational Technologies*, July, 256–263.	Malach, S.E., and Malach, R.L. (2014). Start your own business assignment in the context of experiential entrepreneurship education. *Journal of Higher Education Outreach and Engagement*, 18(1), 169–186.	Holland, D. (2014). Why didn't I think of that? A classroom exercise for developing entrepreneurial thinking. Entrepreneur and Innovation Exchange, November 6. https:// eiexchange.com/content/32 -why-didnt-i-think-of-that-a -classroom-exercise-f.	Schwartz, R.G., and Teach, R.D. (2002). The congruence™ game: A team-building exercise for students of entrepreneurship. *Simulation and Gaming*, 33(1), 94–108.	Robinson, P.B. (1996). The minefield exercise. *Simulation and Gaming*, 27(3), 350–364.
Key learning objective	Develop an entrepreneurial mindset through the management of a touristic company in a complex and competitive market exercise with other companies/players.	Design a new business to experience the intangible, real-world aspects of the entrepreneurial process.	Construct mental models to enhance entrepreneurial thinking through an open-market trading card activity that introduces barriers to entrepreneurship and strategy.	Demonstrate congruent decision-making in marketing, operations, finance, and human resources in entrepreneurial environments to understand its value and connection to performance.	Formulate a plan for a group to escape from a prisoner of war camp that includes attention to entrepreneurial concepts of vision, mission, strategy, leadership, group dynamics, innovation, and considerations of failure.
Finance	Jacobson, S. (2013). Infusing business finance with ethical dilemmas. *Jesuit Higher Education: A Journal*, 2(2), 127–132.	MacDougall, S.L., and Follows, S.B. (2006). Modeling-building in Excel as pedagogy for the fundamentals of corporate finance. *Journal of Financial Education*, 32, 55–71.	Bruner, R.F. (2006). *Case Studies in Finance: Managing for Corporate Value Creation* (5th edn). McGraw-Hill/Irwin.	Saraoglu, H., Yobaccio, E., and Louton, D. (2000). Teaching dynamic processes in finance: How can we prepare students for an age of rapid and continual chance? *Financial Practice and Education*, 10(2), 231–240.	Brown, K.M. (1990). The use of role play in teaching corporate finance. *Journal of Financial Education*, 19, 37–43.

Discipline / key learning objective	Example 1	Example 2	Example 3	Example 4	Example 5
Key learning objective	Write memos with solutions to ethical dilemmas related to basic business finance.	Utilize a spreadsheet template-building pedagogy and evaluate its effectiveness in terms of learning benefits perceived by students.	Discuss tools and concepts in finance instruction for upper-level undergraduate students and intermediate MBA students through 50 case studies and technical notes.	Explore system dynamics modeling, and present two examples to demonstrate its power and appropriateness as a pedagogical tool that facilitates the teaching of dynamic processes in finance.	Utilize role play to integrate ethics into financial management curriculum.
Human resource management	Armstrong, M.B., Landers, R.N., and Collmus, A.B. (2016). Gamifying recruitment, selection, training, and performance management: Game-thinking in human resource management. In Gangadharbatla, H. and Davis, D.Z. (eds), *Emerging Research and Trends in Gamification* (pp. 140–165). IGI Global.	Taylor, V.F. (2014). Gaining experience using the job classification method: A job evaluation exercise. *Journal of Human Resource Education*, 8, 32–45.	Clardy, A.B. (2014). *Managing Human Resources: Exercises, Experiments, and Applications*. Psychology Press.	Nkomo, S.M., Fottler, M.D., and McAfee, R.B. (2010). *Human Resource Management Applications: Cases, Exercises, Incidents, and Skill Builders*. Cengage Learning.	Gruys, M., and Stewart, S. (2007). Teaching human resource management concepts with experiential exercises. *Journal of Human Resource Education*, 1(1), 38–57.
Key learning objective	Explore opportunities for gamification and serious games in human resource management (HRM) and identify future research in game-thinking in HRM.	Decide on job classification and salary for five position descriptions using The American Society of Civil Engineers' Job Grading Standards.	Evaluate critical experiences across a range of human resource (HR) management practices and responsibilities to apply HR concepts.	Assess knowledge of human resource management concepts and practices and apply knowledge to resolve scenarios.	Demonstrate knowledge of human resource management practices by completing a series of real-world job tasks and reflective questions about the tasks.
International business	de Jong, M., and Warmelink, H. (2017). Oasistan: An intercultural role-playing simulation game to recognize cultural dimensions. *Simulation and Gaming*, 48(2), 178–198.	Punnett, B.J. (2014). *Experiencing International Business and Management: Exercises, Projects, and Cases*. Routledge.	Witte, A.E., and Daly, P. (2014). Proverbial wisdom – a "serious" international business game. *Journal of International Education in Business*, 7(1), 2–13.	Swift, C.O., and Denton, L. (2003). Cross-cultural experiential simulation in the global marketing classroom Bafa-Bafa and its variants. *Marketing Education Review*, 13(3), 41–51.	Ledman, R.E. (2001). The family impact of expatriate assignments: An experimental exercise. *Journal of Management Education*, 25(3), 341–351.

Discipline / key learning objective	Example 1	Example 2	Example 3	Example 4	Example 5
Key learning objective	Interpret experiences of cultural differences using cultural dimensions during a business simulation focused on oil exploration and production in a fictional geopolitically complex region of the world.	Apply international business and management concepts to a variety of real-life scenarios through experiential exercises, projects, and mini case studies.	Construct a linguistic puzzle drawing on diverse language competencies of the group to develop awareness of cultural self, study world values, and examine the importance of rule-based behavior and fair play.	Discover the strong feelings associated with being part of one culture and then being forced to interact with another through the Bafá-Bafá game and its variations.	Identify issues related to workers on international assignment, including culture and language training and impact on families, and apply management concepts to them.
Management	Herrmann, C., Othmer, J., Mennenga, M., Nohr, R., Böhme, S., and Heinemann, T. (2011). Business game for total life cycle management. In Hesselbach, J. and Herrmann, C. (eds) *Globalized Solutions for Sustainability in Manufacturing* (pp. 531–536). Springer.	Moore, S., and Ryan, A. (2006). Learning to play the drum: An experiential exercise for management students. *Innovations in Education and Teaching International, 43*(4), 435–444.	Bumpus, M.A. (2005). Using motion pictures to teach management: Refocusing the camera lens through the infusion approach to diversity. *Journal of Management Education, 29*(6), 792–815.	Bacon, D., Stewart, K., and Giclas, H. (1996). The ice cream experiment: An exercise in understanding customer perceptions of quality. *Journal of Management Education, 20*(2), 265–275.	Steger, J.A. (1968). A simple but effective business game for undergraduates. *The Journal of Business Education, 43*(5), 202–205.
Key learning objective	Develop a holistic life cycle strategy that considers the interdependencies of four different management disciplines: product, production, after-sales, and end-of-life management.	Analyze an in-class experience learning to play the drum and participation in a drum circle for aspects of the experience that can be translated to other learning experiences in the management classroom.	Provide motion picture options that feature diverse actors in leading roles that are applicable for teaching topics other than diversity and advocate an infusion approach to diversity in the management classroom.	Discuss the complex nature of customer perceptions of quality through an experiential exercise involving data collection and analysis of an ice cream taste test.	Explain research findings that, regardless of the complexity or simplicity of management games, enhance learning and increase student interest and motivation.

Discipline / key learning objective	Example 1	Example 2	Example 3	Example 4	Example 5
Marketing	Lee, S.H., and Hoffman, K.D. (2015). Learning the ShamWow: Creating infomercials to teach the AIDA model. *Marketing Education Review*, 25(1), 9–14.	Forman, H. (2012). Implementing a board game simulation in a marketing course: An assessment based on "real world" measures. *Journal of the Academy of Business Education*, 13, 41–54.	Hall, S.E. (2014). Incorporating relevance and rigor in a game environment: Barracuda Cove investment game. *Marketing Education Review*, 24(1), 47–52.	Ducoffe, S.S., and Tucker, M. (2004). Is the price right? A marketing exercise in setting a selling price. *Marketing Education Review*, 14(1), 13–19.	Butler, D.D., and Herbig, P. (1992). Export to win: A useful international marketing simulation. *Journal of Marketing Education*, 14(3), 58–62.
Key learning objective	Assess infomercials as examples of classic promotional theories in marketing, specifically through the AIDA model (Attention–Interest–Desire–Action).	Develop interorganizational collaboration skills through a board game using traditional industry-based metrics for gauging skill acquisition.	Apply marketing and business concepts through a product investment game modeled after the reality television show *Shark Tank*.	Determine price levels and product amounts to sell followed by iterations allowing for price changes after examining the decisions of other competing teams.	Analyze international marketing choices and consequences through a computer-generated export simulation.
Operations management	Klotz, D. (2011). The bicycle assembly line game. *Decision Sciences Journal of Innovative Education*, 9(3), 371–377.	Piercy, N. (2010). Experiential learning: The case of the production game. *Innovations in Education and Teaching International*, 50(2), 202–213.	Heriot, K.C., Cook, R., Jones, R.C., and Simpson, L. (2008). The use of student consulting projects as an active learning pedagogy: A case study in a production/ operations management course. *Decision Sciences Journal of Innovative Education*, 6(2), 463–481.	Sun, H. (1998). A game for the education and training of production/operations management. *Education+Training*, 40(9), 411–416.	Van Ackere, A., Larsen, E. R., and Morecroft, J.D. (1993). Systems thinking and business process redesign: An application to the beer game. *European Management Journal*, 11(4), 412–423.

Discipline / key learning objective	Example 1	Example 2	Example 3	Example 4	Example 5
Key learning objective	Discover principles of continuously operating processes, such as output rate, capacity relative to market demand and inventory, through a real-time group assembly line activity.	Demonstrate application of theoretical business and operations management concepts in practice by simulating the workings of an actual manufacturing organization.	Apply learning from production and/or operations management courses to provide consulting for an organization.	Discover the basic principles of and the differences between two production planning methods (material requirement planning and just-in-time) through a car production process with manual paperwork and a set of poker cards.	Develop systems thinking for business process design through a well-known logistical system activity called the "beer game."
Organizational behavior	Teckchandani, A., and Schultz, F.C. (2014). The vision thing: An experiential exercise introducing the key activities performed by leaders. *Journal of Leadership Studies*, 8(1), 63–69.	Lewis, A.C., and Grosser, M. (2012). The change game: An experiential exercise demonstrating barriers to change. *Journal of Management Education, 36,* 669–697.	Gibson, D.E. (2006). Emotional episodes at work: An experiential exercise in feeling and expressing emotions. *Journal of Management Education, 30*(3), 477–500.	Joireman, J., Daniels, D., George-Falvy, J., and Kamdar, D. (2006). Organizational citizenship behaviors as a function of empathy, consideration of future consequences, and employee time horizon: An initial exploration using an in-basket simulation of OCBs. *Journal of Applied Social Psychology, 36*(9), 2266–2292.	Blanton, K.K., and Barbuto, J.E. (2005). Cultural constraints in the workplace: An experiential exercise utilizing Hofstede's dimensions. *Journal of Management Education, 29,* 654–666.

Discipline / key learning objective	Example 1	Example 2	Example 3	Example 4	Example 5
Key learning objective	Create a three-tiered hierarchical organizational structure to experience the activities performed by leaders and managers and serve as a platform for discussing important issues, such as planning and strategy, culture, teams, communication, and organizational structure.	Discover leadership challenges in the change management process through a simulation that explores communication, intergroup dynamics, trust, power, and motivation.	Explore and discuss emotional "episodes" from personal experiences at work to learn about how organizations generate display rules for emotional expression and what this means for individual and organizational effectiveness.	Use an in-box simulation to evaluate organizational citizenship behaviors as a function of empathy in terms of their cost and benefit to the employee and the organization in both the short term and the long term.	Apply cultural dimensions in the context of a simulation involving subcultures in the sales organization of a multinational organization.
Strategic management	Norman, P.M. (2018). An exercise to integrate strategic and financial analysis. *Management Teaching Review*, 3(3), 252–264.	Schaefer, R.A.B. and Crosswhite, A.M. (2018). Top management team crisis communication after claims of sexual harassment. *Management Teaching Review*, 3(2), 148–171.	MacMillan, K., and Komar, J. (2018). Population ecology (organizational ecology): An experiential exercise demonstrating how organizations in an industry are born, change, and die. *Journal of Management Education*, 42, 375–397.	Patz, A.L. (2014). Strategy learning in a total enterprise simulation. In *Proceedings of the 2014 ABSEL conference: Developments in Business Simulation and Experiential Learning*, March. https://absel-ojs-ttu.tdl.org/absel/index.php/absel/issue/view/41.	Seethamraju, R. (2011). Enhancing student learning of enterprise integration and business process orientation through an ERP business simulation game. *Journal of Information Systems Education*, 22(1), 19.
Key learning objective	Develop greater appreciation that financial outcomes are driven by complex, interrelated factors.	Create a response to a public claim of workplace sexual harassment and share reactions within a simulated press conference.	Discover how populations of organizations change in predictable ways over time through a simulation.	Assess what is learned and by whom in a total enterprise (TE) simulation.	Investigate the influence of an enterprise resource planning (ERP) simulation game on learning effectiveness, skills development, and decision-making.

Discipline / key learning objective	Example 1	Example 2	Example 3	Example 4	Example 5
Supply chain management	Foster, S., and Hopkins, J. (2011). ERP simulation game: Establishing engagement, collaboration and learning. In *Proceedings of the 2011 PACIS Conference*, July. https://aisel.aisnet.org/pacis2011/62/.	Merkuryev, Y., Merkuryeva, G., Bikovska, J., Hatem, J., and Desmet, B. (2009). Business simulation game for teaching multi-echelon supply chain management. *International Journal of Simulation and Process Modelling*, 5(4), 289–299.	Zhou, L., Xie, Y., Wild, N., and Hunt, C. (2008). Learning and practising supply chain management strategies from a business simulation game: A comprehensive supply chain simulation. In *Proceedings of the 2008 Winter Simulation conference*, December. https://www.informs-sim.org/wsc08papers/317.pdf.	Kanet, J.J., and Stößlein, M. (2008). Using a supply chain game to effect problem-based learning in an undergraduate operations management program. *Decision Sciences Journal of Innovative Education*, 6(2), 287–295.	Corsi, T.M., Boyson, S., Verbraeck, A., Van Houten, S.P., Han, C., and Macdonald, J.R. (2006). The real-time global supply chain game: New educational tool for developing supply chain management professionals. *Transportation Journal*, 45(3), 61–73.
Key learning objective	Develop a range of business and "soft" skills using a real-world ERP system.	Evaluate different aspects of supply chain management, including general supply chain mechanisms, non-cyclic and cyclic inventory replenishment policies, through a rules-based simulation.	Test a comprehensive set of supply chain (SC) management strategies in a business simulation that has a built-in management information system (MIS).	Combine the case-oriented problem-based learning approach with a competitive supply chain management strategy game for students to see the impact of their decisions instantaneously in cash flow balance and overall team standing.	Make distribution decisions in a complex, global, real-time supply chain simulation.

management, and organizational behavior. For each discipline, five example experiential exercises are provided. For each exercise, the exercise author, title, publication source, and learning objectives are shared to facilitate your review and consideration of these exercises. This reference tool provides a starting point for finding exercises in a discipline, and a source of inspiration for creating new experiential exercises for the classroom. Whether you are adopting, adapting, or creating an experiential exercise, this book provides the foundational theories, models, evidence-based best practices, and examples to help any educator integrate experiential exercises into their teaching practice.

CONCLUSION

This chapter provides a detailed look at how three different experiential exercises were planned and implemented with distinct audiences (undergraduate, graduate, professional) at diverse institutions of higher education. The educators who facilitated these exercises are also diverse, sharing their unique perspectives in bringing the exercises to life. While different mindsets, environments, and experiences were involved in the creation of these exercises, the exercises are unified by a number of common factors: (1) the foundational theories of experiential learning (presented in Chapter 1); (2) the high-impact, evidence-based best practices that enhance learning (discussed in Chapter 2); and (3) the model that provided a framework for development and discussion of the example exercises (defined in Chapter 2).

Having the tools and capability to facilitate experiential exercises is incomplete without a discussion of ethical considerations when using them. Ethical issues may arise in situations where learners participate in activities without their knowledge or consent, learners disclose personal information which might cause them embarrassment, or activities evoke strong emotions or trigger painful memories.

Bradford (2019) identified eight areas of ethical concern related to experiential learning, including the following: (1) the degree to which students may freely choose to participate in experiential activities; (2) educator bias in terms of what content or ideas are covered; (3) inadequately debriefing the exercise and thereby limiting the opportunity for reflection and learning; (4) the risks associated with students exposing personal information in class; (5) the (not uncommon) use of deception in experiential learning; (6) the use of explicit role instructions and the impact of role playing on the role player; (7) the negative impact of feedback, particularly if students are not trained to provide behavioral feedback; and (8) the uncontrollable nature of experiential learning in terms of what students construct from and react to during an activity.

Bradford (2019) encourages educators to take the necessary steps to create a supportive learning environment, to monitor the personal impact of learning activities, and to reflect upon their assumptions and intentions for using a specific activity. Reflection-in-action during exercises and reflection-on-action after exercises, including making appropriate adjustments, help to ensure that educators identify and appropriately respond to ethically sensitive situations. We encourage educators to use the processes and evidence-based best practices discussed in Chapter 2, particularly the high-impact micro contextual factors such as educator beliefs and instructional approaches (for example, building caring and respectful relationships with students, creating clear expectations for learning, establishing relevance, and providing some autonomy and choice) to ensure that exercises are conducted ethically and in a supportive learning environment. See Lund Dean et al.'s (2019) "Experiential learning and the moral duty of business schools" for a discussion of approaches educators can take as a community to anticipate and mitigate possible harms associated with experiential learning.

Experiential exercises are increasingly in demand in both academic and professional learning environments because of the benefits they offer in terms of dynamic, engaging learning, and the robust empirical support for experiential pedagogy. There are many opportunities to safely and effectively integrate a wide variety of classroom-based experiential exercises into classes, courses, degree programs, and professional development workshops. We hope you find the guidance, tools, and examples here useful in your work as an educator, and in the higher mission of helping people to learn and grow.

APPENDIX 3.1: SUPPLEMENTAL RESOURCES FOR THE EMBRACING A GROWTH MINDSET EXERCISE

Learning More About Growth Mindset

Dweck, C.S. (2007). The perils and promises of praise. *Educational Leadership, 65*(2), 34.

Dweck, C.S., and Yeager, D.S. (2019). Mindsets: A view from two eras. *Perspectives on Psychological Science, 14*(3), 481–496. DOI: 10.1177/1745691618804166.

Sisk, V.F., Burgoyne, A.P., Sun, J., Butler, J.L., and Macnamara, B.N. (2018). To what extent and under which circumstances are growth mind-sets important to academic achievement? Two meta-analyses. *Psychological Science, 29*(4), 549–571. DOI:10 .1177/0956797617739704.

Learning More About Designing Growth Mindset Exercises

Yeager, D.S., Romero, C., Paunesku, D., Hulleman, C.S., Schneider, B., et al. (2016). Using design thinking to improve psychological interventions: The case of the growth mindset during the transition to high school. *Journal of Educational Psychology, 108*(3), 374–391. DOI: http://doi.org/10.1037/edu0000098.

APPENDIX 3.2: SUPPLEMENTAL RESOURCES FOR THE GLOBAL STRATEGY MEETING EXERCISE

Cultural Resource Examples

Ambler, T., Witzel, M., and Xi, C. (2016). *Doing Business in China.* Routledge.

Aperian Global (2019). GlobeSmart profile. https://www.aperianglobal .com/modes-of-delivery/globesmart-profile-2/.

Country Navigator (2019). Business meeting etiquette: 12 tips for doing business around the world. https://countrynavigator.com/ blog/global-talent/business-meeting-etiquette/.

eDiplomat (2020). Cultural etiquette. http://www.ediplomat.com/np/ cultural_etiquette/cultural_etiquette.htm.

French, A.M.M. (2010). *United States Protocol: The Guide to Official Diplomatic Etiquette*. Rowman & Littlefield.
Hofstede Insights (2018). Compare countries. https://www. hofstede-insights. com/product/compare-countries.
Hurn, B.J. (2007). The influence of culture on international business negotiations. *Industrial and Commercial Training*, *39*(7), 354–360.
Internations (2019). International etiquette for business people. https://www.internations.org/guide/global/international-etiquette -for-businesspeople-15300.
Knight, R. (2015). How to run a meeting of people from different cultures. https://hbr.org/2015/12/how-to-run-a-meeting-of-people -from-different-cultures.
Martin, J.S., and Chaney, L.H. (2012). *Global Business Etiquette: A Guide to international Communication and Customs*. ABC-CLIO.
Morrison, T., Conaway, W.A., and Borden, G.A. (1994). *How to do Business in Sixty Countries: Kiss, Bow, or Shake Hands*. Holbrook, MA: Adams Media Corporation.
Sabath, A.M. (2005). *International Business Etiquette: Europe*. iUniverse.

Wine Industry Resource Examples

Bhasin, H. (2018). Top wine brands across the globe. *Marketing 91*, October 16. https://www.marketing91.com/top-wine-brands -across-the-globe/.
Cain, S. (2020). Millennials are passing on wine when dining out. How the wine industry is changing its approach. *Fortune*, February 21. https://fortune.com/2020/02/21/millennials-wine-industry -habits/.
Catchpole, A. (2014). Top 10 wine trends for 2014. *The Drinks Business*, January 23. http://www.thedrinksbusiness.com/2014/01/ top-10-wine-trends-for-2014/.
NBBJ Staff (2013). Fetzer acquisition architect to speak at April wine conference. *North Bay Business Journal*, February 4. http://www .northbaybusinessjournal.com/68103/fetzer-acquisition-architect -to-speak-at-april-wine-conference/.
Rabobank (2012). Wine market contains hidden gems. *Western Farm Press*, November 30. http://westernfarmpress.com/grapes/wine -market-contains-emerging-hidden-gems.

Schachner, M. (2011). Concha y Toro is acquiring California based Fetzer Vineyards. *Wine Enthusiast*, March 3. http://www.winemag .com/March-2011/Concha-y-Toro-is-acquiring-California-based -Fetzer-Vineyards/.

Wine Business (n.d.). Home page for the wine industry. https://www .winebusiness.com/

Wine Folly (n.d.). Learn about wine. https://winefolly.com/

Wine Folly (2014). Taxes and the 3-tier system (Why wine costs so much!). WineFolly, August 29. https://winefolly.com/lifestyle/ three-tier-system/.

Wine Industry (n.d.). Advisor. https://wineindustryadvisor.com/

Wine Institute (n.d.). The voice for wine in public policy. https:// wineinstitute.org.

Annotated bibliography

Beard, C., and Wilson, J.P. (2018). *Experiential Learning: A Practical Guide for Training, Coaching and Education* **(4th edn). Kogan Page.**

This book provides a combination of learning theory, case studies from international organizations using experiential activities, and practical tools for experiential education. Since the cases in this book focus on training in organizations, professional trainers would benefit most from this volume. However, there is application to traditional higher education environments in terms of the theory and some of the tools. This resource complements the discussion of learning theory and provides additional insights on the integration of games and sensory experiences in a classroom environment.

The authors introduce a model they created called the learning combination lock. It is a diagnostic tool which looks at considerations for learning in the external environment (that is, the classroom and learning activities), through the senses, and in the internal environment (that is, emotions, reasoning and intelligence, and response to change). The tool helps educators to work through practical considerations for where learning takes place, what is learned, how learners will receive the experience, how emotions will be engaged, what learners need to know, and how learners can be encouraged to change. The authors argue that effective learning requires balance in six dimensions of the learning experience: belonging, doing, sensing, feeling, thinking, and being. The experiential learning activities discussed are diverse, including indoor and outdoor environments, creative approaches, incorporation of affective learning strategies, the evaluation of experiential learning, and considerations for both for-profit and not-for-profit organizations. Cases in the book include a focus on ethical and behavioral challenges in facilitating learning experiences. This fourth edition of the book has added discussion on the use of digital games and the design of multi-sensory experiences.

Branch, R.M., and Dousay, T.A. (2015). *Survey of Instructional Design Models* **(5th edn). Association for Educational Communications and Technology. http://members.aect.org/ publications/SurveyofInstructionalDesignModels.pdf.**

This free online book is published periodically to chronicle the history and evolution of thinking about instructional design models. It provides a comprehensive overview of the field and a deep discussion of key design theories and models. The models presented appeal to different audiences. The classroom models are intended for educators working independently to create and deliver learning experiences. Product models are intended for cross-functional expert teams designing and producing multimedia instructional products for wide distribution, typically no one on the team is involved in implementation or use of the product. System models are intended for multidisciplinary expert teams; however, these teams have a much broader scope. Typically, they are creating a complex interrelated set of courses or an entire curriculum to achieve specific training goals (for example, military training).

The book starts with definitions and an overview of the generic ADDIE model (that is, analyze, design, develop, implement, evaluate), including a review of the assumptions underlying this model. Then the book features a brief history on how and why instructional design models have evolved over time. This section highlights the ongoing: (1) desire to improve instruction; (2) search for models that help practitioners manage complex situations; and (3) search for models that best suit various contexts or situations. These factors have led to the development of more than 100 instructional design models. Finally, a taxonomy for instructional design models is described and the most significant and unique models in each category are reviewed in detail (that is, classroom-oriented, product oriented, and system oriented).

Burch, G.F., Batchelor, J.H., Heller, N.A., Shaw, J., Kendall, W., and Turner, B. (2016). Do experiential learning pedagogies effect student learning? A meta-analysis of 40 years of research. *Academy of Management Best Paper Proceedings*, *2016*(1), 1672–1677. https:// doi.org/10.5465/ambpp.2016.127.

This article discusses the findings of a meta-analysis of 53 studies of the evaluation of experiential pedagogies published over 40 years. Hypotheses tested the effect on student learning outcomes, understanding of social issues, development of personal insight, and cognitive development. The research included various forms of experiential learning with the exception of service-learning, as a previous meta-analysis had been performed on this method. The article is of interest to researchers of learning pedagogies as well as educators who employ experiential learning pedagogies in the classroom. The study supports the use of experiential learning exercises to enhance student learning.

The analysis found that most scholars who authored the articles accepted the concept of experiential learning, as defined by D.A. Kolb in 1984 (knowledge is created through the transformation of experience), and believe it to be beneficial to learning outcomes. In terms of the analysis, experiential learning was found to have a positive effect on student learning in all 53 studies that were analyzed. It also had a positive effect on understanding social issues, developing personal insight, and cognitive development. Learning outcomes were found to be a standard deviation higher in experiential learning environments. The effects varied across moderators, but were assessed to be generally robust across all of them. The moderators included level of cognitive processing, type of assessment used to measure the outcome (objective versus subjective), whether students received feedback during the activity, duration of the activity, whether the activity involved a simulation, the type of simulation, if a simulation was used, age, gender, and nationality of participants (United States or non-United States).

Chin, J., Dukes, R., and Gamson, W. (2009). Assessment in simulation and gaming: A review of the last 40 years. *Simulation and Gaming*, *40*(4), 553–568.

The state of assessment in simulation and gaming over the past 40 years is discussed in this article. The authors discuss how educators who use games and simulations have had to defend the educational value of these activities in the past, and that the journal has been a place where many of these arguments have been discussed through the years. They share that while there is more acceptance of the educational value of these activities, educators need to continue to be mindful of using assessments to measure the specific impact of their games and simulations. The primary focus of this article is on the challenge with assessments for games and simulations, and suggestions on how to build assessment into the design process during creation of these activities. The article is written for educators who design and use simulations and gaming in classroom environments to advance learning. Readers will find the discussion of two specific games (SIMSOC and Global Justice Game) of interest, as they are critically assessed in terms of the assessment strategies that need to be considered. Assessment strategy is a key component of the model for use of experiential exercises in this book.

The research reviewed is drawn from *Simulation and Gaming* journal using the keyword "assessment" and a sample of meta-studies on evidence of educational effectiveness prior to 1990 when the term was not formally used in this field. The authors concluded in their findings that past efforts to demonstrate educational value were not formally called assessments, even though assessments of learning have long been used in the field. The original skepticism of the traditional education community regarding the use of gaming and simulation in classrooms has spurred more formal assessment practices in recent years. Two games, SIMSOC and Global Justice Game, are discussed in terms of specific considerations for assessment. A primary focus of the discussion is regarding the role of agency versus structure in gaming and simulations. The authors conclude that a balance between agency and structure is important to allow for discovery while also maintaining a realistic sense of obstacles that must be overcome. Furthermore, they say that assessment goals should move beyond simple cognitive development to goals that empower students to thereby increase their sense of agency.

Clark, R.E., Kirschner, P.A., and Sweller, J. (2012). Putting students on the path to learning: The case for fully guided instruction. *American Educator, 36*(1), 6–11.

This article provides a useful summary of Kirschner, Sweller, and Clark's article "Why minimal guidance during instruction does not work: An analysis of the failure of constructivist, discovery, problem-based, experiential and inquiry-based teaching" (Kirschner et al., 2006). The article is written for educators who engage in discovery learning, problem-based learning, inquiry-learning or other forms of constructivist learning to discuss the research-based benefits of step-by-step and explicit instruction. This perspective may be helpful when creating instructions and directions for experiential exercises in the classroom.

The Kirschner et al. (2006) article examines various perspectives on the impact of instructional guidance during teaching over the last 50 years. On one side of the spectrum, there are those who argue that all people – novices and experts alike – learn best when provided with loose instruction (that is, unguided or partly guided segments). On the other side, there is a conviction that ideal learning environments for experts and novices differ and require different degrees of guided instruction (that is, experts may thrive without much guidance; nearly everyone else thrives with full, explicit guidance). After examining each side of the argument, the authors assert that partial guidance (that is, providing loose or no instruction or guidance) is not effective or efficient. They draw on robust research that supports the use of step-by-step instruction with full explanations to achieve learning objectives. The implications for implementing a classroom experiential exercise is that the educator should be thorough in providing instructions for each step of an exercise and actively provide guidance where necessary.

Ducoffe, S.S., and Tucker, M. (2004). Is the price right? A marketing exercise in setting a selling price. *Marketing Education Review*, *14*(1), 13–19. https://doi.org/0.1080/10528008.2004.11488848.

This article presents an experiential exercise in pricing designed for students on a marketing course. The authors discuss the benefits of using an interdisciplinary, experiential exercise to teach the intricacies of pricing decisions. The article is intended for marketing educators who would like to incorporate this experiential exercise in their classrooms. The authors discuss challenges they have faced in facilitating the activity, and solutions to manage these. This article provides a discipline-specific exercise and contextual considerations for teaching these concepts to students in a marketing class.

The activity discussed in this article incorporates perspectives from the supply and demand theory of economics, income statement and cash flow analysis from finance and accounting, and pricing principles and consumer analysis from marketing. During the activity, student teams determine price levels and product amounts to sell. They must go through an iterative process of examining the decisions of competing teams and adjusting prices for the market. This activity allows students to make pricing decisions in a competitive market, developing their understanding of how companies must react quickly to changes in competitor prices, product supply in the market, and consumer demand.

Dunn, C.L. (2016). A portable factory: Experiential learning of manufacturing concepts. *Journal of Emerging Technologies in Accounting*, *13*(1), 141–159. https://doi.org/10.2308/jeta-51393.

This article presents an experiential exercise which focuses on the manufacturing process and may be used by accounting educators to add a hands-on activity to their courses. It discusses the importance of decision-makers in every business discipline understanding this process. Because business students may not have manufacturing experience, the activity provides a useful visual representation to enhance learning of concepts that would otherwise be abstract in "resources, events, agents" (REA) accounting, such as machine operation, labor operation, and labor type. REA is a model of how an accounting system can be re-engineered for the computer age. The exercise turns the classroom into a temporary factory that produces laminated bookmarks, so that students can see these concepts in action. Dunn also discusses potential applications for cost/ managerial accounting, operations management, or human resources management.

Fink, L.D. (2013). *Creating Significant Learning Experiences: An Integrated Approach to Designing College Courses* **(revised and updated ed.). Jossey Bass.**

This book is an update to the original publication from 2003. Fink provides an integrated approach (that is, a model that is relational, not linear) for educators to use a taxonomy of "significant learning" comprised of ways to deepen the learning experience. The book is primarily intended for educators in higher education to assist them in deepening learning experiences. A secondary audience is administrators who support educators. There is specific discussion on how administrators can provide the resources and support needed for educators to produce significant learning experiences for students. This resource complements the discussion in this book of tools and strategies to enhance the effectiveness of experiential exercises in the classroom.

Fink's model involves gathering information regarding situational factors that may influence the selection of content and design of the experience. Then, decisions must be made regarding the learning goals, the teaching and learning activities, and feedback and assessments. Fink's taxonomy of learning goals includes six interacting types of learning: foundational knowledge, application, integration, human dimension, caring, and learning how to learn. The discussion addresses research on the learning process, active learning and student engagement. Later in the book, Fink discusses the tensions in higher education between institutional demands for research, teaching loads, and insufficient support for educator development that can lead to less effective learning environments. He argues that there is an ongoing need for educator development in teaching that provides alternatives to traditional lectures and discussions.

Holman, D., Pavlica, K., and Thorpe, R. (1997). Rethinking Kolb's theory of experiential learning in management education: The contribution of social constructionism and activity theory. *Management Learning*, *28*(2), 135–148. doi:10.1177/ 1350507697282003.

This article critically evaluates D.A. Kolb's 1984 theory of experiential learning from social constructionist and activity theory perspectives. The authors discuss different perspectives in the field on the concepts of self and thought, including Kolb's. The article appeals to researchers and theorists in learning and management education. It supports the importance of experiential exercises as a component of management development.

The authors argue that while social relationships are often deemed secondary in the analysis of learning, they should be considered primary based upon the theories discussed. Kolb's experiential learning theory is placed within the cognitive psychological tradition, where the authors argue that it is affiliated with a tradition that tends to overlook or mechanically explain social, historical, and cultural aspects of identity. The analysis supports experiential learning as an important part of the development of a person (a manager, in the context of this discussion), and their thoughts, as the environment in which the person is working has a direct effect on beliefs and behaviors. The authors propose activity theory as an alternative way of understanding the social, historical, and cultural aspects of identity. This analysis reconceptualizes experiential learning theory and concludes that learning is an argumentative and rhetorical process in which the manager acts as an author.

Hoover, J.D., Giambatista, R.C., Sorenson, R.L., and Bommer, W.H. (2010). Assessing the effectiveness of whole person learning pedagogy in skill acquisition. *Academy of Management Learning and Education*, 9(2), 192–203. https://doi.org/10.5465/amle.9.2.zqr192.

Management education has been criticized for its perceived lack of relevance to the skills needed in the workforce today. The authors discuss the criticisms and offer an example of the "whole person learning" approach that they offer in an executive skills course that may bridge this gap in management education. The model that they present provides a holistic perspective on teaching and learning in business schools. This model is useful for educators who want to enhance interactive learning, especially through experiential learning activities in the classroom.

   Whole person learning refers to the perspective that a human being exists in a network of relationships and interdependent systems. This approach necessarily addresses the intersection of relationships and systems in the learning process. The authors discuss their choice of experiential learning as a method that supports whole person learning. They discuss its use in the classroom and provide an empirical assessment of skill improvement over a five-year period. The skills assessed included communication, teamwork, leadership/initiative, decision-making, and planning/organizing. The pedagogical approach was found to be effective for the development of all these skills. Guidance is provided for implementing the pedagogy into MBA curricula.

Kayes, D.C. (2002). Experiential learning and its critics: Preserving the role of experience in management learning and education. *Academy of Management Learning and Education*, 1(2), 137–149. doi:10.5465/amle.2002.8509336.

Experiential learning in management education has been criticized on both empirical and theoretical grounds for placing emphasis on individual learning at the expense of other social, political, and cultural aspects of learning. Kayes addresses these criticisms, providing a reconceptualized perspective on experiential learning, especially in the relationship between personal and social knowledge. This article is designed to address critics of experiential learning and may be of interest to both researchers and educators of management education. The article supports the use of experiential exercises in the classroom, and offers additional theoretical perspectives on how it develops students.

Kayes looks at the primary distinctions in the literature in the episte-
mologies informing experiential education and then critically evaluates
the criticisms in terms of their theoretical basis. Ultimately, he proposes
that personal and social knowledge are developed in tandem with a vac-
illation between them. One cannot be developed in isolation of the other,
he argues. The implications for management education are to place
greater emphasis on language and conversation in the learning process.

**Keys, B., and Wolfe, J. (1990). The role of management games and
simulations in education and research. *Journal of Management*,
16(2), 307–336. https://doi.org/10.1177/014920639001600205.**

This article is a review of the evolution of gaming activities in management education. It provides a historical perspective that is foundational
to understanding the continued modern-day challenges and opportunities
with integration of experiential activities, such as games, in the management curriculum. While the article is dated, it remains among one of the
most cited articles in business education, and provides a historical review
of the inclusion of gaming in management education.

Keys and Wolfe track the inception of games for training in military
contexts and their evolution from the military contexts to modern-day
management training around the 1940s. Most of the discussion focuses
on the evolution from the 1950s to the publication date (1990), including
challenges to its use in both management education and research and the
opportunities it presents for integrative learning in business schools. The
authors define the terms and parameters of the management gaming field.
They explain several models of experiential learning that are relevant for
the use of games. The review includes studies on the educational value
of management games. The findings conclude that they are generally
effective.

**Kolb, A.Y., and Kolb, D.A. (2005). Learning styles and learning
spaces: Enhancing experiential learning in higher education.
Academy of Management Learning and Education, *4*(2), 193–212.
doi:10.5465/amle.2005.17268566.**

This article examines developments in theory and research on experiential learning. The principles for the enhancement of experiential learning
in higher education that are discussed in this article expand on the discussions in D.A. Kolb's 1984 book about experiential learning (see annota-

tion for the second edition of the 1984 book below) and how to maximize the value of experiential exercises. The authors suggest how experiential learning can be applied throughout the educational environment by institutional development programs, including longitudinal outcome assessment, curriculum development, student development, and educator development. The article may be of particular interest to researchers and theorists in experiential learning.

Kolb and Kolb explore how experiential learning can enhance learning, and introduce the concept of the learning space. The learning space refers to the interdependent nature of student learning and their learning environment (that is, student and classroom). The authors discuss this interdependence through the examples of three case studies in distinct programs, including an MBA program and an undergraduate arts program. They found that the differences between management education and the arts were particularly notable. Students in the MBA program tended to occupy the "southern" end of the classroom space (for example, lecture space), where they focus on thinking as a prominent learning style, while the arts students tended to occupy the "northern" end of the classroom space, focusing more on feeling and reflection. Ultimately, the authors offer a chart reflecting the different spaces in the classroom and how they align themselves with one or more learning styles: feeling, reflecting, thinking, acting. This article provides a compelling argument for intentional design of learning activities within the classroom space.

Kolb, D.A. (2014). *Experiential Learning: Experience as the Source of Learning and Development* (2nd edn). FT Press.

The second edition of this book reviews three decades of research and practice since the original publication. The book is written for a wide audience, including educators, researchers, and administrators. It is a comprehensive resource on the topic of experiential learning in higher education and organizations alike.

This edition builds on the origins of experiential learning theory that were defined by Dewey, Lewin, Piaget, Vygotsky, and others, discussing models proposed by Lewin, Dewey, and Piaget specifically. Kolb finds that while each model offers a unique perspective, they share three characteristics: (1) learning is best conceived as a process, not in terms of the outcomes; (2) learning is a continuous process grounded in experience; and (3) the process of learning requires resolution of conflicts between opposing ways of dealing with the world. Kolb offers a comprehensive structural model to discuss learning styles and structures of knowledge from a multidisciplinary perspective, which is discussed further in Chapter 1 of this volume. The current organizational and education landscape is discussed in terms of the application and uses of experiential learning.

Ledman, R.E. (2001). The family impact of expatriate assignments: An experimental exercise. *Journal of Management Education*, *25*(3), 341–351. https://doi.org/10.1177/105256290102500306.

This article outlines an experiential exercise focused on issues related to employees in international assignments (that is, expatriates). It is designed for educators who teach international human resources management or international business. The experiential activity is useful to develop perspectives on the human impact of expatriate assignments and the subsequent impact on organizations.

The scenario discussed in the article captures research-based issues that these employees face, and the resulting impacts on their families, as students take on the role of family members discussing whether the expatriate assignment should be accepted and, if so, whether the family should also relocate. This activity has particular value in understanding the expatriate experience, as research reveals that family concerns are a principal reason why employees decline international assignments or come home early. The discussion in the article highlights the importance of managers understanding these issues to maximize the benefits of international assignments. Topics addressed in the exercise include the need for intercultural training in language and culture for both the employee and the family. The exercise can be completed in 50 minutes and may be used with undergraduate or graduate students.

Lewis, A.C., and Grosser, M. (2012). The change game: An experiential exercise demonstrating barriers to change. *Journal of Management Education*, *36*(5), 669–697. https://doi.org/10.1177/1052562911435474.

The article discusses leading change as an essential skill for managers in organizations. It also shares the concern that students may underestimate the difficulty of convincing others to work toward change. This is why the exercise is designed to teach both the theories on leading change and the need for students to develop their change leadership skills. The exercise is designed for educators of management to use in helping students experience the difficulties of leading change in organizations. This 45-minute exercise can be used with a range of courses in management curricula, and it can scale from small to large classes.

During the activity, students are divided into managers and workers, and must cooperate to complete a task and earn a reward. The exercise simulates resistance to change by giving the workers an incentive to stay with the status quo. Through the experience, students are able to identify opportunities for further skill development in change management. Debrief topics include communication, intergroup dynamics, trust, power, and motivation. The authors find that many groups tend to fail completion of the task due to resistance to change, creating a valuable opportunity to discuss success strategies in leading change in organizations.

Lund Dean, K., and Fornaciari, C.J. (2002). How to create and use experiential case-based exercises in a management classroom. *Journal of Management Education*, *26*(5), 586–603. https://doi.org/10.1177/105256202236728.

While the case-discussion teaching method is popular for its ability to provide real-world, decision-oriented scenarios for student analysis, it has limitations that are explored in this article. The article is written for management educators who are interested in experiential exercises that incorporate case studies. It complements the discussion in this book by providing an experiential alternative for using cases in the classroom.

Lund Dean and Fornaciari argue that overuse of cases can reduce their effectiveness, making them formulaic and repetitive. They also discuss how cases can de-emphasize the process of organizational decision-making. To maximize the benefits of the use of cases and reduce the limitations, the authors suggest case-based role play as an alternative, interactive technique. They say that by converting the case into a role play it places the student in a more beneficial position to "learn by doing." While many cases could be converted, the authors cite key considerations for choosing appropriate cases, including having a limited number of actors or roles within the case study, clearly identifiable actors with strong role-based characteristics, a limited number of feasible decision paths and scenarios, minimal background detail, a focus on a particular organization and its issues, and a focus on bounded issues that students can reasonably resolve. Preparation and facilitation considerations are also discussed, along with sample debrief questions and modification options.

McCarthy, P.R., and McCarthy, H.M. (2006). When case studies are not enough: Integrating experiential learning into business curricula. *Journal of Education for Business, 81*(4), 201–204. https:// doi.org/10.3200/JOEB.81.4.201-204.

This article provides a critical analysis of the continued popularity of the case study method in business education. The authors argue that case analysis is not a sufficient substitute for experiential learning, especially in an era where job-related field experiences are not generally required. This article is intended for educators in the field of business. It provides a perspective on the limitations of case studies to provide direct personal encounters with the topic of learning, and outlines the benefits of hands-on experiential learning activities for student development.

McCarthy and McCarthy discuss the value that experiential education has in providing students with a direct and personal encounter with the topic being studied. It allows them to make real-time decisions, rather than hypothetical ones. It also allows them to integrate their academic study with direct learning experiences. Given the many benefits of experiential education, the authors make a case for mandatory experiential programs that create an opportunity for students to have direct personal encounters, such as job shadowing, in all major areas within the business curriculum. The authors implemented this method in three courses and found that students indicated that experiential learning was "more helpful" or "helpful" to a higher degree than case studies.

Mohr, K.A., and Mohr, E.S. (2017). Understanding Generation Z students to promote a contemporary learning environment. *Journal on Empowering Teaching Excellence, 1*(1), Article 9, 84–94.

The article is written for educators to enhance their understanding of who Gen Y and Gen Z students are as learners, including their values and expectations. The newest generation of students is placing greater demands on educators to innovate teaching and learning. While some educators have expressed concern that these students lack the motivation to learn, this article argues that students from Gen Y and Gen Z are interested in learning, and that they just need to be better understood as learners. Mohr and Mohr advocate for a trifold approach that includes understanding the characteristics and needs of these generations, modifying assignments to better engage with their learning needs, and actively promoting the real-world value of assignments to enhance commitment to them. The discussion in this article expands on the considerations for experiential exercises using technology, especially with undergraduate students who are digital natives.

The authors discuss the defining characteristics of Gen Y and Gen Z learning styles to be highly acculturated to cyber and digital technologies, proactive in information-seeking, independent, and with a preference for autonomy. Mohr and Mohr say that educators who respond to these preferences may better engage their classes in learning, but must also consider the potential drawbacks to discipline and rigor in learning. The authors suggest that the solution for balancing engagement and rigor is to respond to student preferences, while providing clear instructions and expectations. The implication is that educators of Gen Y and Gen Z students must pay attention to both what is learned and how it is learned, providing guidance on the learning process itself.

Norman, P.M. (2018). An exercise to integrate strategic and financial analysis. *Management Teaching Review*, 3(3), 252–264.

Norman highlights the pivotal role courses in strategic management tend to play in business education as vehicles for integrating functional knowledge from other courses. However, while financial analysis is an important business competency, the author states that it is often missing from capstone courses. This article introduces an exercise that integrates strategic and financial analysis. It is designed for educators in business education to integrate financial analysis in strategy courses so that students will have a greater appreciation that financial outcomes are the result of factors that are both complex and interrelated.

The exercise aims to help students discover the connections between organizational strategy and financial outcomes. The learning outcomes include correctly calculating a number of financial ratios, interpreting ratios in the context of the firm's external environment and internal circumstances, and linking ratios and trends in the ratios to a firm's strategic choices. Ultimately, the exercise emphasizes that financial outcomes are the result of interdependent decisions, actions, and external events.

Redfern, A. (2018). *The Essential Guide to Classroom Practice: 200+ Strategies for Outstanding Teaching and Learning*. Routledge. https://doi.org/10.4324/9781315755557.

This robust volume provides more than 200 practical and effective strategies that educators can apply in the classroom to maximize learning. While some of the examples in the book relate specifically to secondary education, all the strategies can effectively be used across higher education. The tips in this book are intended for educators and are useful to enhance experiential exercises through high-quality teaching practices.

Strategies in the book range from simple tools, such as considerations for improving questioning techniques, to high-level principles that shape the instructional approach. Each strategy is discussed in terms of its benefits and considerations for use. The principal topics of discussion throughout the book include creating a plan for learning, developing thinking skills, engaging learners, encouraging collaborative learning, challenging and supporting, and providing feedback and assessment. Each chapter also includes a quick top ten list for reference.

Roberts, J.W. (2016). *Experiential Education in the College Context*. Routledge. https://doi.org/10.4324/9781315774992.

This book is designed for educators who are interested in adding to or refining their instructional approaches for experiential education in a college context. It is divided into two parts. The first is an exploration of the landscape of experiential education, looking at definitions, models, and methodologies. The second part reviews principles and practices of experiential education, such as design, facilitation, and assessment considerations.

The pedagogical approaches discussed were selected for this book based upon their effectiveness in engaging students and supporting high-impact learning. The practices cross disciplines and are organized around four essential categories: active learning, integrated learning, project-based learning, and community-based learning. The last chapter looks at how experiential exercise can be integrated on a campus.

Salas, E., Wildman, J.L., and Piccolo, R.F. (2009). Using simulation-based training to enhance management education. *Academy of Management Learning and Education*, 8(4), 559–573. https://doi.org/10.5465/amle.8.4.zqr559.

The authors argue that business students, whether they be undergraduate or graduate students, benefit by having practical management experiences before they enter (or re-enter) the workforce. However, there is often limited or no opportunity in business education for these experiences. Simulation-based training (SBT) offers advantages as an experiential learning approach for management education.

SBT involves the use of an artificial environment that is created to manage an individual's or a team's experiences with reality. The artificial environment may be a role play, physically based simulations, or computer-based simulations. The authors discuss research-based findings on the many advantages of using SBT, such as superior training in complex and applied competencies, accelerated student learning, and providing a more complex and realistic learning environment. A useful chart is included to provide an overview of guidelines and implementation tips for SBT in management education.

Schaefer, R.A.B., and Crosswhite, A.M. (2018). Top management team crisis communication after claims of sexual harassment. *Management Teaching Review*, 3(2), 148–171. https://doi.org/10 .1177/2379298118760163.

Schaefer and Crosswhite describe an experiential exercise for learning about managing management responses to workplace sexual harassment claims. The exercise places students in positions to respond to the public claim and to interact with the press at a press conference. The latter portion of the activity teaches students about crisis communication from a management perspective. This is an important topic for experiential learning, according to the authors, because the scenario has application at undergraduate, graduate, and executive-level business education.

The role play is designed to be used in a variety of courses that cover management, group dynamics, human resources, public relations, and/or strategy. The presentation of the exercise in the article speaks to its use in an undergraduate or graduate management course. However, the authors include instructions for use in an executive course. The instructions include exercise objectives, description of the exercise, and adaptations, and all materials needed to conduct the 50-minute exercise and debrief sessions.

Stefaniak, C.M. (2016). Using "the wave" to facilitate participants' understanding of the implicit pressures associated with the auditing profession. *Current Issues in Auditing, 10*(1), 11–117. https://doi.org/ 10.2308/ciia-51370.

This case is designed for auditing students in a classroom setting or junior auditors in a training session. It presents a collaborative, experiential learning exercise to facilitate understanding of the social complexities and pressures associated with auditing. This is important for student learning, as understanding the process of auditing through texts alone may not convey the real-world pressures that occur in the process.

Throughout the exercise, students must evaluate the flow of information through an accounting system. The title of the exercise, "the wave," is a reference to the way information flows through a system. Students experience the challenging position auditors are placed in, where they must decide how to handle a problem within a system. There are real-world social and psychological pressures built into the scenario. Students have to navigate these pressures and make difficult choices that impact people and groups in the exercise. The exercise requires only three volunteers and about 25 minutes of class time. There is no pre-work. Ultimately, the exercise stimulates dialogue about the auditing process, pressures, and professional responsibilities.

Tromley, C., Giapponi, C., and McDevitt, R. (2014). Cultural identity and ethical decision making: An experiential exercise. *Organization Management Journal, 11*(1), 17–30. https:// doi.org/10.1080/15416518.2014.903104.

This experiential exercise explores the relationship between an ethical decision and cultural identity. It includes a short case that may also be used as a role play. Instructions are included for both formats. The authors discuss the theories that inform the activity (that is, Hofstede's cultural dimensions, and Janis and Mann's decision-making model), making it of interest to researchers and professors alike. Ultimately, the article provides a useful case study and activity to explore cultural identity and ethical decision-making in a classroom environment.

The process described in the model is drawn from Janis and Mann's (1977) work *Decision Making: A Psychological Analysis of Conflict, Choice and Commitment* detailing the decision process in an environment of conflict, choice, and commitment. The model is enhanced by the inclusion of content variables derived from the ethics literature. The resulting integrated model aids in understanding the complexity of the decision process used by individuals facing ethical dilemmas and suggests variable interactions that could be field-tested. A better understanding of the process will help managers develop policies that enhance the likelihood of ethical behavior in their organizations.

Wurdinger, S.D., and Bezon, J.L. (2009). Teaching practices that promote student learning: Five experiential approaches. *Journal of Teaching and Learning*, **6(1), 1–13. https://doi.org/10.22329/jtl.v6i1 .505.**

This article discusses five innovative teaching approaches – project-based learning, problem-based learning, service-learning, place-based education, and active learning – that can enhance student learning. Wurdinger and Bezon provide practical considerations for educators to understand how to use and apply experiential learning in the classroom. Most importantly, the authors discuss how experiential learning changes the classroom culture to create active learning.

The authors state that their intent is to help inspire and motivate students to learn, resulting in more exciting classrooms and a better-educated society. The lecture format is argued to be a key contributor to student disengagement in higher education. Overuse of the format can lead to students engaging in other tasks, such as texting friends, rather than listening to the information that the educator provides. More active learning methods may inspire and motivate students to learn, which would improve the overall learning environment and potentially increase retention rates.

Resources for experiential exercises

PROFESSIONAL ASSOCIATIONS BY DISCIPLINE

- American Educational Research Association (Service-Learning and Experiential Education Special Interest Group): http://www.aera.net.
- Association for Business Simulation and Experiential Learning: https://absel.org.
- Association for Experiential Education: http://www.aee.org.
- Council for Adult and Experiential Learning: https://www.cael.org.
- Experiential Learning Leadership Institute: https://www.suu.edu/siel/elli/.
- Institute for Experiential Learning: http://www.experientiallearninginstitute.org.
- National Society for Experiential Education: http://www.nsee.org.

TEACHING CONFERENCES IN HIGHER EDUCATION

- AEE Regional and Annual Conferences: https://www.aee.org/conferences.
- American Educational Research Association (AERA): http://www.aera.net/EventsMeetings.
- American Educational Research Association (Service-Learning and Experiential Education Special Interest Group): https://www.aera.net/SIG041/Service-Learning-and-Experiential-Education.
- Annual NSEE Conference: https://www.nsee.org/annual-conference.
- Association of American Colleges and Universities (AAC&U): https://www.aacu.org/events.
- Conference on Higher Education Pedagogy: https://chep.teaching.vt.edu.
- Council for Adult and Experiential Learning Conference: https://www.cael.org/conference.

- ELLI Conference (The Experiential Learning Leadership Institute): https://www.suu.edu/siel/elli/conference/.
- Experiential Learning Conference (Institute for Experiential Learning): http://www.experientiallearninginstitute.org/events/conference-registration/.
- Frontiers in Education (FIE): http://fie-conference.org.
- Institute for Experiential Learning Symposiums and Workshops: https://www.experientiallearninginstitute.org/events.
- International Conference on Experiential Learning (European Centre for the Development of Vocational Training): https://www.cedefop.europa.eu/en/events-and-projects/events/10th-international-conference-experiential-learning.
- Leadership in Higher Education Conference: https://www.magnapubs.com/leadership-in-higher-education-conference/.
- Lilly Conferences, Evidence Based Teaching and Learning: https://www.lillyconferences.com.
- Teaching Professor Conference: https://www.magnapubs.com/teaching-professor-conference/.

JOURNALS, BOTH ACADEMIC AND PROFESSIONAL, BY DISCIPLINE

- *Journal of Experiential Education* (SAGE): http://journals.sagepub.com/home/jee.

Accounting

- *Accounting Education* (Taylor & Francis): https://www.tandfonline.com/toc/raed20/current.
- *Issues in Accounting Education* (American Accounting Association): https://aaahq.org/issues-in-accounting-education.
- *Journal of Accounting Education* (Elsevier): https://www.journals.elsevier.com/journal-of-accounting-education.

Business

- *Business Education Forum* (National Business Education Association): https://nbea.org.

- *Journal for Advancing Business Education* (International Accreditation Council for Business Education): https://iacbe.org/news/journal-for-advancing-business-education/.
- *Journal for Global Business Education* (International Society of Business Education): https://isbeusa.wordpress.com/journal/.
- *Journal of Applied Research for Business Instruction* (Delta Pi Epsilon) (Association for Business Teaching and Research): https://www.arberesearch.org.
- *Journal of Business Education* (Taylor & Francis): https://www.tandfonline.com/toc/vjeb19/current.
- *Journal of Economics Education Research* (Taylor & Francis): https://www.tandfonline.com/toc/vece20/current.
- *Journal of Teaching in International Business* (Taylor & Francis): https://www.tandfonline.com/toc/wtib20/current.
- *NABTE Review* (National Association of Business Teacher Education): https://www.nabte.org/publications.html.

Finance

- *Financial Management* (Financial Management Association): https://www.fma.org/financial-management.
- *Journal of Financial Education* (Financial Education Association): http://jfined.org.

Management

- *Journal of Management Education* (SAGE): https://journals.sagepub.com/home/jme.
- *Management Teaching Review* (SAGE): https://journals.sagepub.com/home/mtr.
- *Organization Management Journal* (Emerald): https://www.emeraldgrouppublishing.com/journal/omj.

Marketing

- *Journal of Marketing Education* (SAGE): https://journals.sagepub.com/home/jmd.
- *Marketing Education Review* (Taylor & Francis): https://www.tandfonline.com/toc/mmer20/current.

SEMINAL WORKS RELATED TO EXPERIENTIAL LEARNING THEORY

Dewey, J. (1938). *Experience and Education*. Macmillan.

Dewey, J. (1954). *The Public and Its Problems*. Ohio University Press.

Dewey, J. (1961). *Democracy and Education*. Macmillan.

Dewey, J. (1973). *The Philosophy of John Dewey: Two Volumes in One*. Ed. by J.J. McDermott. University of Chicago Press.

Freire, P. (1970). *Pedagogy of the Oppressed*. Continuum.

Illeris, K. (2018). *Contemporary Theories of Learning* (2nd edn). Routledge.

Rogers, C. (1969). *Freedom to Learn*. Charles E. Merrill.

Rogers, C. (1989). The interpersonal relationship in the facilitation of learning. In H. Kirschenbaum and V. Land Henderson (eds), *The Carl Rogers Reader* (pp. 304–322). Houghton Mifflin.

Rogers, C. (1995). *On Becoming a Person*. Houghton Mifflin.

Rogers, C. (2002). Defining reflection: Another look at John Dewey and reflective thinking. *College Teachers Record, 104*(4), 842–866.

References

Abraham, S., and Karns, L. (2009). Do business schools value the competencies that businesses value? *Journal of Education for Business*, *84*(6), 350–356. https://doi.org/10.3200/JOEB.84.6.350-356.

Abrami, P.C., Bernard, R.M., Borokhovski, E., Wade, A., Surkes, M.A., et al. (2008). Instructional interventions affecting critical thinking skills and dispositions: A stage 1 meta-analysis. *Review of Educational Research*, *78*(4), 1102–1134. https://doi.org/10.3102/0034654308326084.

Ackerman, C. (2018). What is self-efficacy theory in psychology? Definition and examples. *Positive Psychology Program*. https://positivepsychologyprogram .com/self-efficacy/.

Agogo, D.A., and Anderson, J. (2019). Teaching tip "the data shuffle": Using playing cards to illustrate data management concepts to a broad audience. *Journal of Information Systems Education*, *30*(2), 84–96.

Alfieri, L., Brooks, P.J., Aldrich, N.J., and Tenenbaum, H.R. (2011). Does discovery-based instruction enhance learning? *Journal of Educational Psychology*, *103*(1), 1–18. https://doi.org/10.1037/a0021017.

Aloni, N. (2011). Humanistic education: From theory to practice. In W. Veugelers (ed.), *Education and Humanism: Linking Autonomy and Humanity* (pp. 35–46). Sense Publishers. https://doi.org/10.1007/978-94-6091-577-2_3.

Ambrose, S.A., Bridges, M.W., DiPietro, M., Lovett, M.C., and Norman, M.K. (2010). *How Learning Works: 7 Research-Based Principles for Smart Teaching*. Jossey-Bass.

Anderson, L.W., Krathwohl, D.R., Airasian, P.W., Cruikshank, K.A., Mayer, R.E., et al. (2001). *A Taxonomy for Learning, Teaching, and Assessing: A Revision of Bloom's Taxonomy of Educational Objectives* (complete edn). Longman. https://doi.org/10.4324/9781003118299-22.

Andresen, L., Boud, D., and Cohen, R. (2000). Experience-based learning. In G. Foley (ed.), *Understanding Adult Education and Training* (2nd edn, pp. 225–239). Allen & Unwin.

Angelo, T.A., and Cross, K.P. (1993). *Classroom Assessment Techniques: A Handbook for College Teachers* (2nd edn). Jossey-Bass.

Antunes, D., and Thomas, H. (2007). The competitive (dis)advantages of European business schools. *Long Range Planning*, *40*(3), 382–404. https://doi .org/10.1016/j.lrp.2007.04.003.

Arbaugh, J.B., and Hwang, A. (2015). What are the 100 most cited articles in business and management education research and what do they tell us? *Organization Management Journal*, *12*(3), 154–175. https://doi.org/10.1080/ 15416518.2015.1073135.

Argyris, C., and Schön, D. (1974). *Theory in Practice: Increasing Professional Effectiveness*. Jossey-Bass.

Armstrong, S.J., and Mahmud, A. (2008). Experiential learning and the acquisition of managerial tacit knowledge. *Academy of Management Learning and Education*, 7(2), 511–526. https://doi.org/10.5465/AMLE.2008.32712617.

Aronson, J., Fried, C.B., and Good, C. (2002). Reducing the effects of stereotype threat on African American college students by shaping theories of intelligence. *Journal of Experimental Social Psychology*, 38(2), 113–125. https://doi.org/10.1006/jesp.2001.1491.

Association for Experiential Education (2012). *Experiential Education: The Principles of Practice*. https://www.aee.org/what-is-ee.

Association for Experiential Education (n.d.). About AEE. https://www.aee.org/about.

Association to Advance Collegiate Schools of Business (AACSB) (2013). Eligibility procedures and accreditation standards for business accreditation. AACSB International. https://www.aacsb.edu/accreditation/standards/business.

Association to Advance Collegiate Schools of Business (AACSB) (2018). Eligibility procedures and accreditation standards for business accreditation. AACSB International. https://www.aacsb.edu/accreditation/standards/business.

Audet, J., and Marcotte, G. (2018). Student trade missions: An experiential learning opportunity. *American Journal of Business Education*, 11(1), 1–14. https://doi.org/10.19030/ajbe.v11i1.10116.

Augier, M., and March, J.G. (2007). The pursuit of relevance in management education. *California Management Review*, 49(3), 129–146. https://doi.org/10.2307/41166398.

Augier, M., and March, J.G. (2011). *The Roots, Rituals, and Rhetorics of Change: North American Business Schools after the Second World War*. Stanford University Press. https://doi.org/10.2307/j.ctvqr1f02.

Austin, M.J., and Rust, D.Z. (2015). Developing an experiential learning program: Milestones and challenges. *International Journal of Teaching and Learning in Higher Education*, 27(1), 143–153.

Bandura, A. (1997). *Self-efficacy: The Exercise of Control*. W.H. Freeman & Company.

Bandura, A. (1999). Self-efficacy: Toward a unifying theory of behavioral change. In R.F. Baumeister (ed.), *The Self in Social Psychology* (pp. 285–298). Psychology Press.

Barkley, E.F. (2010). *Student Engagement Techniques: A Handbook for College Faculty*. Jossey-Bass.

Barrows, H.S. (2002). Is it truly possible to have such a thing as PBL? *Distance Education*, 23(1), 119–122. https://doi.org/10.1080/0158791022012426.

Barrows, H.S., and Tamblyn, R. (1980). *Problem-Based Learning: An Approach to Medical Education*. Springer.

Beaudin, B.P., and Quick, D. (1995). *Experiential Learning: Theoretical Underpinnings*. Colorado State University, High Plains Intermountain Center for Agricultural Health and Safety.

Beck-Dudley, C.L. (2018). The future of work, business education and the role of AACSB. *Journal of Legal Studies Education*, *35*(1), 165–170. https://doi.org/ 10.1111/jlse.12073.

Bell, R. (2015). Developing the next generation of entrepreneurs: Giving students the opportunity to gain experience and thrive. *International Journal of Management Education*, *13*(1), 37–47. https://doi.org/10.1016/j.ijme.2014.12 .002.

Bell, R., and Bell, H. (2016). An enterprise opportunity for entrepreneurial students. *Education and Training*, *58*(7/8), 751–765. https://doi.org/10.1108/ET -12-2014-0150.

Benek-Rivera, J., and Mathews, V.E. (2004). Active learning with jeopardy: Students ask the questions. *Journal of Management Education*, *28*(1), 104–118. https://doi.org/10.1177/1052562903252637.

Benson, G.E., and Chau, N.N. (2017). Negotiation skill development exercise. *Marketing Education Review*, *27*(2), 80–85. http://doi.org/10.1080/10528008 .2017.1296754.

Bevan, D., and Kipka, C. (2012). Experiential learning and management education. *Journal of Management Development*, *31*(3), 193–197. https://doi.org/10 .1108/02621711211208943.

Bickerstaffe, G. (1981). Crisis of confidence in the business-schools. *International Management*, *36*(8), 19–23.

Biggs, J.B. (1979). Individual differences in study processes and the quality of learning outcomes. *Higher Education*, *8*(4), 381–394. https://doi.org/10.1007/ BF01680526.

Biggs, J.B., and Collis, K.F. (1982). *Evaluating the Quality of Learning: The SOLO Taxonomy (Structure of the Observed Learning Outcome)*. Academic Press.

Biggs, J.B., and Tang, C. (2011). *Teaching for Quality Learning at University* (4th edn). Open University Press, McGraw Hill Education.

Billsberry, J., Ambrosini, B., Garrido-Lopez, M., and Stiles, D. (2019). Towards a non-essentialist approach to management education: Philosophical underpinnings from phenomenography. *Academy of Management Learning and Education*, *18*(4), 626–638. https://doi.org/10.5465/amle.2017.0401.

Bobbitt, L.M., Inks, S.A., Kemp, K.J., and Mayo, D.T. (2000). Integrating marketing courses to enhance team-based experiential learning. *Journal of Marketing Education*, *22*(1), 15–24. https://doi.org/10.1177/0273475300221003.

Bonwell, C.C., and Eison, J.A. (1991). *Active Learning: Creating Excitement in the Classroom*. ASH-ERIC Higher Education Report No. 1. George Washington University. https://files.eric.ed.gov/fulltext/ED336049.pdf.

Boud, D. (1989). Some competing traditions in experiential learning. In S. Weil and I. McGill (eds), *Making Sense of Experiential Learning: Diversity in Theory and Practice* (pp. 39–49). Open University Press.

Boud, D., and Feletti, G. (1997). Changing problem-based learning. Introduction to the second edition. In D. Boud and G. Feletti (eds), *The Challenge of Problem Based Learning* (2nd edn, pp. 1–14). Kogan Page.

Boud, D., Keogh, R., and Walker, D. (1985). Introduction: What is reflection in learning? In D. Boud, R. Keogh, and D. Walker (eds), *Reflection: Turning Experience into Learning* (pp. 7–17). Kogan Page.

Bourgeois, E. (2002). A constructivist approach to adult learning. In A. Bron and M. Schemman (eds), *Social Science Theories in Adult Education Research* (pp. 130–153). LIT Verlag.

Bradford, D.L. (2019). Ethical issues in experiential learning. *Journal of Management Education*, 43(1), 89–98. https://doi.org/10.1177/1052562918807500.

Branch, R.M., and Dousay, T.A. (2015). *Survey of Instructional Design Models* (5th edn). Association for Educational Communications and Technology. http://members.aect.org/publications/SurveyofInstructionalDesignModels.pdf.

Brandes, D., and Ginnis, P. (1986). *A Guide to Student Centered Learning*. Blackwell.

Bransford, J.D., Brown, A.L., and Cocking, R.R. (2000). *How People Learn: Brain, Mind, Experience, and School* (expanded edn). National Academy Press.

Breunig, M. (2005). Turning experiential education and critical pedagogy theory into praxis. *Journal of Experiential Education*, 28(2), 106–122. https://doi.org/10.1177/105382590502800205.

Bronfenbrenner, U. (1977). Toward an experimental ecology of human development. *American Psychologist*, 32(7), 513–531. https://doi.org/10.1037/0003-066x.32.7.513.

Brophy, J., and Good, T.L. (1984). Teacher behavior and student achievement. Occasional Paper No. 73. https://files.eric.ed.gov/fulltext/ED251422.pdf.

Brown, K.G., Arbaugh, J.B., Hrivnak, G., and Kenworthy, A. (2013). Overlooked and unappreciated: What research tells us about how teaching must change. In B. Holtom and E. Dierdorff (eds), *Disrupt or be Disrupted: Evidence-Based Strategies for Graduate Management Education* (pp. 219–258). Wiley & Sons. https://doi.org/10.5465/ambpp.2013.11320abstract.

Brown, P.C., Roediger, H.L., and McDaniel, M.A. (2014). *Make it Stick: The Science of Successful Learning*. Belknap Press. https://doi.org/10.4159/9780674419377.

Burch, G.F., Batchelor, J.H., Heller, N.A., Shaw, J., Kendall, W., and Turner, B. (2014). Experiential learning – What do we know? A meta-analysis of 40 years of research. *Developments in Business Simulation and Experiential Learning: Proceedings of the Annual ABSEL Conference*, 41(2014), 279–283. https://absel-ojs-ttu.tdl.org/absel/index.php/absel/article/view/2127/2096.

Burch, G.F., Batchelor, J.H., Heller, N.A., Shaw, J., Kendall, W., and Turner, B. (2016). Do experiential learning pedagogies effect student learning? A meta-analysis of 40 years of research. *Academy of Management Best Paper Proceedings*, 2016(1), 1672–1677. https://doi.org/10.5465/ambpp.2016.127.

Burch, G.F., Giambatista, R., Batchelor, J.H., Burch, J.J., Hoover, J.D., and Heller, N.A. (2019). A meta-analysis of the relationship between experiential learning and learning outcomes. *Decision Sciences Journal of Innovative Education*, 17(3), 239–273. https://doi.org/10.1111/dsji.12188.

Burke, M.J., and Day, R.R. (1986). A cumulative study of the effectiveness of managerial training. *Journal of Applied Psychology, 71*(2), 232–245. https://doi.org/10.1037/0021-9010.71.2.232.

Cajiao, J., and Burke, M.J. (2016). How instructional methods influence skill development in management education. *Academy of Management Learning and Education, 15*(3), 508–524. https://doi.org/10.5465/amle.2013.0354.

Cambridge Dictionary (2019). Cambridge University Press. https://dictionary.cambridge.org/us/dictionary/english/context.

Cameron, K.S., and Whetten, D.A. (1983). A model for teaching management skills. *Exchange· Organizational Behavior Teaching Journal, 8*(2), 21–27. https://doi.org/10.1177/105256298300800207.

Caza, A., Brower, H., and Wayne, J. (2015). Effects of a holistic, experiential curriculum on business students' satisfaction and career confidence. *International Journal of Management Education, 13*(1), 75–83. https://doi.org/10.1016/j.ijme.2015.01.006.

Challenge Success (2018). *A 'Fit' over Rankings: Why College Engagement Matters More Than Selectivity.* https://ed.stanford.edu/sites/default/files/challenge_success_white_paper_on_college_admissions_10.1.2018-reduced.pdf.

Chatelier, S. (2015). Towards a renewed flourishing of humanistic education? *Discourse: Studies in the Cultural Politics of Education, 36*(1), 81–94. https://doi.org/10.1080/01596306.2013.834635.

Cheit, E.F. (1985). Business schools and their critics. *California Management Review, 27*(3), 43–62. https://doi.org/10.2307/41165141.

Chemers, M.M., Hu, L.-t., and Garcia, B.F. (2001). Academic self-efficacy and first year college student performance and adjustment. *Journal of Educational Psychology, 93*(1), 55–64. https://doi.org/10.1037/0022-0663.93.1.55.

Chen, P., and Schmidtke, C. (2017). Humanistic elements in the educational practice at a United States sub-baccalaureate technical college. *International Journal for Research in Vocational Education and Training, 4*(2), 117–145. https://doi.org/10.13152/IJRVET.4.2.2.

Chick, N. (2020). Thinking about one's thinking. *Metacognition.* https://cft.vanderbilt.edu/guides-sub-pages/metacognition/.

Chin, C.K., Khor, K.H., and Teh, T.K. (2015). Is gallery walk an effective teaching and learning strategy for biology? In E.G.S. Daniel (ed.), *Biology Education and Research in a Changing Planet* (pp. 55–59). Springer. https://doi.org/10.1007/978-981-287-524-2_6.

Chmielewski-Raimondo, D., McKeown, W., and Brooks, A. (2016). The field as our classroom: Applications in a business-related setting. *Journal of Accounting Education, 34*(March), 41–58. https://doi.org/10.1016/j.jaccedu.2015.11.002.

Clark, J., and White, G.W. (2010). Experiential learning: A definitive edge in the job market. *American Journal of Business Education, 3*(2), 115–118. https://doi.org/10.19030/ajbe.v3i2.390.

Coakley, L.A., and Sousa, K.J. (2013). The effect of contemporary learning approaches on student perceptions in an introductory business course. *Journal* of the Scholarship of Teaching and Learning, *13*(3), 1–22. https://files.eric.ed .gov/fulltext/EJ1017021.pdf.

Colby, A., Ehrlich, T., Sullivan, W.M., and Dolle, J.R. (2011). *Rethinking Undergraduate Business Education: Liberal Learning for the Profession.* Jossey-Bass.

Collie, R.J., Martin, A.J., and Granziera, H. (2018). Being able to adapt in the classroom improves teachers' well-being. *The Conversation US.* Retrieved from: https://theconversation.com/ being-able-to-adapt-in-the-classroom-improves-teachers-well-being-95788.

Crosby, A. (1995). A critical look: The philosophical foundations of experiential education. In K. Warren, M. Sakofs, and J.S. Hunt (eds), *The Theory of Experiential Education* (3rd edn, pp. 3–14). Kendall/Hunt.

Crossan, M., Mazutis, D., Seijts, G., and Gandz, J. (2013). Developing leadership character in business programs. *Academy of Management Learning and Education, 12*(2), 285–305. https://doi.org/10.5465/amle.2011.0024a.

Cunliffe, A.L. (2008). Orientations to social constructionism: Relationally responsive social constructionism and its implications for knowledge and learning. *Management Learning, 39*(2), 123–139. https://doi.org/10.1177/ 1350507607087578.

Datar, S.M., Garvin, D.A., and Cullen, P.G. (2011). Rethinking the MBA: Business education at a crossroads. *Journal of Management Development, 30*(5), 451–462. https://doi.org/10.1108/02621711111132966.

de Boer, H., Donker, A.S., Kostons, D.D.N.M., and van der Werf, G.P.C. (2018). Long-term effects of metacognitive strategy instruction on student academic performance: A meta-analysis. *Educational Research Review, 24*(June), 98–115. https://doi.org/10.1016/j.edurev.2018.03.002.

de Bruijn-Smolders, M., Timmers, C.F., Gawke, J.C.L., Schoonman, W., and Born, M.P. (2016). Effective self-regulatory processes in higher education: Research findings and future directions. A systematic review. *Studies in Higher Education, 41*(1), 139–158. https://doi.org/10.1080/03075079.2014 .915302.

Deeter-Schmelz, D. (2015). Corporate–academic partnerships: Creating a win– win in the classroom. *Journal of Education for Business, 90*(4), 192. https:// doi.org/10.1080/08832323.2015.1014457.

Dehler, G.H., and Welsh, M.A. (2014). Against spoon-feeding for learning: Reflections on students' claims to knowledge. *Journal of Management Education, 38*(6), 875–893. https://doi.org/10.1177/1052562913511436.

Dent, A.L., and Koenka, A.C. (2016). The relation between self-regulated learning and academic achievement across childhood and adolescence: A meta-analysis. *Educational Psychology Review, 28*(3), 425. https://doi.org/ 10.1007/s10648-015-9320-8.

DeSimone, F., and Buzza, J. (2013). Experiential learning: Improving the efficacy of an undergraduate business degree. *American Journal of Business Education, 6*(1), 7–24. https://files.eric.ed.gov/fulltext/EJ1054187.pdf.

Desjarlais, M., and Smith, P. (2011). A comparative analysis of reflection and self-assessment. *International Journal of Process Education, 3*(1), 3–18.

Devasagayam, R., Johns-Masten, K., and McCollum, J. (2012). Linking information literacy, experiential learning and student characteristics: Pedagogical possibilities in business education. *Academy of Educational Leadership Journal, 16*(4), 1–18.

Dewey, J. (1938). *Experience and Education*. Macmillan.

Donker, A.S., de Boer, H., Kostons, D., Dignath van Ewijk, C.C., and van der Werf, M.P.C. (2014). Effectiveness of learning strategy instruction on academic performance: A meta-analysis. *Educational Research Review, 11*(January), 1–26. https://doi.org/10.1016/j.edurev.2013.11.002.

Dunn, T.G., and Shriner, C. (1999). Deliberate practice in teaching: What teachers do for self-improvement. *Teaching and Teacher Education, 15*(6), 631–651. https://doi.org/10.1016/S0742-051X(98)00068-7.

Dweck, C.S. (1999). *Self-Theories: Their Role in Motivation, Personality, and Development*. Taylor & Francis Group.

Dweck, C.S. (2008). *Mindset: The New Psychology of Success*. Ballantine Books.

Dweck, C.S., and Yeager, D.S. (2019). Mindsets: A view from two eras. *Perspectives on Psychological Science, 14*(3), 481–496. https://doi.org/10.1177/1745691618804166.

Eckhaus, E., Klein, G., and Kantor, J. (2017). Experiential learning in management education. *Business, Management and Education, 15*(1), 42–56. https://doi.org/10.3846/bme.2017.345.

Edfelt, R. (1988). US management education in comparative perspective. *Comparative Education Review, 32*(3), 334–354. https://doi.org/10.1086/446781.

EFMD Quality Improvement System (EQUIS) (2019). 2019 EQUIS standards and criteria. https://efmdglobal.org/wp-content/uploads/EFMD_Global-EQUIS_Standards_and_Criteria.pdf.

Egri, C.P. (2013). From the editors: Context matters in management education scholarship. *Academy of Management Learning and Education, 12*(2), 155–157. https://doi.org/10.5465/amle.2013.0140.

Entwistle, N. (1998). Approaches to learning and forms of understanding. In B. Dart and G. Boulton-Lewis (eds), *Teaching and Learning in Higher Education: From Theory to Practice*. Australian Council for Educational Research.

Ericsson, K.A. (2008). Deliberate practice and acquisition of expert performance: A general overview. *Academic Emergency Medicine, 15*(11), 988–994. https://doi.org/https://doi.org/10.1111/j.1553-2712.2008.00227.x.

Ericsson, K.A., Krampe, R.T., and Tesch-Römer, C. (1993). The role of deliberate practice in the acquisition of expert performance. *Psychological Review, 100*(3), 363–406. https://doi.org/10.1037/0033-295X.100.3.363.

Estes, C.A. (2004). Promoting student-centered learning in experiential education. *Journal of Experiential Education, 27*(2), 141–160. https://doi.org/10.1177/105382590402700203.

Eyler, J. (2009). The power of experiential education. *Liberal Education, 95*(4), 24–31. https://files.eric.ed.gov/fulltext/EJ871318.pdf.

Farashahi, M., and Tajeddin, M. (2018). Effectiveness of teaching methods in business education: A comparison study on the learning outcomes of lectures, case studies and simulations. *International Journal of Management Education, 16*(1), 131–142. https://doi.org/10.1016/j.ijme.2018.01.003.

Faria, A.J. (1987). A survey of the use of business games in academia and business. *Simulation and Games, 18*(2), 207–224. https://doi.org/10.1177/104687818701800204.

Faria, A.J. (1998). Business simulation games: Current usage levels – an update. *Simulation and Gaming, 29*(3), 295–308. https://doi.org/10.1177/1046878198293002.

Faria, A.J., Hutchinson, D., Wellington, W.J., and Gold, S. (2009). Developments in business gaming: A review of the past 40 years. *Simulation and Gaming, 40*(4), 464–487. https://doi.org/10.1177/1046878108327585.

Fencl, H., and Scheel, K. (2005). Engaging students: An examination of the effects of teaching strategies on self-efficacy and course climate in a non-majors physics course. *Journal of College Science Teaching, 35*(1), 20–24. https://www.jstor.org/stable/42992548.

Fenwick, L., and Cooper, M. (2013). Learning about the effects of context on teaching and learning in pre-service teacher education. *Australian Journal of Teacher Education, 38*(3), 96–110. https://doi.org/10.14221/ajte.2013v38n3.6.

Fenwick, T.J. (2001). *Experiential Learning: A Theoretical Critique from Five Perspectives* (Information Series No. 385). ERIC Clearinghouse on Adult, Career, and Vocational Education. https://files.eric.ed.gov/fulltext/ED454418.pdf.

Finch, D., Peacock, M., Lazdowski, D., and Hwang, M. (2015). Managing emotions: A case study exploring the relationship between experiential learning, emotions, and student performance. *International Journal of Management Education, 13*(1), 23–36. https://doi.org/10.1016/j.ijme.2014.12.001.

Fink, L.D. (2003a). *Creating Significant Learning Experiences: An Integrated Approach to Designing College Courses*. Jossey-Bass.

Fink, L.D. (2003b). *A Self-Directed Guide to Designing Courses for Significant Learning*. https://www.deefinkandassociates.com/GuidetoCourseDesignAug05.pdf.

Forster, G., and Robson, A. (2019). Developing the "oven-ready" postgraduate: Squeezing a quart into a pint pot to meet the employability agenda. In A. Diver (ed.), *Employability via Higher Education: Sustainability as Scholarship*. Springer. https://doi.org/10.1007/978-3-030-26342-3_23.

Foster, M.K. (2020). Embracing a growth mindset: An experiential exercise to explore beliefs about learning. *Management Teaching Review*. https://doi.org/10.1177/2379298120930352.

Freire, P. (1970). *Pedagogy of the Oppressed*. Continuum.

Freire, P., Ramos, M.B., and Macedo, D.P. (2012). *Pedagogy of the Oppressed* (30th anniversary edn). Bloomsbury.

Frontczak, N.T. (1998). A paradigm for the selection, use and development of experiential learning activities in marketing education. *Marketing Education Review, 8*(3), 25–33. https://doi.org/10.1080/10528008.1998.11488641.

Fuller, R. (2000). Encouraging self-directed learning through poster presentations. Flexible futures in tertiary teaching. In A. Herrmann and M.M.

Kulski (eds), *Proceedings of the 9th Annual Teaching Learning Forum*. Curtin University of Technology. http://clt.curtin.edu.au/events/conferences/tlf/tlf2000/fuller.html.

Gallup-Purdue (2014). *Great Jobs, Great Lives: The 2014 Gallup-Purdue Index Report*.

Gentry, J.W. (1990). *Guide to Business Gaming and Experiential Learning*. Nichols/GP Publishing.

George, M.P. (2015). Experiential learning to enhance work skills, empathy and entrepreneurship in business schools. *Journal of Contemporary Research in Management, 10*(3), 1–15.

Gerlach, V.S., and Ely, D.P. (1980). *Teaching and Media: A Systematic Approach* (2nd edn). Prentice-Hall.

Gilmore, S., and Anderson, V. (2012). Anxiety and experience-based learning in a professional standards context. *Management Learning, 43*(1), 75–95. https://doi.org/10.1177/1350507611406482.

Godfrey, P.C., Illes, L.M., and Berry, G.R. (2005). Creating breadth in business education through service-learning. *Academy of Management Learning and Education, 4*(3), 309–323. https://doi.org/10.5465/amle.2005.18122420.

Gooding, J., and Metz, B. (2011). After the lab: Learning begins when clean up starts. *Science Scope, 35*(1), 29–33. https://scithoughts-com2.webs.com/Publications/After%20the%20Lab%20Published%20Version.pdf.

Gordon, M. (2009). Toward a pragmatic discourse of constructivism: Reflections on lessons from practice. *Educational Studies, 45*(1), 39–58. https://doi.org/10.1080/00131940802546894.

Gordon, R.A., and Howell, J.E. (1959). *Higher Education for Business*. Columbia University Press.

Gosen, J., and Washbush, J. (2004). A review of scholarship on assessing experiential learning effectiveness. *Simulation and Gaming, 35*(2), 270–293. https://doi.org/10.1177/1046878104263544.

Gosenpud, J.J. (1990). Evaluation of experiential learning. In J. Gentry (ed.), *Guide to Business Simulation and Experiential Learning* (pp. 301–329). Nichols/GP.

Grabinger, R.S., and Dunlap, J.C. (1995). Rich environments for active learning: A definition. *Research in Learning Technology, 3*(2), 5–34. https://doi.org/10.3402/rlt.v3i2.9606.

Groenewald, T. (2004). Towards a definition for cooperative education. In R.K. Coll and C. Eames (eds), *International Handbook for Cooperative Education: An International Perspective of the Theory, Research and Practice of Work-Integrated Learning* (pp. 17–25). World Association for Cooperative Education.

Gundal, R.R., Singh, M., and Cochran, T.K. (2018). Perceptions of integrated experiential learning of graduate marketing students. *Journal of the Scholarship of Teaching and Learning, 18*(2), 74–89. https://doi.org/10.14434/josotl.v18i2.22498.

Hackathorn, J., Solomon, E.D., Blankmeyer, K.L., Tennial, R.E., and Garczynski, A.M. (2011). Learning by doing: An empirical study of active teaching techniques. *Journal of Effective Teaching*, *11*(2), 40–54. https://doi.org/10.1037/ e683152011-599.

Hall, J., and Watson, W.H. (1970). The effects of a normative intervention on group decision-making performance. *Human Relations*, *23*(4), 299–317. https://doi.org/10.1177/001872677002300404.

Hamer, L.O. (2000). The additive effects of semi-structured classroom activities on student learning: An application of classroom-based experiential learning techniques. *Journal of Marketing Education*, *22*(1), 25–34. https://doi.org/10 .1177/0273475300221004.

Hamilton, J.G., and Klebba, J.M. (2011). Experiential learning: A course design process for critical thinking. *American Journal of Business Education*, *4*(12), 1–12. https://doi.org/10.19030/ajbe.v4i12.6608.

Hanson, M. (2015). Business education and the constructivist teaching debate. *Proceedings of 32nd International Business Research Conference*. http:// unsworks.unsw.edu.au/fapi/datastream/unsworks:38118/bin54fcd56c-3ad7 -4786-877c-09e44901ab53?view=true.

Harley, B. (2018). Confronting the crisis of confidence in management studies: Why senior scholars need to stop setting a bad example. *Academy of Management Learning and Education*, *18*(2), 286–297. https://doi.org/10 .5465/amle.2018.0107.

Hartnett, R.T., and Centra, J.A. (1977). Effects of academic departments on student learning. *Journal of Higher Education*, *48*(5), 491–507. https://doi .org/10.2307/1981593.

Harvey, J.H., Ickes, W.J., and Kidd, R.F. (2018). A conversation with Fritz Heider. In J.H. Harvey, W.J. Ickes, and R.F. Kidd (eds), *New Directions in Attribution Research: Volume 1*. Psychology Press. https://doi.org/10.4324/ 9780203780978.

Hattie, J. (2009). *Visible Learning: A Synthesis of Over 800 Meta-Analyses Relating to Achievement*. Routledge. https://doi.org/10.4324/9780203887332.

Hattie, J. (2012). *Visible Learning for Teachers: Maximizing Impact on Learning*. Routledge. https://doi.org/10.4324/9780203181522.

Hattie, J., Biggs, J., and Purdie, N. (1996). Effects of learning skills interventions on student learning: A meta-analysis. *Review of Educational Research*, *66*(2), 99–136. https://doi.org/10.3102/00346543066002099.

Hay, M., and Samra-Fredericks, D. (2019). Bringing the heart and soul back in: Collaborative inquiry and the DBA. *Academy of Management Learning and Education*, *18*(1), 59–80. https://doi.org/10.5465/amle.2017.0020.

Haynes, T.L., Perry, R.P., Stupnisky, R.H., and Daniels, L.M. (2009). A review of attributional retraining treatments: Fostering engagement and persistence in vulnerable college students. In J.C. Smart (ed.), *Higher Education: Handbook of Theory and Research* (pp. 227–272). Springer. https://doi.org/10.1007/978 -1-4020-9628-0_6.

Hedberg, P.R. (2009). Learning through reflective classroom practice: Applications to educate the reflective manager. *Journal of Management Education*, *33*(1), 10–36. https://doi.org/10.1177/1052562908316714.

Henry, J. (1989). Meaning and practice in experiential learning. In S.W. Weil and I. McGill (eds), *Making Sense of Experiential Learning: Diversity in Theory and Practice* (pp. 25–37). Milton Keynes: UK Society for Research into Higher Education and Open University Press.

Herman, W.E. (1995). Humanistic influences on a constructivist approach to teaching and learning. Paper presented at the *Annual Meeting of the American Educational Research Association*, San Francisco, CA, 18–22 April. https://files.eric.ed.gov/fulltext/ED393814.pdf.

Hew, K.F., and Lo, C.K. (2018). Flipped classroom improves student learning in health professions education: A meta-analysis. *BMC Medical Education*, *18*(38), 1–12. https://doi.org/10.1186/s12909-018-1144-z.

Highhouse, S. (2002). A history of the T-group and its early applications in management development. *Group Dynamics: Theory, Research and Practice*, *6*(4), 277–290. https://doi.org/10.1037/1089-2699.6.4.277.

Hmelo-Silver, C.E. (2004). Problem-based learning: What and how do students learn? *Educational Psychology Review*, *16*(3), 235–266. https://doi.org/10.1023/B:EDPR.0000034022.16470.f3.

Hodge, L., Proudford, K.L., and Holt, H. (2014). From periphery to core: The increasing relevance of experiential learning in undergraduate business education. *Research in Higher Education Journal*, *26*, 1–17. https://files.eric.ed.gov/fulltext/EJ1055308.pdf.

Hofstede, G. (1986). Cultural differences in teaching and learning. *International Journal of Intercultural Relations*, *10*(3), 301–320. https://doi.org/10.1016/0147-1767(86)90015-5.

Holman, D., and Mumford, A. (2001). Learning theory in the practice of management development: Evolution and applications. *Management Learning*, *32*(1), 138–143. https://doi.org/10.1177/1350507601321010.

Hoover, J.D., Giambatista, R.C., Sorenson, R., and Bommer, W.H. (2010). Assessing the effectiveness of whole person learning pedagogy in skill acquisition. *Academy of Management Learning and Education*, *9*(2), 192–203. https://doi.org/10.5465/amle.9.2.zqr192.

Hoover, J.D., and Whitehead, C. (1975). An experiential-cognitive methodology in the first course in management: Some preliminary results. In *Developments in Business Simulation and Experiential Learning: Proceedings of the Annual ABSEL Conference* (Vol. 2), 25–30.

Horth, D.M., Miller, L.B., and Mount, P.B. (2016). *Leadership Brand: Deliver on Your Promise*. CCL Press.

Illeris, K. (2007). What do we actually mean by experiential learning? *Human Resource Development Review*, *6*(1), 84–95. https://doi.org/10.1177/1534484306296828.

Inamdar, S.N., and Roldan, M. (2013). The MBA capstone course: Building theoretical, practical, applied and reflective skills. *Journal of Management Education*, *37*(6), 747–770. https://doi.org/10.1177/1052562912474895.

Institute for the Advancement of University Learning (2019). Paper 2: Student approaches to learning. https://moam.info/paper-2-student-approaches-to-learning-oxford-learning-institute_5a1d51c91723ddb8455e4636.html.

Intagliata, J., Ulrich, D., and Smallwood, N. (2000). Leveraging leadership competencies to produce leadership brand: Creating distinctiveness by focusing on strategy and results. *Human Resources Planning*, *23*(4), 12–23.

Janis, I.L., and Mann, L. (1977). *Decision Making: A Psychological Analysis of Conflict, Choice, and Commitment.* Free Press.

Jansen, R.S., van Leeuwen, A., Janssen, J., Jak, S., and Kester, L. (2019). Self-regulated learning partially mediates the effect of self-regulated learning interventions on achievement in higher education: A meta-analysis. *Educational Research Review, 28.* https://doi.org/10.1016/j.edurev.2019.100292.

Jarvis, P. (2006). *Towards a Comprehensive Theory of Human Learning.* Routledge.

Jarvis, P., and Wilson, A.L. (1999). *International Dictionary of Adult and Continuing Education* (2nd edn). Kogan Page.

Johnson, A.P. (2012). Humanistic and holistic learning theory. http://teacher-strategies.homestead.com/Ch_9_humanistic_holistic__1_.pdf

Johnson, D.W., and Johnson, F.P. (2009). *Joining Together: Group Theory and Group Skills* (10th edn). Pearson.

Johnson, D.W., and Johnson, R.T. (1999). *Learning Together and Alone: Cooperative, Competitive and Individualistic Learning.* Allyn & Bacon.

Johnson, D.W., Johnson, R.T., and Smith, K.A. (1991). *Cooperative Learning: Increasing College Faculty Instructional Productivity.* ASHE-ENC Higher Education Report No. 4. George Washington University, School of Education and Human Development. https://files.eric.ed.gov/fulltext/ED343465.pdf.

Johnson, D.W., Johnson, R.T., and Stanne, M.B. (2000). *Cooperative Learning Methods: A Meta-Analysis.* University of Minnesota Press.

Johnston, N., and Sator, A.J. (2017). *Experiential Education in BC Post-Secondary Institutions: Challenges and Opportunities.* British Columbia Council on Admissions and Transfer. https://files.eric.ed.gov/fulltext/ED586098.pdf.

Joplin, L. (1995). On defining experiential education. In K. Warren, M. Sakofs, and J. Hunt (eds), *The Theory of Experiential Education: A Collection of Articles Addressing the Historical, Philosophical, Social, and Psychological Foundations of Experiential Education* (3rd edn, pp. 15–22). Kendall-Hunt. https://files.eric.ed.gov/fulltext/ED385423.pdf.

Jordan, S. (2010). Learning to be surprised: How to foster reflective practice in a high-reliability context. *Management Learning, 41*(4): 391–413. https://doi.org/10.1177/1350507609357388.

Kane, D. (2017). A focus on self-improvement: Five principles of deliberate practice can help teachers consistently improve their teaching. *edutopia.* https://www.edutopia.org/blog/focus-self-improvement-dylan-kane.

Katula, R.A., and Threnhauser, E. (1999). Experiential education in the undergraduate curriculum. *Communication Education, 48*(3), 238–255. https://doi.org/10.1080/03634529909379172.

Katz, D., and Kahn, R.L. (1978). *The Social Psychology of Organizations* (2nd edn). John Wiley & Sons.

Kaye, C.B. (2004). *The Complete Guide to Service Learning.* Free Spirit.

Kelley, H.H. (1973). The processes of causal attribution. *American Psychologist, 28*(2), 107–128. https://doi.org/10.1037/h0034225.

Keys, B., and Wolfe, J. (1990). The role of management games and simulations in education and research. *Journal of Management, 16*(2), 307–336. https://doi.org/10.1177/014920639001600205.

Khatib, M., Sarem, S.N., and Hamidi, H. (2013). Humanistic education: Concerns, implications and applications. *Journal of Language Teaching Research, 4*(1), 45–51. https://doi.org/10.4304/jltr.4.1.45-51.

Khurana, R., and Spender, J.C. (2012). Herbert A. Simon on what ails business schools: More than "a problem in organizational design." *Journal of Management Studies, 49*(3), 619–639. https://doi.org/10.1111/j.1467-6486.2011.01040.x.

Kibbee, J.M., Craft, C.J., and Namus, B. (1961). *Management Games.* Reinhold

Kinsella, E.A. (2006). Constructivist underpinnings in Donald Schön's theory of reflective practice: Echoes of Nelson Goodman. *Reflective Practice, 7*(3), 277–286. https://doi.org/10.1080/14623940600837319.

Kirk, D.J., and Durant, R. (2010). Crossing the line: Framing appropriate responses in the diversity classroom. *Journal of Management Education, 34*(6), 823–847. http://dx.doi.org/10.1177/1052562909337587.

Kirschner, P.A., Sweller, J., and Clark, R.E. (2006). Why minimal guidance during instruction does not work: An analysis of the failure of constructivist, discovery, problem-based, experiential and inquiry-based teaching, *Educational Psychologist, 41*(2), 75–86. https://doi.org/10.1207/s15326985ep4102_1.

Kisfalvi, V., and Oliver, D. (2015). Creating and maintaining a safe space in experiential learning. *Journal of Management Education, 39*(6), 713–740. http://doi.org/10.1177/1052562915574724.

Kitchenham, A. (2008). The evolution of John Mezirow's transformative learning theory. *Journal of Transformative Education, 6*(2), 104–123. https://doi.org/10.1177/1541344608322678.

Kniffin, L.E., Priest, K.L., and Clayton, P.H. (2017). Case-in-point pedagogy: Building capacity for experiential learning and democracy. *Journal of Applied Learning in Higher Education, 7*(Spring), 15–28. https://files.eric.ed.gov/fulltext/EJ1188379.pdf.

Knowles, M.S. (1970). *The Modern Practice of Adult Education: Andragogy versus Pedagogy.* Associated Press.

Knowles, M.S. (1989). *The Making of an Adult Educator.* Jossey-Bass.

Knowles, M.S. (1990). *The Adult Learner: A Neglected Species* (4th edn). Gulf.

Knowles, M.S., Swanson, R.A., and Holton, E.F. (2005). *The Adult Learner* (6th edn). Routledge. https://doi.org/10.4324/9780080481913.

Kolb, A.Y., and Kolb, D.A. (2005). Learning styles and learning spaces: Enhancing experiential learning in higher education. *Academy of Management Learning and Education, 4*(2), 193–212. https://doi.org/10.5465/amle.2005.17268566.

Kolb, A.Y., and Kolb, D.A. (2009a). Experiential learning theory: A dynamic holistic approach to management learning, education and development. In S.J. Armstrong and C. Fukami (eds), *Handbook of Management Learning, Education and Development* (pp. 42–68). SAGE. https://doi.org/10.4135/9780857021038.n3.

Kolb, A.Y., and Kolb, D.A. (2009b). The learning way: Meta-cognitive aspects of experiential learning. *Simulation and Gaming, 40*(3), 297–327. https://doi.org/10.1177/1046878108325713.

Kolb, D.A. (1984). *Experiential Learning: Experience as the Source of Learning and Development*. Prentice-Hall.

Kosnik, R.D., Tingle, J.K., and Blanton, E.L. (2013). Transformational learning in business: The pivotal role of experiential learning projects. *American Journal of Business Education, 6*(6), 613–630. https://doi.org/10.19030/ajbe.v6i6.8166.

Kozlowski, S.W.J., and Klein, K.J. (2000). A multilevel approach to theory and research in organizations: Contextual, temporal, and emergent processes. In K.J. Klein and S.W.J. Kozlowski (eds), *Multilevel Theory, Research, and Methods in Organizations: Foundations, Extensions, and New Directions* (pp. 3–90). Jossey-Bass.

Krathwohl, D.R. (2002). A revision of Bloom's taxonomy: An overview. *Theory into Practice, 41*(4), 212. https://doi.org/10.1207/s15430421tip4104_2.

Kulik, C.-L.C., Kulik, J.A., and Bangert-Drowns, R.L. (1990). Effectiveness of mastery learning programs: A meta-analysis. *Review of Educational Research, 60*(Summer), 265–307. https://doi.org/10.2307/1170612.

Kulik, J.A., and Kulik, C.-L.C. (1989). The concept of meta-analysis. *International Journal of Educational Research, 13*(3), 227–340. https://doi.org/10.1016/0883-0355(89)90052-9.

Lainema, T., and Lainema, K. (2007). Advancing acquisition of business know-how: Critical learning elements. *Journal of Research on Technology in Education, 40*(2), 183–198. https://doi.org/10.1080/15391523.2007.10782504.

Lazowski, R.A., and Hulleman, C.S. (2016). Motivation interventions in education: A meta-analytic review. *Review of Educational Research, 86*(2), 602–640. https://doi.org/10.3102/0034654315617832.

Le, Q.V., and Raven, P.V. (2015). An assessment of experiential learning of global poverty issues through international service projects. *Journal of Teaching in International Business, 26*(2), 136–158. https://doi.org/10.1080/08975930.2015.1051692.

Leavitt, H.J. (1989). Educating our MBAs: On teaching what we haven't taught. *California Management Review, 31*(3), 38–50. https://doi.org/10.2307/41166569.

Lemar, J. (2016). *Project-Based Learning vs. Problem-Based Learning vs. X-BL*. July 13. https://www.edutopia.org/blog/pbl-vs-pbl-vs-xbl-john-larmer.

Levashina, J., Hartwell, C.J., Morgeson, F.P., Campion, M.A. (2014). The structured employment interview: Narrative and quantitative review of the research literature. *Personnel Psychology, 67*(1), 241–293. https://doi.org/10.1111/peps.12052.

Lewin, K. (1951). *Field Theory in Social Science*. Harper & Row.

Lewin, K. (1997). *Resolving Social Conflicts and Field Theory in Social Science*. American Psychological Association. https://doi.org/10.1037/10269-000.

Linder, C., and Marshall, D. (2003). Reflection and phenomenography: Towards theoretical and educational development possibilities. *Learning and Instruction, 13*(3), 271–284. https://doi.org/10.1016/S0959-4752(02)00002-6.

Lizzio, A., Wilson, K., and Simons, R. (2002). University students' perceptions of the learning environment and academic outcomes: Implications for theory and practice. *Studies in Higher Education, 27*(1), 27. https://doi.org/10.1080/03075070120099359.

Lohmann, G., Pratt, M.A., Benckendorff, P., Strickland, P., Reynolds, P., and Whitelaw, P.A. (2019). Online business simulations: Authentic teamwork, learning outcomes and satisfaction. *Higher Education, 77*(3), 455–472. https://doi.org/10.1007/s10734-018-0282-x.

Lund Dean, K., and Forray, J.M. (2015). Breaking through without crashing through. *Journal of Management Education, 39*(5), 543–548. https://doi.org/10.1177/1052562915597941.

Lund Dean, K., Wright, S.L., and Forray, J.M. (2019). Experiential learning and the moral duty of business schools. *Academy of Management Learning and Education, 19*(4). https://doi.org/10.5465/amle.2018.0335.

Lutterman-Aguilar, A., and Gingerich, O. (2002). Experiential pedagogy for study abroad: Educating for global citizenship. *Frontiers: The Interdisciplinary Journal of Study Abroad, 8*(1), 41–82. https://doi.org/10.36366/frontiers.v8i1.94.

Maddox, K.N., Armstrong, T.I., and Wheatley, W.J. (1991). Ethical dilemmas in experiential learning: Issues and strategies. *Developments in Business Simulation and Experiential Exercises: Proceedings of the Annual ABSEL Conference, 18*, 57–60. https://absel-ojs-ttu.tdl.org/absel/index.php/absel/article/view/1708/1677.

Mandt, E.J. (1982). The failure of business education – and what to do about it. *Management Review, 71*(8): 47–52.

Margolis, H., and McCabe, P.P. (2006). Improving self-efficacy and motivation: What to do, what to say. *Intervention in School and Clinic, 41*(4), 218–227. https://doi.org/10.1177/10534512060410040401.

Marton, F., and Saljo, R. (1976). On qualitative differences in learning. *British Journal of Educational Psychology, 46*(2), 115–127. https://doi.org/10.1111/j.2044-8279.1976.tb02304.x.

Mayer, R.E. (2009). Constructivism as a theory of learning versus constructivism as a prescription for instruction. In S. Tobias and T. Duffy (eds), *Constructivist Instruction: Success or Failure?* (pp. 184–200). Routledge.

McCarthy, M. (2016). Experiential learning theory: From theory to practice. *Journal of Business and Economics Research, 14*(3). 91–100. https://doi.org/10.19030/jber.v14i3.9749.

McGuire, S.Y., and McGuire, S. (2015). *Teach Students How to Learn: Strategies You Can Incorporate into any Course to Improve Student Metacognition, Study Skills, and Motivation.* Stylus.

McNamara, S., and McNamara, A. (2019). Authentic simulated startups: Bringing the real world into the classroom. *Journal of Education for Business, 94*(4), 209–216. https://doi.org/10.1080/08832323.2018.1496897.

McTighe, J., and Wiggins, G. (2004). *Understanding by Design – Professional Development Workbook*. Association for Supervision and Curriculum Development (ASCD).

Meertens, J.V. (2018). Cultural differences in the classroom. *XPat Journal*, Spring, 58–59.

Merseth, K.K. (1991). The early history of case-based instruction: Insights for teacher education today. *Journal of Teacher Education, 42*(4), 243–249. https://doi:10.1177/002248719104200402.

Meyer, B.B., and Wenger, M.S. (1998). Athletes and adventure education: An empirical investigation. *International Journal of Sport Psychology, 29*(3), 243–266.

Mezirow, J. (1978). Perspective transformation. *Adult Education, 28*(2), 100–110. https://doi.org/10.1177/074171367802800202.

Mezirow, J. (1991). *Transformative Dimensions of Adult Learning*. Jossey-Bass.

Mezirow, J. (1997). Transformative learning: Theory to practice. *New Directions for Adult and Continuing Education, 74*(Summer), 5–12. https://doi.org/10.1002/ace.7401.

Mezirow, J. (1998). On critical reflection. *Adult Learning Quarterly, 48*(3), 185–198. https://doi.org/10.1177/074171369804800305.

Mezirow, J. (2000). *Learning as Transformation: Critical Perspectives on a Theory in Progress*. Jossey-Bass.

Michaelsen, L.K., Knight, A.B., and Fink, L.D. (2004). *Team-Based Learning: A Transformative Use of Small Groups in College Teaching*. Stylus.

Michaelson, L.K., and Sweet, M. (2008). The essential elements of team-based learning. *New Directions for Teaching and Learning, 2008*(116), 7–27. https://doi.org/10.1002/tl.330.

Michel, N., Carter III, J.J., and Varela, O. (2009). Active versus passive teaching styles: An empirical study of student outcomes. *Human Resource Development Quarterly, 20*(4), 397–418. https://doi.org/10.1002/hrdq.20025.

Miles, R.E. (1985). The future of business education. *California Management Review, 27*(3), 63–73. https://doi.org/10.2307/41165142.

Miller, B.A. (2014). *Building your Leadership Brand*. HDI. https://www.thinkhdi.com/library/supportworld/2014/leadership-brand.aspx.

Mintzberg, H. (2004). *Managers, not MBAs: A Hard Look at the Soft Practice of Managing and Management Development*. Berrett-Koehler.

Molenda, M. (2015). In search of the elusive ADDIE model. *Performance Improvement, 54*(2), 40–42. https://doi.org/10.1002/pfi.21461.

Moon, J. (2004). *A Handbook of Reflective and Experiential Learning: Theory and Practice*. Routledge.

Muller, H.J., Porter, J.L., and Rehder, R.R. (1988). Have the business schools let down US corporations? *Management Review, 77*(10), 24–31.

Munro, J. (2012). *Social-Cultural Influences on Learning*. https://students.education.unimelb.edu.au/selage/pub/readings/psyexlearn/PELculturaleffects.pdf.

Murray, H.G. (2007). Low-inference teaching behaviors and college teaching effectiveness: Recent developments and controversies. In R.P. Perry and J.C.

Smart (eds), *The Scholarship of Teaching and Learning in Higher Education: An Evidence-Based Perspective* (pp. 145–200). Springer.

Murray, H.G., and Renaud, R.D. (1995). Disciplinary differences in classroom teaching behaviors. *New Directions for Teaching and Learning, 1995*(64), 31–39. https://doi.org/10.1002/tl.37219956406.

National Association of Colleges and Employers (2017). Job outlook 2018: The attributes employers want to see on new college graduates' resumes. https://www.naceweb.org/about-us/press/2017/the-key-attributes-employers-seek-on-students-resumes/.

National Society for Experiential Education (2013). Eight principles of good practice for all experiential learning activities. https://www.nsee.org/8-principles.

National Society for Experiential Education (n.d.). Vision, missions and goals. https://www.nsee.org/vision-mission-and-goals.

Nesbit, J.C., and Adesope, O.O. (2006). Learning with concept and knowledge maps: A meta-analysis. *Review of Educational Research, 76*(3), 413–448. https://doi.org/10.3102/00346543076003413.

Neves, J., and Hillman, N. (2019). *Student Academic Experience Survey.* Higher Education Policy Institute. https://www.advance-he.ac.uk/sites/default/files/2019-06/Student%20Academic%20Experience%20Survey%202019%20Results%20Report.pdf.

Newby, T.J., Stepich, D.A., Lehman, J.D., Russell, J.D., and Ottenbreit-Leftwich, A. (2000). *Educational Technology for Teaching and Learning* (4th edn). Pearson.

Ng, K., Van Dyne, L., and Ang, S. (2009). From experience to experiential learning: Cultural intelligence as a learning capability for global leader development. *Academy of Management Learning and Education, 8*(4), 511–525. https://doi.org/10.5465/amle.8.4.zqr511.

Nicolaides, A., and Yorks, L. (2008). An epistemology of learning through. *Emergence: Complexity and Organization, 10*(1), 50–61.

Nilson, L.B. (2010). *Teaching at its Best: A Research-Based Resource for College Instructors.* John Wiley & Sons.

Noddings, N. (1990). Constructivism in mathematics education. In R.B. Davis, C.A. Maber, and N. Noddings (eds), *Constructivist Views on the Teaching and Learning of Mathematics* (pp. 7–18 and 195–210). National Council of Teachers of Mathematics. https://doi.org/10.2307/749909.

Noyd, R.K. (2001). *A Primer on Writing Effective Learning-Centered Course Goals.* https://www.utm.edu/departments/rgc/_pdfs/Noyd%20-%20Writing%20Good%20Learning%20Goals.pdf.

Offstein, E.H., and Chory, R.M. (2019). In defense of the lecture: Revisiting and reassessing its place within management pedagogy. *Organization Management Journal, 16*(4), 1–13. https://doi.org/10.1080/15416518.2019.1681255.

Pariseau, S.E., and Kezim, B. (2007). The effect of using case studies in business statistics. *Journal of Education for Business, 83*(1), 27–31. https://doi.org/10.3200/JOEB.83.1.27-31.

Perry, R.P., and Smart, J.C. (2007). *The Scholarship of Teaching and Learning in Higher Education: An Evidence-Based Perspective.* Springer. https://doi.org/10.1007/1-4020-5742-3.

Petriglieri, G., and Petriglieri, J.L. (2010). Identity workspaces: The case of business schools. *Academy of Management Learning and Education, 9*(1), 44–60. https://doi.org/10.5465/amle.9.1.zqr44.

Pettigrew, A., and Starkey, K. (2016). From the guest editors: The legitimacy and impact of business schools: Key issues and a research agenda. *Academy of Management Learning and Education, 15*(4), 649–664. https://doi.org/10.5465/amle.2016.0296.

Pfeffer, J. (2018). *Dying for a Paycheck.* Harper Business.

Pfeffer, J., and Fong, C.T. (2002). The end of business schools? Less success than meets the eye. *Academy of Management Learning and Education, 1*(1), 78–95. https://doi.org/10.5465/amle.2002.7373679.

Pintrich, P.R. (2002). The role of metacognitive knowledge in learning, teaching, and assessing. *Theory Into Practice, 41*(4), 219. https://doi.org/10.1207/s15430421tip4104_3.

Pope, M. (2019). The right way to choose a college. *Wall Street Journal,* March 22. https://www.wsj.com/articles/the-right-way-to-choose-a-college-11553266896?st=vfa1c2hvgopwrbk.

Porter, J. (2017). Why you should make time for self-reflection (even if you hate doing it). *Harvard Business Review Digital Articles,* 2–4. http://search.ebscohost.com/login.aspx?direct=true&db=buh&AN=122087632&site=ehost-live.

Priem, R.L. (2018). Towards becoming a complete teacher of strategic management. *Academy of Management Learning and Education, 17*(3), 374–388. https://doi.org/10.5465/amle.2017.0237.

Prince, M.J., and Felder, R.M. (2006). Inductive teaching and learning methods: Definitions, comparisons, and research bases. *Journal of Engineering Education, 95*(2), 123–138. https://doi.org/10.1002/j.2168-9830.2006.tb00884.x.

Ramburuth, P. and Daniel, S. (2011). Integrating experiential learning and cases in international business. *Journal of Teaching in International Business, 22*(1), 38–50. https://doi.org/10.1080/08975930.2011.585917.

Ramsden, P. (1979). Student learning and perceptions of the academic environment. *Higher Education, 8,* 411–427. https://doi.org/10.1007/BF01680529.

Ramsden, P. (2003). *Learning to Teach in Higher Education* (2nd edn). Routledge Falmer. https://doi.org/10.4324/9780203507711.

Reichheld, F.F. (2003). The one number you need to grow. *Harvard Business Review, 81*(12), 46–54.

Reivich, K., and Shatté, A. (2002). *The Resilience Factor: 7 Keys to Finding your Inner Strengths and Overcoming Life's Hurdles.* Random House.

Revans, R.W. (1982). *The Origin and Growth of Action Learning.* Chartwell Bratt. https://doi.org/10.1108/eb051529.

Reynolds, M. (2009). Wild frontiers – reflections on experiential learning, *Management Learning, 40*(4), 387–392. https://doi.org/10.1177/1350507609335848.

Richardson, M., Abraham, C., and Bond, R. (2012). Psychological correlates of university students' academic performance: A systematic review and meta-analysis. *Psychological Bulletin*, *138*(2), 253–387. https://doi.org/10.1037/a0026838.

Richardson, V. (1997). Constructivist teaching and teacher education: Theory and practice. In V. Richardson (ed.), *Constructivist Teacher Education: Building a World of New Understandings* (pp. 3–14). Falmer Press.

Riley, J., and Ward, K. (2017). Active learning, cooperative active learning and passive learning methods in an accounting information systems course. *Issues in Accounting Education*, *32*(2), 1–16. https://doi.org/10.2308/iace-51366.

Roberts, J. (2018). From the editor: The possibilities and limitations of experiential learning research in higher education. *Journal of Experiential Education*, *41*(1), 3–7. https://doi.org/10.1177/1053825917751457.

Roberts, N. (2006). Disorienting dilemmas: Their effects on learners, impact on performance and implications for adult educators. In M.S. Plakhotnik and S.M. Nielsen (eds), *Proceedings of the Fifth Annual College of Education Research Conference: Urban and International Education Section* (pp. 100–105). https://digitalcommons.fiu.edu/cgi/viewcontent.cgi?article=1249&context=sferc.

Rodgers, W., Simon, J., and Gabrielsson, J. (2016). Combining experiential and conceptual learning in accounting education: A review with implications. *Management Learning*, *48*(2), 187–205. https://doi.org/10.1177/1350507616669479.

Rogers, C.R. (1969). *Freedom to Learn*. Charles E. Merrill.

Rogers, C.R. (1983). *Freedom to Learn for the 80s*. Merrill.

Ross, L. (1977). The intuitive psychologist and his shortcomings: Distortions in the attribution process. *Advances in Experimental Social Psychology*, *10*, 173–220. https://doi.org/10.1016/S0065-2601(08)60357-3.

Rousseau, D.M. (2012). Designing a better business school: Channeling Herbert Simon, addressing the critics and developing actionable knowledge for professionalizing managers. *Journal of Management Studies*, *49*(3), 600–618. https://doi.org/10.1111/j.1467-6486.2011.01041.x.

Rubin, R.S., and Dierdorff, E.C. (2013). Building a better MBA: From a decade of critique toward a decennium of creation. *Academy of Management Learning and Education*, *12*(1), 125–141. https://doi.org/10.5465/amle.2012.0217.

Rust, C. (2002). The impact of assessment on student learning: How can the research literature practically help to inform the development of departmental assessment strategies and learner-centred assessment practices? *Active Learning in Higher Education*, *3*(2), 145–158. https://doi.org/10.1177/1469787402003002004.

Salas, E., Tannenbaum, S.I., Kraiger, K., and Smith-Jentsch, K.A. (2012). The science of training and development in organizations: What matters in practice. *Psychological Science in the Public Interest*, *13*(2), 74–101. https://doi.org/10.1177/1529100612436661.

Salas, E., Wildman, J.L., and Piccolo, R.F. (2009). Using simulation-based training to enhance management education. *Academy of Management Learning and Education*, *8*(4), 559–573. https://doi.org/10.5465/amle.8.4.zqr559.

Saunders, P. (1997). Experiential learning, cases and simulations in business communications. *Business Communications Quarterly, 60*(1), 97–114. https://doi.org/10.1177/108056999706000108.

Schary, D.P., Jenny, S.E., Morrow, G.S., and Wozniak, T. (2018). Bringing challenge course activities into the classroom: Pedagogical strengths, obstacles and recommendations. *Journal of Outdoor Recreation, Education, and Leadership, 10*(3), 238–252. https://doi.org/10.18666/JOREL-2018-V10-I3-8533.

Schneider, M., and Preckel, F. (2017). Variables associated with achievement in higher education: A systematic review of meta-analyses. *Psychological Bulletin, 143*(6), 565–600. https://doi.org/10.1037/bul0000098.

Schön, D.A. (1983). *The Reflective Practitioner.* Basic Books.

Schön, D.A. (1987). *Educating the Reflective Practitioner.* Jossey-Bass.

Schön, D.A. (1995). The new scholarship requires a new epistemology. *Change: The Magazine of Higher Learning, 27*(6), 27–34. https://doi.org/10.1080/00091383.1995.10544673.

Schramm, H. (n.d.). Using dynamic adaptive cases to bring practical experience into the classroom. Vienna University of Economics and Business, Working Paper. https://pdfs.semanticscholar.org/152f/235d667339cc200df58511c42c599066b76c.pdf.

Schunk, D.H. (2012). *Learning Theories: An Educational Perspective* (6th edn). Pearson.

Schunk, D.H., and Pajares, F. (2002). The development of academic self-efficacy. In A. Wigfield and J.S. Eccles (eds), *Development of Achievement Motivation* (pp. 15–31). Academic Press. https://doi.org/10.1016/B978-012750053-9/50003-6.

Schwartz, B.M., and Gurung, R.A.R. (2012). *Evidence-Based Teaching for Higher Education.* American Psychological Association. https://doi.org/10.1037/13745-000.

Scott, W.R. (2003). *Organizations: Rational, Natural, and Open Systems.* Prentice Hall.

Scott, W.R., and Davis, G.F. (2007). *Organizations and Organizing: Rational, Natural, and Open System Perspectives.* Pearson-Prentice Hall.

Seaman, J., Brown, M., and Quay, J. (2017). The evolution of experiential learning theory: Tracing lines of research in the JEE. *Journal of Experiential Education, 40*(4), NP1–NP21. https://doi.org/10.1177/1053825916689268.

Serva, M.A., and Fuller, M.A. (2004). Aligning what we do and what we measure in business schools: Incorporating active learning and effective media use in the assessment of instruction. *Journal of Management Education, 28*(1), 19–38. https://doi.org/10.1177/1052562903252648.

Shingles, R. (2015). Writing effective learning objectives. *The Innovative Instructor: Best Practice*, December. https://cer.jhu.edu/files/InnovInstruct-BP_learning-objectives.pdf.

Silberman, M.L. (2007). *The Handbook of Experiential Learning.* Pfeiffer.

Sisk, V.F., Burgoyne, A.P., Sun, J., Butler, J.L., and Macnamara, B.N. (2018). To what extent and under which circumstances are growth mind-sets important to academic achievement? Two meta-analyses. *Psychological Science, 29*(4), 549–571. https://doi.org/10.1177/0956797617739704.

Sitzmann, T., and Ely, K. (2011). A meta-analysis of self-regulated learning in work-related training and educational attainment: What we know and where we need to go. *Psychological Bulletin, 137*(3), 421–442. http://dx.doi.org/10.1037/a0022777.

Sitzmann, T., Ely, K., Brown K.G., and Bauer, K.N. (2010). Self-assessment of knowledge: A cognitive learning or affective measure? *Academy of Management Learning and Education, 9*(2), 169–191. https://doi.org/10.5465/amle.9.2.zqr169.

Slavich, G.M., and Zimbardo, P.G. (2012). Transformational teaching: Theoretical underpinnings, basic principles, and core methods. *Educational Psychology Review, 24*(4), 569–608. https://doi.org/10.1007/s10648-012-9199-6.

Slavin, R.E. (1994). *Educational Psychology Theory and Practice* (4th edn). Allyn & Bacon.

Smith, G.F. (2003). Beyond critical thinking and decision making: Teaching business students how to think. *Journal of Management Education, 27*(1), 24–51. https://doi.org/10.1177/1052562902239247.

Smith, K.A., Sheppard, S.D., Johnson, D.W., and Johnson, R.T. (2005). Pedagogies of engagement: Classroom-based practices. *Journal of Engineering Education, 94*(1), 87–101. https://doi.org/10.1002/j.2168-9830.2005.tb00831.x.

Smith, T.E., and Knapp, K.E. (2011). *Sourcebook of Experiential Education: Key Thinkers and Their Contributions.* Routledge. https://doi.org/10.4324/9780203838983.

Snyder, K.D. (2003). Ropes, poles, and space: Active learning in business education. *Active Learning in Higher Education, 4*(2), 159–167. https://doi.org/10.1177/1469787403004002004.

Sobel, D. (2003). *Place-Based Education: Connecting Classrooms and Communities.* Orion.

Splan, R.K., Brooks, R.M., and Porr, C.S. (2016). Student reflections on personal and professional growth after a 16-week immersive, experiential learning program in equine science. *NACTA Journal, 60*(1), 60–64. https://doi.org/10.2307/nactajournal.60.1.60.

Springer, L., Stanne, M.E., Donovan, S.S. (1999). Effects of small-group learning on undergraduates in science, mathematics, engineering, and technology. *Review of Educational Research, 69*(1), 21–51. https://doi.org/10.3102/00346543069001021.

Stajkovic, A.D., and Luthans, F. (1998). Self-efficacy and work-related performance: A meta-analysis. *Psychological Bulletin, 124*(2), 240–261. https://doi.org/10.1037/0033-2909.124.2.240.

Stewart, A.C., Houghton, S.M., and Rogers, P.R. (2012). Instructional design, active learning, and student performance: Using a trading room to teach strategy. *Journal of Management Education, 36*(6), 753–776. https://doi.org/10.1177/1052562912456295.

Stone, C.L. (1983). A meta-analysis of advance organizer studies. *Journal of Experimental Education, 51*(4), 194. https://doi.org/10.1080/00220973.1983 .11011862.

Strobel, J., and van Barneveld, A. (2009). When is PBL effective? A meta-synthesis of meta-analyses comparing problem-based learning to conventional classroom learning. *Interdisciplinary Journal of Problem Based Learning, 3*(1), 44–58. https://doi.org/10.7771/1541-5015.1046.

Sunderman, G.L. (2006). Do supplemental educational services increase opportunities for minority students? *Phi Delta Kappan, 88*(2), 117–122. https://doi .org/10.1177/003172170608800208.

Swanson, E., McCulley, L.V., Osman, D.J., Lewis, N.S., and Solis, M. (2019). The effect of team-based learning on content knowledge: A meta-analysis. *Active Learning in Higher Education, 20*(1), 39–50. https://doi.org/10.1177/ 1469787417731201.

Taylor, V.F. (2018). Afraid of the deep: Reflections and analysis of a role-play exercise gone wrong. *Journal of Management Education, 42*(6), 772–782. https://doi.org/http://dx.doi.org/10.1177/1052562918802875.

Tight, M. (2019). Systematic reviews and meta-analyses of higher education research. *European Journal of Higher Education, 9*(2), 133–152. https://doi .org/10.1080/21568235.2018.1541752.

Tomkins, L., and Ulus, E. (2016). Oh, was that "experiential learning"?! Spaces, synergies and surprises with Kolb's learning cycle. *Management Learning, 47*(2), 158–178. https://doi.org/10.1177/1350507615587451.

Turner, J.C., and Meyer, D.K. (2000). Studying and understanding the instructional contexts of classrooms: Using our past to forge our future. *Educational Psychologist, 35*(2), 69–85. https://doi.org/10.1207/S15326985EP3502_2.

Tyler, R.W., and Hlebowitsh, P.S. (2013). *Basic Principles of Curriculum and Instruction.* University of Chicago Press. https://doi.org/10.7208/chicago/ 9780226086644.001.0001.

Tyson, D.F., Linnenbrink-Garcia, L., and Hill, N.E. (2009). Regulating debilitating emotions in the context of performance: Achievement goal orientations, achievement-elicited emotions, and socialization contexts. *Human Development, 52*(6), 329–356. https://doi.org/10.1159/000242348.

Ulrich, D., and Smallwood, N. (2007). Five steps to building your personal leadership brand. *Harvard Management Update, 12*(12), 3–5.

Umbach, P.D., and Porter, S.R. (2002). How do academic departments impact student satisfaction? Understanding the contextual effects of departments. *Research in Higher Education, 43*(2), 209–234. https://doi.org/10.1023/A: 1014471708162.

Ungaretti, T., Thompson, K.R., Miller, A., and Peterson, T.O. (2015). Problem-based learning: Lessons from medical education and challenges for management education. *Academy of Learning and Education, 14*(2), 173–186. https://doi.org/10.5465/amle.2013.0245.

Vaara, E., and Faÿ, E. (2012). Reproduction and change on the global scale: A Bourdieusian perspective on management education. *Journal of Management Studies, 49*(6) 1023–1051. https://doi.org/10.1111/j.1467-6486.2012.01049.x.

Vernon, D.T., and Blake, R.L. (1993). Does problem-based learning work? A meta-analysis of evaluative research. *Academic Medicine, 68*(7), 550–563. https://doi.org/10.1097/00001888-199307000-00015.

Vogel, R., Hattke, F., and Petersen, J. (2017). Journal rankings in management and business studies: What rules do we play by? *Research Policy, 46*(10), 1707–1722. https://doi.org/10.1016/j.respol.2017.07.001.

von Bertalanffy, L. (1972). The history and status of general systems theory. *Academy of Management Journal, 15*(4), 407–426. https://doi.org/10.5465/255139.

von Bertalanffy, L. (2008). An outline of general system theory. *Emergence: Complexity and Organization,* 10(2), 103–123.

Waddock, S., and Lozano, J.M. (2013). Developing more holistic management education: Lessons learned from two programs. *Academy of Management Learning and Education, 12*(2), 265–284. https://doi.org/10.5465/amle.2012.0002.

Wadsworth, B.J. (1996). *Piaget's Theory of Cognitive and Affective Development: Foundations of Constructivism* (5th edn). Longman Publishing.

Walvoord, B.E., and Anderson, V.J. (2010). *Effective Grading: A Tool for Learning and Assessment in College* (2nd edn). Jossey-Bass.

Wang, M.C., Haertel, G.D., and Walberg, H.J. (1993). Toward a knowledge base for school learning. *Review of Educational Research, 63*(3), 365–376. https://doi.org/10.3102/00346543063003249.

Wang, M.C., Haertel, G.D., and Walberg, H.J. (1997). *What Helps Students Learn? Spotlight on Student Success.* https://files.eric.ed.gov/fulltext/ED461694.pdf.

Warren, K. (1995). The student-directed classroom: A model for teaching experiential education theory. In K. Warren (ed.), *The Theory of Experiential Education* (pp. 249–258). Kendall/Hunt Publishing Company.

Watson, H.J. (1981). *Computer Simulation in Business.* John Wiley.

Whetten, D.A. (2009). An examination of the interface between context and theory applied to the study of Chinese organizations. *Management and Organization Review, 5*(1), 29–55. https://doi.org/10.1111/j.1740-8784.2008.00132.x.

Whetten, D.A., and Cameron, K.S. (1983). Management skills training: A needed addition to the management curriculum. *Organizational Behavior Teaching Journal, 8*(2), 10–15. https://journals.sagepub.com/doi/10.1177/105256298300800205.

Wick, C., Pollock, R., Jefferson, A., and Flanagan, R. (2006). *The Six Disciplines of Breakthrough Learning: How to Turn Training and Development into Business Results.* Pfeiffer.

Wiggins, G., and McTighe, J. (2005). *Understanding by Design* (2nd edn). Pearson Education.

Wilhelmson, L., Åberg, M.M., Backström, T., and Olsson, B.K. (2015). Enabling transformative learning in the workplace: An educative research intervention. *Journal of Transformative Education, 13*(3), 219–238. https://doi.org/10.1177/1541344615574599.

Williams, B. (2005). Case based learning – a review of the literature: Is there scope for this educational paradigm in prehospital education? *Emergency Medical Journal*, *22*(8), 577–581. http://dx.doi.org/10.1136/emj.2004.022707.

Wilson, K.L., Lizzio, A.L.F., and Ramsden, P. (1997). The development, validation and application of the Course Experience Questionnaire. *Studies in Higher Education*, *22*(1), 33–53. https://doi.org/10.1080/03075079712331381121.

Windschitl, M. (2002). Framing constructivism in practice as the negotiation of dilemmas: An analysis of the conceptual, pedagogical, cultural and political challenges facing teachers. *Review of Educational Research*, *72*(2), 131–175. https://doi.org/10.3102/00346543072002131.

Wraga, W.G. (2017). Understanding the Tyler rationale: Basic principles of curriculum and instruction in historical context. *Espacio, Tiempo y Educación*, *4*(2), 227–252. https://doi.org/10.14516/ete.156.

Wren, D.A., Buckley, M.R., and Michaelsen, L.K. (1994). The theory/applications balance in management pedagogy: Where do we stand? *Journal of Management 20*(1), 141–157. https://doi.org/10.1177/014920639402000107.

Wright, M.C., Assar, N., Kain, E.L., Kramer, L., Howery, C.B., et al. (2004). Greedy institutions: The importance of institutional context for teaching in higher education. *Teaching Sociology*, *32*(2), 144–159. https://doi.org/10.1177/0092055X0403200201.

Wright, S., Forray, J.M., and Lund Dean, K. (2019). From advocacy to accountability in experiential learning practices. *Management Learning*, *50*(3), 261–281. https://doi.org/10.1177/1350507618814645.

Wurdinger, S.D. (2005). *Using Experiential Learning in the Classroom*. Scarecrow Education.

Wurdinger, S.D., Haar, J., Hugg, B., and Bezon, J. (2007). A qualitative study using project-based learning in a mainstream middle school. *Improving Schools*, *10*(2), 150–161. https://doi.org/10.1177/1365480207078048.

Yeager, D.S., Walton, G.M., Brady, S.T., Akcinar, E.N., Paunesku, D., et al. (2016a). Teaching a lay theory before college narrows achievement gaps at scale. *Proceedings of National Academy of Sciences USA*, *113*(24), E3341–E3348. https://doi.org/10.1073/pnas.1524360113.

Yeager, D.S., Romero, C., Paunesku, D., Hulleman, C.S., Schneider, B., et al. (2016b). Using design thinking to improve psychological interventions: The case of the growth mindset during the transition to high school. *Journal of Educational Psychology*, *108*(3), 374–391. http://doi.org/10.1037/edu0000098.

Ylvisaker, M., Hibbard, M., and Feeney, T. (2006). What is an advance organizer? LearNet. http://projectlearnet.org/tutorials/advance_organizers.html.

Yorio, P., and Ye, F. (2012). A meta-analysis on the effects of service-learning on the social, personal and cognitive outcomes of learning. *Academy of Management Learning and Education*, *11*(1), 9–27. https://doi.org/10.5465/amle.2010.0072.

Zell, E., and Krizan, Z. (2014). Do people have insight into their abilities? A meta-synthesis. *Perspectives on Psychological Science*, *9*(2), 111–125. https://doi.org/10.1177/1745691613518075.

Zimmerman, J.L. (2001). Can American business schools survive? Simon School of Business Working Paper No. FR 01-16, September 1. http://dx.doi.org/10.2139/ssrn.283112.

Zohar, A., and Ben David, A. (2009). Paving a clear path in a thick forest: A conceptual analysis of a metacognitive component. *Metacognition and Learning*, *4*(3), 177–195. https://doi.org/10.1007/s11409-009-9044-6.

Index

Abrami, P.C. 37
abstract conceptualization 16
abstract skills 20–21
academic achievement 110
accounting 30–31, 185, 217
accreditation requirements 1
achievement approach to learning 23,
    25, 64, 77, 104
acknowledgement 45
action learning 3
action research agenda 19
active engagement in learning
    processes 117
active experimentation 16
active learning 2–3
activity and learning objectives 156
adaptive system 60
adjust and adapt 81–4, 134
    global strategy meeting exercise
        167
    growth mindset exercise 150–51
    leadership brand exercise 179–80
    to presentations 179
    in timing 82
Adult Learner, The (Knowles) 19
adult learning theory 17–19
affective outcomes 32
alignment 75, 77–80, 133
    global strategy meeting exercise
        162–4
    growth mindset exercise 147–8
    leadership brand exercise 174–6
Ambrose, S.A. 71, 75, 85
American business education 22
Analysis, Design, Development,
    Implementation, and
    Evaluation model (ADDIE
    model) 50–51, 54–5, 57
Anderson, V.J. 64–5, 75

Angelo, T.A. 75
Annenberg Learner 132
applied problem–solving 37
assessment(s) 28, 32, 35, 36, 39, 45,
    48, 51, 52, 53, 56, 72, 128, 132
    approaches/methods 64, 65, 125,
        129
    and evaluation 45
    exercise 77
    of individual roles 158–9
    selection/creation 72, 74–6,
        132–3
        global strategy meeting
            exercise 161–2
        growth mindset exercise
            146–7
        leadership brand exercise
            174
Association for Business Simulation
    and Experiential Learning
    (ABSEL) 21
Association for Experiential
    Education (AEE) 42–3
Association of American Colleges and
    Universities (AACU) 132–3
Association of MBAs (AMBA) 23–4
Association to Advance Collegiate
    Schools of Business (AACSB)
    21, 23–4, 64, 141
attitude change, approaches to 143
attributions, appropriate 104, 119–20,
    131
Audet, J. 26–7
authenticity 44

Backward Design model 50–51, 52–3,
    55–6
banking model of education 2

Barrows, H.S. 19, 37
Beck-Dudley, C.L. 24
behavioral–based questions 171
behavioral changes 33–4
beliefs 106, 109
best practices 48
    Effective Experiential Exercise
        Design Model description
        62–87
    for facilitating experiential
        learning activities 42–8
Biggs, J.B. 68, 78, 88, 105–6
Boud, D. 7
Bourgeois, E. 14
Bradford, D.L. 193–4
Branch, R.M. 51, 54
Bronfenbrenner, U. 89
Brown, P.C. 75
Burch, G.F. 34–6, 39
business 26
    brief 162
    educators 42
    ethics 185
    games and simulations 20–21
    knowledge 25, 27
    management simulation 13
    schools 20, 22–3
    skills 25
    statistics 31
business education
    call for reform in 22–3
    evidence from outside of business
        schools 35–9
    evidence of effectiveness in 26–7,
        32
    history and future of experiential
        learning in 19–25
    in–class and field–based
        experiential exercises in
        27
    meta–analyses in 32–5
    research and scholarship for 22
    systematic reviews in 32–5

call for reform in business education
    22–3
Cambridge Dictionary 87

Cameron, K.S. 21–2
case–based learning 3
change theory 21
checklist 61–2, 87
chief executive officer (CEO) 153,
        156, 158–9, 167
class discussions 166–7
class–room assessment techniques 72
*Classroom Assessment Techniques:
    A Handbook for College
    Teachers* (Angelo and Cross)
    75
classroom–based activities *see*
        classroom–based experiential
        exercises
classroom–based experiential
        exercises 1, 8–10, 16, 194
classroom context 87
classroom–oriented instructional
        design models 50–51
    ADDIE model 50–51, 54
    Backward Design model 50–51,
        52–3
    contextual factors considered by
        model 58
    Effective Experiential Design
        model 58–62
    Integrated Design model 50–52
    model comparison 56–7
    PIE model 50–51, 53
    strengths and weaknesses 55,
        57–8
    Systematic Planning model
        50–51, 53–4
cognitive conflict 14
cognitive constructivism 11–12
cognitive dimensions 69
cognitive learning 32
collaborative learning 2–3, 40
Collis, K.F. 68
communication
    adaptation 162
    marketing and 158
community citizenship 27
comprehensive institutions 117–18
concept mapping 40
confidence *see* self–efficacy

conscientiousness 105–6
constructive alignment 78
constructivism 10–12
  cognitive 11–12
  Piaget's theory of 88
  social 11–12
content
  characteristics 66
  reflection 6
context 60–61, 62–6, 87–128
  adjustment and adaptation 134
  alignment 133
  applying what we know about
    121–7
  approach to learning 104–5
  appropriate attribution 104
  assessment 62–4, 141–2, 128
    global strategy meeting
      exercise 153–4
    growth mindset exercise
      140–42
    leadership brand exercise
      170–71
  assessments selection/creation
    132–3
  classroom 87
  contextual factors 65–6
    affecting experiential
      exercises 90
  department characteristics,
    impact of 117
  educator characteristics, impact
    of 106, 110
    educator characteristics and
      teaching practices 109
    learner characteristics 109
    relationships between
      context, learning
      approach, and
      learning outcomes
      107–8
  experiential learning 88
  general learning context, impact
    of 113, 117
  growth mindset exercise 102
  in higher education 87
  impact assessment 123, 129
  impact of 92–5
implementation 133–4
  checklist 135–7
  instructional 87
instructional approaches 122
  impact of 110–13
intelligence and prior
  achievement 100–101
learner characteristics, impact of
  96, 100, 106
  relationships between
    context and outcomes
    97–9
learning
  activities selection/creation
    130–31
  objectives 128, 130
learning context 87–8
  impact 119–21
  theoretical foundations
    88–91
metacognition 102
personality 105–6
practices/conditions related to
  context and effect sizes
  114–16
professional and societal
  influences, impact of
  118–19
reflection and revising 135
school/university characteristics,
  impact of 117–18
self–efficacy 102–3
specific learning context, impact
  of 95–6
strategies, mindsets, and
  motivation 101
subject/content characteristics,
  impact of 113
contextual factors 93, 137
  affecting experiential exercises
    90
contingency
  studies 26
  variables 33
conventional business disciplines 20
cooperative education 3, 7, 20

cooperative learning 3, 31, 40, 66, 103, 131
coordination 21
Course Experience Questionnaire 96
Creating Significant Learning Experiences (Fink) 75
Creating Significant Learning Experiences model 56
criterion–referenced assessment 132
critical thinking 26, 27, 29, 31, 37
criticisms 70
Critics of Experiential Learning Methods 39, 42
cross–cultural
  cues 162, 168
  global strategy meeting exercise implementation 159
  leadership skills 155
  strategic meeting game 152–3
cross–departmental instructional development 117
Cross, K.P. 75
cultural/culture 155
  differences in teaching and learning 119
  intelligence 26
  resources 168
  society and 118

Daniel, S. 16
data management 28
Dean, L. 194
debrief 127, 134, 144, 149, 151, 157
  experience in small groups 160–61
  key observations as class 160–61
decision–making 21, 170
deep approach to learning 104, 107, 120
demands
  from business community for workplace skills 1
  for learning outcomes 23–4
department 125, 129
  characteristics 64, 66
  impact 117
Desjarlais, M. 16

developmental formative feedback 132
Dewey, J. 5–6, 10, 12, 19
disciplinary–specific considerations for marketing, finance, and supply chain 168
discipline–based content 20
discovery learning 2–3
distal variables 93
Dousay, T.A. 51, 54
Dunlap, J.C. 43

Earl G. Graves School of Business and Management 141
ecological theory of human development 89–90
educational accrediting bodies 23
educator–led discussions 37
educators 82, 85, 117, 119–20, 124, 129, 135
  assigns individual roles within the groups 158
  beliefs 83, 128
  business 42
  characteristics 63, 65, 122
    impact 106, 110
    relationships between context, learning approach, and learning outcomes 107–8
  and teaching practices 109
  using evidence–based best practices 120
  following humanistic theory 17
  making notes during priority presentations 160
  role in experiential learning 5, 7, 9, 14–15, 43, 46
  self–directed learning of 17–18
educator's perspective
  adjusting and adaptation 180
  assessment selection/creation 146
  breaks 166–7
  context assessment 141–2, 154, 170–71
    general context 141

specific context 141
ensuring alignment 147–8, 176
implementation 148, 166–7,
        178–9
learning activities selection/
        creation 143, 145, 173–4
motivation 140, 153, 169–70
reflection and revision 151–2,
        181–2
timing 166–7
educator–student relationships 119–20
Effective Experiential Exercise
        Design Checklist 50, 58–9,
        61–2
Effective Experiential Exercise
        Design Model 50, 56, 58–9,
        61–2, 139
adaptation 81–4
adjustment 81–4
alignment 75, 77–9, 80
assessments selection/creation
        72, 74–6
comparison of key learning
        outcome taxonomies
        69–70
context assessment 62–4
contextual factors 65–6
exercise 77, 81
implementation 79–80
learning
        activities selection/creation
        68, 71, 73
        objectives 64, 66–8
reflection 84–6
revising 84–6
theoretical and practical
        foundations 60–62
timing 81
Effective Grading (Walvoord and
        Anderson) 75
effective instructional methods 111
Ely, D.P. 51, 53
emotional engagement 131
emotional states 103
enhanced learning outcomes 1
ensuring alignment in growth mindset
        exercise 147–8

entrepreneurial mindset 26–7
entrepreneurship 26, 28–9, 186
Ericsson, K.A. 85
ethical concerning areas 193–4
ethical literacy 26
European Quality Improvement
        System (EQUIS) 23–4
evidence–based best practices 83,
        120, 194
evidence–based high–impact
        contextual factors 121
evidence–based suggestions 48
evidence of effectiveness 25–6
        in business education 26–7, 32
exercise
        resources for global strategy
                meeting exercise 168–9
        sequence 81
exosystems 89
Experience and Education (Dewey)
        19
Experiential Exercise Implementation
        Checklist 127
experiential exercises 127, 194
        by business discipline 185–92
        contextual factors affecting 90
        global strategy meeting exercise
                138, 152–69
        growth mindset exercise 138–51
        implementation in classroom
                50–51
                classroom–oriented design
                        models 51–8
                Effective Experiential
                        Exercise Design
                        Model 50, 58–9,
                        62–87
        implementation in teaching
                practice 182
        leadership brand exercise 138,
                169–82
        learning objectives 134
        specific contextual factors to
                increase learning in 100
experiential learning
        activities 7–10

best practices for facilitating
　　activities 42–8
　　National Society for
　　　　Experiential
　　　　Education (NSEE)
　　　　44–5
　　recommendations based on
　　　　experiential learning
　　　　literature 43–8
characteristics 2–7
context 88
definition 1–2
evidence of effectiveness 25–42
　　in business education 26–32
　　critics of experiential
　　　　learning methods
　　　　39–42
　　evidence from outside of
　　　　business schools 35–9
　　systematic reviews and
　　　　meta-analyses in
　　　　business education
　　　　32–5
history and future in business
　　education 19–25
　　calls for reform 22–3
　　demands for learning
　　　　outcomes 23–4
　　increased emphasis on
　　　　experiential methods
　　　　24–5
leadership brand creation 172
requirement for implementation
　　110
theoretical foundations in
　　classroom 10–19
　　constructivism 11–12
　　humanistic learning theory
　　　　16–17
　　Knowles's theory of adult
　　　　learning 17–19
　　Kolb's experiential learning
　　　　theory 15–16
　　Mezirow's transformative
　　　　learning theory 13–15
　　Schön's theory of reflective
　　　　practice 12–13

experiential learning theory (ELT) 10,
　　15–16
experiential methods 24–5

feedback 72, 74–5
field–based experiential
　　exercises 27
　　learning 3, 7–8
finance 158, 186
Fink, L.D. 51, 55, 58, 68, 71, 75
forecasting 21
formative assessment 72, 111, 132
formative evaluation 112
Foster, M.K. 139, 140
Freire, P. 2

gallery walk technique 172–3, 180,
　　182
Gallup–Purdue 113
general context 64, 88, 94, 122, 125,
　　129, 141 *see also* specific
　　context
　　impact of 113, 117
　　of learning situation 66
Gerlach, V.S. 51, 53
global business mindset 26
global strategy meeting exercise 138,
　　152–3 *see also* growth mindset
　　exercise; leadership brand
　　exercise
　　adjustment and adaptation 167
　　assessments 163
　　　　selection/creation 161–2
　　context assessment 153–4
　　ensuring alignment 162–4
　　exercise resources 168–9
　　implementation 164–7
　　learning activities 163
　　learning activities selection/
　　　　creation 156, 157
　　activity and learning
　　　　objectives 156
　　assignment of individual
　　　　roles 158–9
　　cross–cultural global strategy
　　　　meeting exercise
　　　　implementation 159

debrief experience in small groups 160–61
debrief key observations as class 160–61
formation of small groups 158
reinforcement of learning 161
small group presentations of top strategic priorities to CEO 159–60
learning objectives 155–6, 163
reflection and revision 168
sequence and timing of activities for 165
Gooding, J. 169
Google 170, 177
images 169, 172
Gordon/Howell Report 22
Gosen, J. 34
Gosenpud, J.J. 7, 32–3
Grabinger, R.S. 43
graduate exercise 138
great disruption in higher education 24
growth mindset exercise 101–2, 120, 131, 138, 139–40 *see also* global strategy meeting exercise; leadership brand exercise
adjusting and adaptation 150–51
assessments selection/creation 146–7
context assessment 140–62
ensuring alignment 147–8
implementation 148–50
interventions 102
learning activities selection/creation 143–5
learning objectives 142–3
reflection and revision 151
students with 119

Hamer, L.O. 8
Harvard Business School case method 23
Harvard's Graduate School of Business Administration 20
Hattie, J. 85, 92–3, 111–12
high–impact
contextual factors 121, 128, 138
instructional approaches 111–12
micro contextual factors 127, 134
educator factors 109
student factors 109
Hmelo–Silver, C.E. 36
Hofstede, G. 119
Hoover, J.D. 6
How Learning Works: 7 Research–Based Principles for Smart Teaching (Ambrose et al.) 75, 140
human development, ecological theory of 89–90
humanistic education 17
humanistic learning theory 16–17
humanistic theory 10
human resource management 187

immediacy of cross–cultural communications 154
implementation
in classroom 50–51, 79–81, 133–5
classroom–oriented design models 51–8
Effective Experiential Exercise Design Model 50, 58–9, 62–87
context 133–4
checklist 135–7
cross–cultural global strategy meeting exercise 159
educator's perspective 148, 166–7, 178–9
Effective Experiential Exercise Design Model 79–80
global strategy meeting exercise 159
growth mindset exercise 148–50

leadership brand exercise 176–9
    in teaching practice 182
in–class experiential exercises 27
informed consent 43
inquiry–learning 2, 3, 9
instructional approaches 63, 65–6, 83,
    85, 93, 111–13, 124, 129
    context 87, 122
    impact of 110–13
instructional media 53
instructional methods 63, 65, 124,
    129–30
    techniques, and activities 53
instructional strategy 164
instructional systems design models
    51
instructional technology 53
Integrated Design model 50–52, 55–7
intelligence and prior achievement
    100–101
intention 44, 107, 108
international business 187
interpersonal behaviors 106, 109
interpersonal skills 24, 26
Interservice Procedures for
    Instructional Systems
    Development model (IPISD
    model) 54
introductory business course 29
iRubric 132

Jarvis, P. 6

Kane, D. 85
Kelley, H.H. 104
Klein, K.J. 90
Knapp, K.E. 10
Knowles, M.S. 17–18, 48
    theory of adult learning *see* adult
        learning theory
Kolb, David 12, 15–16, 48
    experiential learning theory
        see experiential learning
        theory (ELT)
Kosnik, R.D. 25
Kozlowski, S.W.J. 90
Krizan, Z. 36

leadership 29, 170
    skills 24
    texts 172
leadership brand exercise 138,
        169–70, 179 *see also* growth
        mindset exercise; global
        strategy meeting exercise
    adjustment and adaptation
        179–80
    alignment 174–6
    assessments selection/creation
        174
    context assessment 170–71
    development 172
    implementation 176–9
    learning
        activities selection/creation
            171–4
        objectives 171
    reflection and revision 180–82
learner–centered pedagogy 6–7
learners 6–7, 123, 129
    characteristics 63, 65
        high–impact micro
            contextual educator
            factors 109
        impact of 96, 100, 106
        relationships between
            context and outcomes
            97–9
    interpersonal relations among 14
    open–mindedness and
        adaptability 16
learning
    achievement approach to 104
    active engagement in 117
    approaches 104–5
    collaborative 2–3, 40
    cooperative 3, 40
    context 87–8
        contextual factors affecting
            experiential exercises
            90
        impact of 92–5, 119–21
        theoretical foundations of
            88–91
    deep approach to 104, 107, 120

objectives 64, 66–8, 83, 128, 130
   global strategy meeting
      exercise 155–6, 163
   growth mindset exercise
      142–3
   leadership brand exercise
      171
   three–part 67
   Tyler's model for 64, 66
outcomes 7, 174
   in classes 36–7
   direct and indirect impact of
      context 95
   from Schön's perspective 12
   reinforcement of 161
   theories 10
      Humanistic learning theory
         16–17
      Knowles's theory of adult
         learning 18–20
      Kolb's experiential learning
         theory 15–16
      Mezirow's transformative
         learning theory 13–15
learning activities selection/creation
   68, 71, 73, 130–31
   global strategy meeting exercise
      156, 157
   activity and learning
      objectives 156
   assignment of individual
      roles 158–9
   cross–cultural global
      strategy meeting
      exercise
      implementation 159
   debrief experience in small
      groups 160–61
   debrief key observations as
      class 160–61
   formation of small groups
      158
   reinforcement of learning
      161
   small group presentations of
      top strategic priorities
      to CEO 159–60

   growth mindset exercise 143–5
   leadership brand exercise 171–4
lecture–based model of education 21
Lemar, J. 9
Lewin, K. 19, 21, 88
live cases 3, 8
loosely structured experiential
   activities 8
low–inference instructional
   approaches 112
lower–level learning objective 130

macro contextual factors 137
macrosystems 89
Maddox, K.N. 47
Make it Stick (Brown) 75
management 33, 87, 188
   data 28
   education 22
   of effort and time 101
   human resource 187
   operations 189
   strategic 191
   supply chain 192
   training types 34
Marcotte, G. 26, 27
Margolis, H. 103
marketing 28–9, 189
   and communications 158
   and finance 168
mastery experiences 103
mastery learning 121
McCabe, P.P. 103
McTighe, J. 51–2, 68
Meertens, J.V. 118
mesosystems 89
meta–analyses 100
   based on type of experiential
      learning methods 40–41
   in business education 32–5
   in higher education 93
   of variables 92
metacognition 102

metacognitive learning skills 101, 120, 131
Metz, B. 169
Mezirow, J. 5, 10, 12–15, 48
    transformative learning theory
        see theory *under*
        transformative learning
micro contextual factors 119–20, 137
microsystems 89
micro variables *see* specific context
Molenda, M. 54
monitoring and continuous improvement 45
Morgan State University 141
motivation 101, 140
multilevel approach to organizational phenomenon 90
Murray, H.G. 113

NASA Moon Landing survival exercise 9
National Association of Colleges and Employers survey (NACE survey) 23
National Society for Experiential Education (NSEE) 42–3
    principles of good practice 44–5
National Training Laboratories 21
negative emotions 81–2
Newby, T.J. 53
Nilson, L.B. 67–8, 71, 75
Noddings, N. 12
North American business education 22
Noyd, R.K. 67

open systems theory 60
operations management 189
organizational behavior 30, 190
organizational strategy, setting 164
outdoor adventure education 4

passive lecture methods 2
pedagogies of engagement 2
peer–to–peer teaching 130
personality 105–6
Piaget's theory of constructivism 88

place–based learning 4
Planning, Implementing and Evaluating model (PIE model) 50–51, 53, 55–6
positive general attitudes 33
positive perceptions of specific learning context 95
post–exercise 74
practices/conditions related to context and effect sizes 112, 114–16
Preckel, F. 92–3, 105, 110–12
pre–exercise 72, 74
premise reflection 6
pre–prepared questions 134
pre–reflection 5
prescriptive model 87
presentation skills 24
Priem, R.L. 35
Primer on Writing Effective Learning–Centered Course Goals (Noyd) 67
prior achievement, intelligence and 100–101
problem–based activities 9–10
problem–based learning (PBL) 4, 19–20, 26, 37–8, 41
problem–solving 32
process reflection 6
production 158
professional and societal influences, impact of 118–19
professional training exercise 138
profession/society 126, 129
project–based activities 9–10
project–based learning 4
project management 24
proximal variables *see* specific context

quality field–based exercises 7

Ramburuth, P. 16
recruiting strategy proposal 9
reflection 5–7, 44, 135
    growth mindset exercise 151
    leadership brand exercise 180–82
    and revising 84–6

global strategy meeting
  exercise 168
reflection–in–action 5, 13, 82, 84, 194
reflection–on–action 5, 12, 194
reflective observation 16
reflective practice theory 10, 12–13
reinforcement of learning 161
Renaud, R.D. 113
research–oriented institutions 117–18
research for business education 22
revising 84–6, 135, 168
  global strategy meeting exercise
    168
  growth mindset exercise 151
  leadership brand exercise 180–82
Reynolds, P. 25
rich environments for active learning
  (REALs) 43
Roberts, J. 24
Rogers, C.R. 17
role playing 37
RubiStar 132
Rubric Maker 132
rubrics 132

Salas, E. 71
Schary, D.P. 9
Schneider, M. 92–3, 105, 110–12
scholarship for business education 22
Schön, D.A. 5, 10, 12–13, 48, 82
  theory of reflective practice *see*
    reflective practice theory
School of Medicine at McMaster
  University in Canada 19
Seaman, J. 19
self–assessed knowledge 36
self–assessments 161–2, 172, 176–7
  reflections 176
self–awareness 172
self–directed learning 17
self–efficacy 26, 102–3, 119–20
self–improvement 26
self–regulated learners 101
self–regulated learning processes 101,
  104
self–serving bias 104
semi–structured classroom activities 8

sensitivity training 21
service–learning 4, 41
Shingles, R. 67
Sitzmann, T. 36
small groups
  debrief experience in 160–61
  discussions 171, 176
  formation of 158
  presentations of top strategic
    priorities to CEO 159–60
Smallwood, N. 169
Smith, P. 10, 16
social constructivism 11–12
society and culture 118
solution, access, value, education
  (SAVE) 67
sound institutional approach 118
specific context 63–4, 88, 93–4, 123,
  127–9, 141 *see also* general
  context
  impact of 95–6
specific, measurable, attainable,
  realistic, time–based action
  plan (SMART action plan)
  171, 175
Stanford Graduate School of
  Education 117
Stone, C.L. 111
strategic management 191
strategy–level decisions 154
Strobel, J. 38
Structure of Observed Learning
  Outcomes Taxonomy (SOLO
  Taxonomy) 68
student
  engagement 27
  perceptions of context 96
  practices associated with student
    learning outcomes 46–7
  preference for active learning
    methods 1
student–centered learning 4
student–educator interaction 119
student–teacher relationships 106
summative assessments 72, 111
supply chain 158
  management 192

supportive learning environment 194
surface approaches 108
Survey of Instructional Design Models
    (Branch and Dousay) 51
systematically planning instruction 57
Systematic Planning model 50–51,
    53–5

Tang, C. 78, 88, 105–6
Tavistock Institute of Human
    Relations in United Kingdom
    21
taxonomy 68
Taylor, F. 20
Taylor, V.K. 169
teacher–centered educational systems
    118–19
teaching 96, 106, 112, 114, 117, 121
    and assessment methods 105
    approaches of experiential
        learning 3–4
    constructive alignment 78
    constructivism advocating 11
    implementation in teaching
        practice 182
    implications for 14, 90
    metacognition and 102
    peer-to-peer 130
    responsibilities 25
    strategy 52
    teaching-oriented organizations
        117–18
    teaching practices, educator
        characteristics and 109
    theory of adult learning 18
    traditional active teaching
        methodologies 32
Teaching at Its Best (Nilson) 75
Teach Students How to Learn
    (McGuire and McGuire) 102
team–based learning 4, 41
teamwork 24
technical rationality 12–13

Technology Agility 25
T–group methods 21
Tight, M. 92
Tomkins, L. 2
transformative learning
    phases 14
    theory 10, 13–15
twin sins 57
Tyler's model for learning objectives
    64, 66

Ulrich, D. 169
Ulus, E. 2
undergraduate exercise 138

Valid Assessment of Learning in
    Undergraduate Education
    rubrics (VALUE rubrics) 133
van Barneveld, A. 38
verbal persuasion 103
vicarious learning 121, 130
Visible Learning (Hattie) 102
Vygotsky, L. 11

Walker, J.L. 152, 153
Walvoord, B.E. 75
Wang, M.C. 93
Warren, K. 43
Washbush, J. 34
WHERETO 57
Whetten, D.A. 21–2
Whitehead, C. 6
Wick, C. 71
Wiggins, G. 51–2, 68
Wilson, A.L. 6
wine industry resources 168
Wright, M.C. 117–18
Wright, S.L. 47
Wurdinger, S.D. 9

Ylvisaker, M. 111

Zell, E. 36